LA METHODE

Also by Jacques Pépin

La Technique

Jacques Pépin
LA METHODE

An Illustrated Guide
to the Fundamental Techniques
of Cooking

Photographs by Léon Perer

MACMILLAN LONDON

First published in the United States by Times
Books

First published in the United Kingdom 1983 by
MACMILLAN LONDON LIMITED

Published in paperback in the United Kingdom
1983 by
PAPERMAC
a division of Macmillan Publishers Limited
4 Little Essex Street London WC2R 3LF
and Basingstoke

Associated companies in Auckland, Dallas, Delhi,
Dublin, Hong Kong, Johannesburg, Lagos,
Manzini, Melbourne, Nairobi, New York,
Singapore, Tokyo, Washington and Zaria

ISBN 0 333 35905 4 (hardcover)
ISBN 0 333 35381 1 (Papermac)

Printed in Hong Kong by South China Printing Co.

To my "Aristarque,"
Helen McCully,
who had great style and courage

Contents

Publisher's Note

The colour plates contained in the American edition between pages 55 and 70 inclusive have been omitted from this edition.

Introduction

My last book, *La Technique*, ended with fifteen hundred photographs painfully selected from six thousand, with my publisher screaming stop, stop, stop and my editor buried under a mountain of photographs and captions. It had taken two years of conceiving, writing and rewriting, testing, tasting, shooting, shopping, chopping, and, finally, I let go so the book could go to press, but I never really stopped producing that book. I kept extensive lists of unsaid thoughts, of new ways I'd discovered of doing things, of old ways I hadn't been able to cover, and the result is this second volume. This book is actually a continuation of *La Technique*, and it feels good to have been able to cover everything I wanted to cover, to know that all the techniques that didn't make it into the first volume are included here. In truth, I probably won't be truly content until I can publish a composite volume bringing together all of the important techniques of cooking in a perfectly organized and entirely restructured tome including those techniques that too soon I'll realize have also been left out of this book.

The question is bound to arise, "Do I need *La Technique* to use this volume?" And the answer is "No." Although both books are part of the same thought, and the two, taken as a whole, bring you the closest you can come to a cook's apprenticeship short of working with a professional chef in a restaurant, each technique is a separate entity and can be used alone. This new volume doesn't depend on the first any more than the first depends on this one. The techniques do not progress from easy to hard but are like the pieces of a puzzle—all are equally important.

La Méthode is not a recipe book although we have included more recipes in this book than in *La Technique*. The recipes are provided as vehicles and examples to understand and carry out techniques. It was never our intention to illustrate recipes, although often we do, for example in Brown Stocks (technique 6), where it is important to show the texture and degree of concentration that the stock should have. Our intention is to describe certain processes that involve manual skills and are impossible to explain in words. These processes, or techniques, or *tours de main*, will not teach you recipe-making but will teach you how to cook. Don't be discouraged if you can't master one of these techniques instantly—some will be perfectly simple, but others require practice and patience. Remember that any technique you master will leave you better equipped to perform with ease and proficiency, and in time you will find that when you revisit your favorite cookbooks you will experience them in a new light.

Equipment

IF YEARS AGO THE VARIETY WAS SCARCE, today, cooking equipment comes in all types, shapes, prices and materials. The enormous interest in food, heightened by cooking schools, cookbooks, newspapers and magazine articles, etc., has spurred the manufacturers into bringing many different types of paraphernalia onto the market, and a lot of it is good. However, it is often hard for people to differentiate. What pots should one buy? Should they be copper? Stainless steel? Heavy aluminum? No-stick? Black cast iron? Enameled cast iron? It is difficult to choose because ultimately there is no ideal pot. Every material has its good and bad points. The thick, heavy hand-hammered copper (Dehillerin in Paris, Michel et Clément in Lyon, Lamalle or Bridge in New York are known supply houses) is the best to conduct, diffuse and retain heat. While attractive, it is very heavy, very expensive and needs constant polishing. Pots lined with tin become a problem when retinning is needed; it is expensive and finding someone who does is difficult.

Heavy aluminum pans, customarily used in professional kitchens (such as heavy-duty Wearever or Magnalite and brushed aluminum), are much lighter and easier to handle. Heavy aluminum is the best heat conductor after copper and it's tough. However, it tends to discolor food, especially when acidic ingredients such as wine, vinegar and tomatoes are used. (When using a whisk for an emulsion, such as hollandaise, you will often have a brownish dirty color mixed with your sauce.) At home the discoloration happens regularly just from boiling water. The pan is not used often enough and moisture in the air will cause darkening. The same heavy aluminum pot used in a restaurant kitchen may not discolor since it is used over and over again and is washed between each use, preventing any buildup.

The no-stick lined pans are very good for omelets but too delicate for general use. (The plain steel omelet skillet is better if used often; if not, it will stick.) They will lose their releasing quality and the coating will eventually peel off, and may even be harmful to your health. In addition, you are prevented from using a whisk or a scouring pad, since this will destroy the surface, making them unsatisfactory for normal use. The coating used in such pans as Calphalon pans is much stronger and withstands a great deal of beating, making that pot one of the best on the market.

Stainless steel cleans easily, keeps shiny, does not discolor food but, unfortunately, does develop "hot spots" or patches of burn. The transfer of heat is fast but stainless steel does not retain heat well. Fortunately, stainless steel pans are now made with thick bottoms, each an aluminum or copper "sandwich" between layers of stainless steel. (Examples are Padarno, Cuisinart, Sitram, Mastercraft, Farberware, etc.)

The dark cast iron skillet and kettle are good, sturdy and practically indestructible. They are not expensive, easy to care for and hold the heat fairly well. However, they are heavy and if not used often will get rusty, stain and discolor food. The enameled cast iron (Copco, Le Creuset, Lauffer) is attractive, cleans well and holds the heat very well. However, it is heavy, expensive and will chip if dropped. Eventually, the inside will darken and discolor.

Earthenware is attractive, good for prolonged oven cooking and can be used as service pieces. Since they are very fragile, and extreme temperature may cause cracking, don't use them for stove-top cooking. For baking, flat, heavy, not too shiny, aluminum cookie sheets are the best. The iron or steel cookie sheets will warp and the heat conductivity is too rapid.

Should you have a plastic or wooden chopping block? The plastic is cleaner, not porous and can be chilled for pastry. The plain wood or laminated wood is attractive, with just enough bounce, and it does not dull the knife's blade. Both types are expensive if they are of the best quality. They should be thick, heavy and wide. Your chopping block won't perform properly if you do not have a high, sturdy table which does not bounce when you use a meat pounder or a cleaver.

What kind of electrical appliances should you get? A food processor (the stronger the better) is a must, as well as an electric mixer. Should you cook with gas, electricity or microwaves? We don't often use microwaves in a home kitchen, and cooking is harder to control on electric tops; although the electric oven is excellent. Gas is our favorite. Professional stoves are a good investment. They are strong, have great capacity and never go out of style (South Bend, Wolf, Garland, Universal Chef). We enjoy seeing the flames and the control is there at all times. Ultimately, the best heat is wood (hard wood). For barbecuing it is a must. Never briquets. Briquets are a derivate of petroleum and they are not good for your health. A steak well charred on a dirty grill over briquets has more tar than several packages of cigarettes.

Good whisks with thick, heavy threads are a must, as well as "piano-wire" whips (very thin, flexible and tightly woven). Both are necessary—the whisk for thick sauces and the whip to whip egg whites and heavy cream. Rubber and wooden spatulas, as well as a series of bowls, wire racks, strainers, metal spoons, skimmers, vegetable peelers, etc., are all part of a necessary impedimenta. Then there are the knives, an extension of your fingers. There is always a controversy about knives. Should they be carbon or stainless? The current trend is toward stainless steel knives. They do not discolor or oxidize when used for cutting lemons, tomatoes or onions. However, stainless steel is a very hard metal and difficult to sharpen, although it keeps a good edge once sharpened. The knives should be very sharp to perform correctly (In addition, you are less likely to cut yourself with a smooth, well-sharpened knife than with a dull tool.) You should have a minimum of three knives. A very large (12- to 14-inch blade) chopping knife, a thinner, 8- to 10-inch slicing knife and a small paring knife. Several paring knives would be even better. (Sabatier, Henckels, Forschner, Zanger, etc., are all good.) Have a good sharpener. A steel or ceramic sharpener (good for stainless steel) is necessary but both sharpen only the tiny cutting edge of the knives (see technique 1). After a year or so, depending on how often you use your knives, this tiny amount of metal will be worn away. The knife must then be sent out to be sharpened professionally unless you have the know-how, and possess a large stone (such as Norton) with which to grind the metal. Send dull knives out to a person who sharpens lawn mowers, scissors or electric saws. Then the knives can again be utilized for one or two years, using the steel periodically.

You will notice that expensive, good equipment is usually well designed and pleasant to look at. Visit pot and pan shops. Many specialize in gadgetry and gimmicks. Some have an enormous, confusing potpourri of paraphernalia, among which, if you have the proper lore, you will discern the good from the bad. Then, there are a few good shops that specialize in good equipment only. When you have chosen a good shop, follow the judgment of the salesperson; once you get to know a place, the people will give you good advice. Have a tag sale and get rid of your bad tools. Buy pieces one by one if you can't afford to spend a lot. Some people will spend a small fortune in a good restaurant without blinking an eye, but won't spend the same amount on a few pieces of equipment. It is worth the investment, since they will go on working for you, your children and, maybe, your grandchildren.

Have your pots, molds, strainers, etc., hung from the wall or the ceiling, as is done in a professional kitchen. They will be easy to get to and you will use them more often.

Even though you may have the best ingredients to start with, nothing is more frustrating when preparing a meal than when your oven does not keep a constant heat, your pan is discolored, your knife is dull, your pots dented, etc., etc. It won't work! Finally, cook, cook, cook and cook again! I know people who have great kitchens with all the latest and best equipment. It is only there for show. The more you cook, the easier it becomes. The more the equipment is used, the better it performs and you will get attached to certain tools.

Basic Techniques

1. How to Sharpen Knives *(Aiguisage des Couteaux)*

A KNIFE IS USELESS if it is not sharp. You can tell if your knife is sharp if it can cut a soft ripe tomato into thin slices with ease. If the knife is dull, it will just crush the tomato.

If you looked at the cutting edge of a knife through a magnifying glass, you'd see that it is made up of hundreds of tiny teeth—like a saw. Through repeated use, these teeth get twisted and bent out of alignment. This is what makes a knife dull; a sharpener gets these little teeth back into alignment.

The harder the metal the knife is made of, the harder it will be to sharpen, but the longer it will hold its edge. A sharpener has to be made of a material that's a shade harder than the metal it is to abrade. (The hardness of metals is measured on the "Rockwell Scale.")

"Steels" are metal sharpeners. They have a fine grain and give a super finish to an already sharp knife. Butchers and professional cooks use a steel constantly, giving the knife a few strokes before each use. A ceramic sharpener is better than a steel for sharpening hard metals such as stainless steel. (Ceramic is harder than the hardest metal on the Rockwell Scale.)

Eventually, repeated sharpening wears away the little teeth of the cutting edge. At this point the knife needs to be ground to thin the blade into a new cutting edge. This is done with an abrasive stone.

USING A CERAMIC SHARPENER

1. Start with the heel of the blade at the tip of the sharpener and slide the knife down the length of the sharpener so the cutting edge abrades against it. Apply steady and strong pressure. Keep the knife at the same angle constantly.

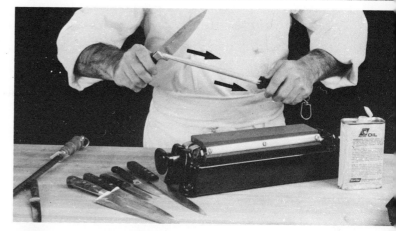

2. End with the point of the blade near the base of the sharpener. This is one steady stroke, one hand moving toward the other, every inch of the cutting edge making contact with the sharpener. Repeat on the other side of the sharpener to sharpen the other side of the knife.

USING A STEEL SHARPENER

3. This photograph is an alternate way of sharpening. In this photo, we are using a steel sharpener with a high-carbon-steel knife. Start with the heel of the blade at the base of the steel and pull the hands away from one another, finishing with the tip of the sharpener at the tip of the blade. Make sure that the whole blade gets worked against the sharpener. Keep the angle about 25 degrees and the pressure the same.

USING A GRINDING STONE

4. Once a year, twice a year, once every two years—depending on the kind of beating your knives get—you will need to grind them down to form a new cutting edge. You can send your knives out and have them ground by a professional or you can do it yourself if you have a sand wheel or a large stone like the one pictured here. This stone is held in place by suction so that you can apply a lot of pressure without having it slide around the way smaller stones do. It has three sides, each of a different coarseness. You begin with the coarsest side and finish with the finest.

5. Rub some mineral oil on the stone to keep stone grindings loose so they can be wiped off with paper and don't seal and glaze the surface of the stone, which would prevent abrasion. Start at the tip of the knife and apply strong pressure down and forward so that the whole side of the blade is in contact with the stone. Move back and forth, applying pressure. Keep the angle constant. Repeat on the other side. As the knife gets sharper and thinner at the end, go to a finer stone. When you are through clean your knife. Keep it sharp with a steel.

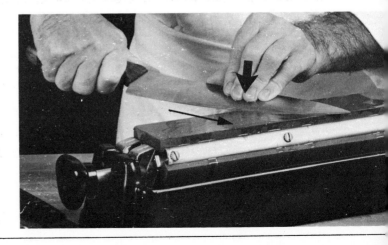

2. How to Peel an Onion *(Epluchage des Oignons)*

IT WOULD SEEM to be extremely simple to peel an onion, but it isn't always so for someone who is inexperienced. People tend not to remove enough of the root and stem, which makes it harder to peel and slice the onion properly.

1. Cut off the root and the stem end on the other side.

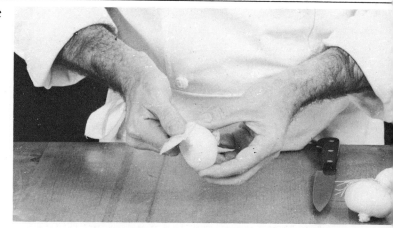

2. Some onions have extremely thin skins which are hard to remove. Some are quite thick. In either case, remove one layer of onion, or several if necessary, so there is no yellow or dry skin visible.

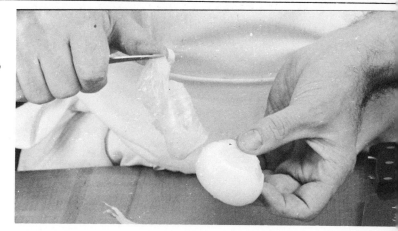

3. How to Julienne *(Julienne)*

TO CUT INTO JULIENNE is to cut into very thin strips. A julienne is aesthetically very pleasing and very nice as a garnish for soups, fish, meat, etc.

A vegetable julienne (such as carrots, leeks and celery) is usually blanched and finished by being cooked a few minutes with fish, veal or whatever it will be served with. Being cut so thin, it cooks very fast.

JULIENNE OF CARROTS (*Julienne de Carottes*)

1. Trim both ends of the carrot to form a flat base to start from. Working toward you, peel a whole strip of carrot in one stroke, from end to end. Rotate the carrot and proceed all the way around. Use long, regular, slow strokes. Your speed will improve with practice. Short nervous strokes (or peeling one half of the carrot then turning the carrot around and peeling the other half) don't produce good results and are very tiring.

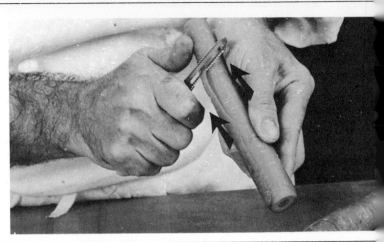

2. Slice the carrot into very thin lengthwise slices. If you do not have a *mandoline* or a similar type of vegetable slicer, and if you're not proficient enough with a knife, use a vegetable peeler. Apply as much pressure as you can so the slices are not too thin.

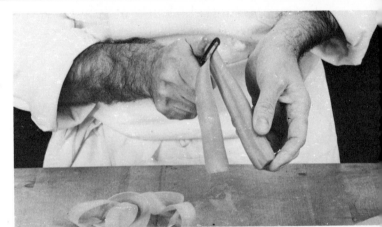

3. Stack 3 or 4 of the thin slices on top of one another, fold and then slice into a fine julienne.

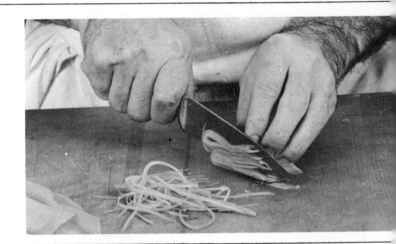

JULIENNE OF LEEKS (*Julienne de Poireaux*)

4. For the julienne of leeks, only the white and the very light green part of the leek is used. Remove the dark green part and the root, keeping the green part in the refrigerator for soups or stocks or to put in a stew. Split the trimmed leek in half.

5. Separate all of the layers of the leek. (Note that in our leek the center is woody. This happens when the leek is old and grows a tough central core. Remove and discard.)

6. Fold a few of the leaves at a time, so that the inside of the leaves shows on the outside.

7. Cut into very thin strips. Wash and then drain.

JULIENNE OF CELERY (*Julienne de Céleri*)

8. Separate the stalks. Use a vegetable peeler to remove the top layer of fiber from the large outer stalks if necessary. (By scratching the celery, you can find out if it is fibrous or not.)

9. Cut each stalk into 4- to 5-inch pieces. Flatten each piece with the palm of your hand. (It will probably crush in the center.)

10. Using the flat of your knife held horizontally to the table, cut the celery into 2 or 3 thin slices.

11. Pile all the slices on top of one another and cut into thin strips. A julienne of celery is never as thin as a julienne of leeks or carrots, but it is used in the same way.

4. Duxelle of Mushrooms *(Duxelle de Champignons)*

A DUXELLE OF MUSHROOMS is a mixture of mushrooms chopped very, very fine and cooked, sometimes with shallots sometimes without, and seasoned with salt and pepper. Duxelle is one of the staples of classic French cooking and is used in many dishes—as a coating, as a stuffing, as a seasoning. With the addition of cream or milk it becomes a purée of mushrooms and is served as a vegetable.

¾ pound mushrooms, finely chopped
2 shallots, peeled and very finely chopped (½ ta-
    blespoon)
1 tablespoon sweet butter
Dash of salt
Dash of pepper

1. One of the best ways to chop mushrooms is in a food processor. However, don't put them into the processor whole. Cut them into coarse slices or chunks first.

2. Place a large handful of mushrooms in the processor. Turn it on and then off. Then on again and off. If the machine is left on for the whole duration, half the mushrooms fly around the blade—not getting properly chopped—while the other half turns into a purée. The on-and-off technique allows the mushrooms to fall back on the blade so that they all get uniformly chopped. (Use this method whenever you chop in a food processor.) Melt the butter in a skillet, add the shallots and cook on medium heat for about ½ minute. Add the chopped mushrooms, a dash of salt and a dash of pepper and cook, mixing occasionally with a wooden spoon, for about 10 minutes. The mushrooms will render some liquid, and will be ready when the liquid has evaporated and the mixture is dry and starts to sizzle. Transfer to a bowl, cover with waxed paper and set aside.

3. If you used mushrooms that were open, large and black inside, older mushrooms (which are often used for a duxelle since they are hard to use for anything else), press them in a cloth towel to extrude some of the dark juices after they have been chopped.

4. As you can see, pressing the mushrooms in a towel does get rid of the juices. From this point, proceed as explained in step 2. If the mushrooms are plump, firm and white, there is no reason to press the juices out.

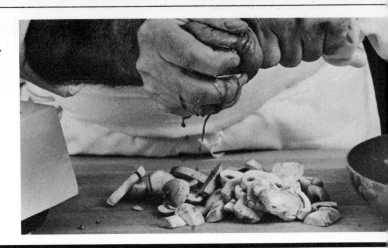

5. How to Peel and Seed a Cucumber
(Evidage des Concombres)

1. To peel a cucumber properly, cut off both ends, then peel toward you, using a vegetable peeler. Remove strips of peel the full length of the cucumber with one stroke. Keep strokes straight and uniform as you work around the cucumber. If you exert uneven pressure, you will take too much flesh off in some places and too little in others and the cucumber will look multicolored.

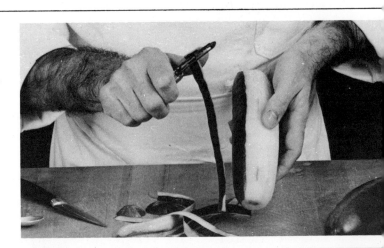

2. To seed the cucumber split it in half using a knife. Then work the edge of a dessert spoon along the seeds, close to the flesh, making a type of incision. When you are through with one side, turn the cucumber and loosen the seeds on the other side. Finally, using the bowl of the spoon, scrape out all the seeds in one stroke.

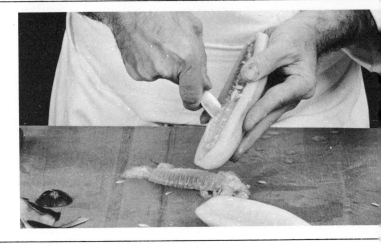

6. Brown Stock (Classic and Fast), Half-Glaze and Meat Glaze *(Fond Brun [Classique et Rapide] Demi-Glace et Glace de Viande)*

COOKS OFTEN GET CONFUSED when they hear names such as "brown stock," *demi-glace* (half-glaze), "brown sauce," *glace de viande* (meat glaze), *sauce espagnole*, *fond lié* (thickened stock), *jus*, "broth," "bouillon," and so forth. In fact, it is confusing. However, it is an area that is too important to French cooking to bypass.

Let's start with the most basic—stock. (We will use the word "stock" instead of broth, bouillon or *jus*.) What is a stock? It is a liquid obtained by boiling bones with water. There are two basic stocks: one white, one brown. The white stock is bones and water boiled together with seasoning. The brown stock is a white stock made from bones that were browned in the oven or on top of the stove. The browned bones give the stock a darker color and a nuttier taste. It is as simple and as complicated as that. (The addition of meat naturally enhances and concentrates the flavor of stock, but is not really necessary, particularly at today's prices—you can get excellent results with bones only by simply reducing the liquid a bit more.)

A stock must cook a certain amount of time, which varies depending on how large the bones are and what type of bone is used. With small pieces of bones, or with thin bones like the bones of a chicken, 3 hours of cooking are sufficient, whereas larger veal or beef bones require up to 10 to 12 hours. Time is essential to extract all the nutrients and taste from the bones. Water is added to the bones, but not a fixed amount. Throughout the cooking water evaporates and more is added regularly to replenish the stock. When the stock is cooked, it is strained and reduced to proper consistency.

We make our brown stock with veal, beef and chicken bones mixed together. The chicken bones, besides being readily available and inexpensive, add a pleasant nutty and sweet taste to the stock. In fact, if we are low on other bones, we'll make up the difference with more chicken bones. It is, of course, better to use fresh bones; however, in a home kitchen you rarely have enough fresh bones on hand. So when you order a roast of beef or veal from your butcher, ask him for a few bones and then freeze them. Once or twice a year, empty the freezer, make large amounts of stock and freeze it in small containers. It should last you for a few months and be very inexpensive. Make great quantities of stock if you have pots and pans large enough, inasmuch as 3 pounds of bones take as much cooking as 20 pounds if you are making a classic brown stock.

Brown stock is a carrier—a vehicle—which permits you to make sauces. It is not a sauce in itself, but is used to "wet" (*mouiller* as we say in France) a stew or deglaze a pan, or add to other bones (game, lamb, etc.) to produce a more concentrated and differently flavored stock (see Saddle of Lamb en

Croûte, technique 84, for an example). Though it is gelatinous when cooked and holds together, a stock is not concentrated enough to be called a sauce. However, the 3 quarts of brown stock (made from the recipe on page 18) reduced by half will yield 1½ quarts of a slightly syrupy and darker liquid which *is* concentrated enough to become a "sauce" and which has a name of its own—*demi-glace* (half-glaze). Furthermore, if that quart and a half of *demi-glace* is reduced to its extreme, it will yield about 2 to 2½ cups of what is called *glace de viande* (meat glaze). The *glace de viande* is not a sauce any longer. It has trancended the condition of a sauce and is now a strengthening and flavoring agent. The *glace de viande* hardens enough when cooled to be unmolded and cut into cubes. Kept loosely wrapped (not in a closed jar) it will keep almost indefinitely if the reduction is correct. These cubes of *glace de viande* are added to sauces to make them stronger and richer. Thus a basic stock, taken to different stages of concentration and volume, changes its name as well as its function.

Stocks should be started in cold water and cooked, uncovered, at a slow, gentle boil. This way, the albumin in the bones and meat will harden and come to the surface of the liquid in the form of a gray foam which can be removed with a skimmer. The fat will also rise to the surface. However, if the stock is covered and boiling too fast, the albumin won't separate and the fat will emulsify back into the liquid (see the discussion of emulsion in the techniques for beurre blanc and hollandaise, techniques 11 and 12) instead of rising to the top. The stock will then be cloudy, less digestible and more caloric.

The classic brown stock is usually seasoned with carrots, onions, thyme, bay leaf, peppercorns, etc., but not salt because if salt is added at the beginning and the stock is then reduced to a glaze, the concentration of salt will be overpowering. A stock, purified by slow cooking and properly skimmed, will be high in proteins, clear, meaty and pratically tasteless. This may seem paradoxical but it's not. The stock has been too lightly seasoned to have much of an identifying taste of its own. And it shouldn't have one if it is to become a *demi-glace* transformed (as we will a little later) into a red wine sauce for beef, a chicken and mushroom sauce or sauce for a sautéed piece of veal. In each of these cases the *demi-glace* must take on the identity of that particular dish. It is the "hidden and modest" friend which enables a cook to produce a well-finished, long-simmered sauce in minutes. It is what we call in English a basic brown sauce. It doesn't have a specific name or identity of its own yet. With the addition of wine it becomes a sauce *Bordelaise,* with Madeira and truffles a sauce *Périgueux,* with vinegar and shallots a sauce *Bercy,* etc. The progression is from a stock to a *demi-glace* or basic brown sauce to a specific sauce.

What is the proper degree of reduction? The key word is "balance." Though a *demi-glace* should be concentrated, an overconcentrated *demi-glace* is just as unpalatable as a weak and bland concoction. To achieve a delicate combination of seasoning and correct concentration takes practice, knowledge and talent.

Making sauces from reduced stocks is particularly well suited for restaurant short-order cooking. It works well with diversified sauces and dishes made one portion at a time. However, it is time-consuming and expensive to make and some cooks do not feel that reductions alone produce a satisfactory result. Besides the question of time and expense, they object to the richness and concentrated taste of the reduction. A truffle sauce for a filet of beef requires a strong reduction but a small delicate quail is overpowered by too potent a sauce.

On occasion a stock will reduce and intensify in flavor but will lack the gelatinous element to thicken to the right consistency. If you feel your sauce has reached the right taste but it is too thin in texture, thicken it lightly with arrowroot. At one time a brown sauce used to be heavily thickened with flour. The classic sauce *Espagnole,* made with a stock, brown *roux* and tomato paste, though rarely made nowadays, is an example. Carème explains that the *roux,* the binding agent, separates after long, slow cooking, and the fat and the scum from the cooking of the *roux* rise to the top and should be skimmed off. The sauce clarifies and purifies through the long cooking until only the "binding elements" of the flour (the glutinous part) remain to hold the sauce together. Although this sauce works with practice and care, it is more logical and faster to use a starch such as arrowroot—which is like a purified flour (binding element only) and has no taste, cooks instantly and doesn't "dirty" the sauce.

Must one use *demi-glace* to cook well? Some types of cooking require it, some do not. Home cooking and some of the best country cooking is often done without brown stock. In our family, and at friends' where we have had some of our most memorable meals, brown stocks are practically never used. Often good cooks modify the principles behind the brown stock and use leftover juices from a roast chicken or a pot roast the way a professional uses *glace de viande.* Roasting and braising give natural strong juices, the equivalent of a strong reduction, which can be used in the same manner.

Following the Classic Brown Stock and the Fast Brown Stock are recipes using these stocks.

CLASSIC BROWN STOCK, HALF-GLAZE AND GLAZE (Fond Brun Classique, Demi-Glace et Glace de Viande)

YIELD: 3 quarts of stock or 1½ quarts *demi-glace* or about 2 cups of *glace de viande*

10 *pounds bones (one-third veal, one-third chicken, one-third beef), cut into 2-inch pieces*
1 *pound carrots, washed and unpeeled, cut into 1-inch chunks (about 4 to 6 carrots depending on size)*
1½ *pounds unpeeled onions, cut into 1-inch pieces (about 4 to 8 onions depending on size)*
3 *large ripe tomatoes, coarsely chopped (1½ pounds)*
1 *large leek, cut in half*
3 *celery ribs, cut in pieces*
2 *bay leaves*
½ *teaspoon thyme leaves*
½ *teaspoon black peppercorns*

1. Place the pieces of bone in a large roasting pan and brown in the oven at 425 degrees for 1½ hours, turning the bones once, halfway through the browning process. Add carrots and onions to the bones and continue cooking in the oven another ½ hour.

2. Remove the bones and vegetables from the oven and transfer to a large stock pot, using a slotted spoon so the drippings of fat are left in the roasting pan.

3. Pour out the fat accumulated in the roasting pan. (The solidified juices left in the pan are in fact a *glace de viande*.)

4. Pour water into the roasting pan, place on top of the stove, bring to a boil and, using a metal spatula, rub the bottom of the pan to melt all the solidified juices.

5. Add this liquid to the kettle and fill it with water. Bring to a boil slowly, then turn the heat down and simmer for 1 hour, removing the scum (technique 9). After 1 hour, add the remaining vegetables and seasonings. Bring to a boil again, then simmer slowly for a generous 10 hours. During the cooking process water will evaporate; replace periodically to keep the same level. The stock can simmer very gently overnight.

6. Strain the liquid through a fine strainer. (It is better to end up with more yield rather than less. When a lot of liquid is left the bones get "well washed" and the strained liquid contains all the nutrients of the stock. If the liquid is over-reduced with the bones, when you strain it, a lot of the *glace* and taste will stick to the bones and be lost.) Return to a clean pot and boil down until it reduces to 3 quarts of liquid. Let the stock cool overnight, then remove the solidified fat on the top. (The bones that have cooked for 10 hours are often recooked, instead of being discarded, to make a *glace de viande.* It is not as rich as the one made only through the reduction of stock but it's free, a bonus—you now have stock or *demi-glace* plus *glace de viande.* To make it, fill the pot containing the cooked bones with cold water, bring to a boil and simmer for another 8 to 10 hours or cook gently overnight. Strain and reduce to a *glace de viande* as described in step 9.)

7. To make *demi-glace*, reduce the stock by half (again), cool and divide into large chunks of about 1 cup each. Wrap in plastic wrap and freeze.

8. Stock, which is gelatinous but not quite as solid as the *demi-glace*, should be poured into plastic containers, covered and frozen.

9. To make a *glace de viande*, strain the *demi-glace* again and reduce to its maximum. As it reduces, transfer the liquid to a smaller, sturdy saucepan. The last hour of reduction is delicate and should be done on very low heat because the mixture has a tendency to burn as it gets thicker. The *glace* will become dark brown and form bubbles on top (like large caramel bubbles) during the last 15 to 20 minutes of cooking. As they break, no steam will escape. If there is any fat left in the mixture it will separate from the glaze and should be removed with a spoon. At that point, the reduction is completed—there is no more moisture in the mixture.

10. Note that the *glace de viande* has the thickness of a caramel. Remember also that it is unsalted.

11. Place the spoon and spatula into the saucepan, cover with water and bring to a boil. There is a lot of leftover, sticky *glace* around the pan and utensils that should be remelted to be used as a stock.

12. When the *glace de viande* is cold, unmold and cut into cubes. They will be hard, rubbery and dark. Keep in an uncovered jar in the refrigerator or in a plastic bag with the top slightly open. It will become very hard and keep almost indefinitely. Use as a seasoning when needed.

FAST BROWN STOCK (*Fond Brun Rapide*)

YIELD: 1 quart of stock or ½ quart *demi-glace*

This is a good, classic way of making a stock and yet it is fast. However, you can only make small amounts of it at a time because the bones get browned in a saucepan on top of the stove, and a saucepan can only accommodate so many bones. The bones are cut into tiny pieces so they brown rapidly and the nutrients and flavors are extracted faster during cooking. In a classic stock, the bones are roasted in the oven, which is a slower way, yet the only way to brown a large quantity of bones.

1 *pound veal bones*
2 *pounds chicken bones (gizzards, legs, necks,*
    wings), cut into 1-inch pieces
2 *carrots, unpeeled, chopped coarsely (1 cup)*
2 *large onions, unpeeled, chopped coarsely (1¼*
    cups)
1 *leek, chopped coarsely (⅓ cup)*
½ *cup celery stems and leaves*
1 *large tomato, cut in pieces*
½ *teaspoon thyme leaves*
1 *bay leaf*

½ *teaspoon black peppercorns*
4 *to 5 cloves garlic, unpeeled*
⅓ *cup parsley stems*

1. Cut the bones into no more than 1-inch pieces and place in a saucepan large enough to accommodate the bones in one layer. Place on the stove for 5 minutes on high heat. When they start sizzling, reduce to medium and continue cooking for 25 minutes, stirring occasionally with a wooden spoon.

2. The pieces should be well browned all around and the juices solidified in the bottom of the pan. Be careful not to burn the *glace* or solidified juices, or the stock will taste bitter.

3. After the bones have cooked for 30 minutes, use the cover to hold the bones in and invert the saucepan to pour out all the liquid fat. Add the carrots and onions to the bones and keep browning for another 10 minutes on medium to low heat. Add the rest of the ingredients and fill the saucepan with water. Bring to a boil slowly and cook uncovered on medium heat for 3 to 4 hours, replacing the water as it evaporates. Remove the scum every 10 to 15 minutes.

4. Strain through a fine *chinois*. Let cool overnight in the refrigerator and remove the fat. Reduce to 2 cups for a *demi-glace*.

STEAK "MARCHAND DE VIN" WITH MARROW (*Steak Marchand de Vin à la Moëlle*)

YIELD: 3 to 4 servings

1 *large shell steak (about 1½ pounds, trimmed)*
¼ *teaspoon salt*
¼ *teaspoon pepper*
1 *tablespoon sweet butter*
1 *tablespoon chopped shallots*
1 *small clove garlic, chopped*
¼ *teaspoon thyme*
1 *cup good dry red wine*
2 *anchovy fillets*
¾ *cup* demi-glace

Sprinkle steak with salt and pepper. Panfry steak in butter over medium to low heat for about 12 minutes, turning the steak every 4 to 5 minutes. Place the steak on a platter and keep warm in a 160-degree oven. Add the shallots to the pan drippings and sauté for 10 to 15 seconds. Add garlic, thyme and red wine. Reduce to ½ cup. Chop anchovy fillets or crush with the blade of a knife to a purée and add to the wine mixture with ¾ cup *demi-glace*. Reduce for 1 to 2 minutes. Taste for seasonings, add salt and pepper if needed and strain the sauce on top of the steak or slice the steak and serve with the sauce around. Add marrow and artichoke bottoms if desired (see technique 13).

FILET OF BEEF WITH TRUFFLE SAUCE (*Filet de Boeuf Périgueux*)

YIELD: 6 servings

3 *tablespoons sweet butter*
1 *¾-pound piece of filet of beef (completely trimmed), from the center, seasoned with*
½ *teaspoon salt*
¼ *teaspoon ground black peppercorns*
1½ *cups* demi-glace
1 *tablespoon chopped truffles*
½ *cup good, dry Madeira wine*
Salt and pepper to taste

Brown meat on all sides in 2 tablespoons butter in a sturdy skillet or saucepan (about 5 minutes). Place the skillet in a 425-degree oven for 18 minutes. Remove, set the meat on a platter and let rest or settle in a warm place for at least 10 to 15 minutes before carving. Place the pan with the drippings on top of the stove and cook on medium heat until the fat is entirely separated from the juices, which should solidify on the bottom of the saucepan. This technique is called "pincer" (see technique 62). Set the skillet on the table for 4 to 5 minutes, inclining the skillet so the fat comes to one corner. Pour fat out and add *demi-glace*. Place on stove on low heat and, with a spatula, loosen all the solidified juices as the sauce boils gently.

Place truffles in a clean saucepan with the Madeira wine. Bring to a boil and reduce by half. Strain the *demi-glace* from the skillet directly on top of the Madeira-truffle mixture. Reduce the sauce until it reaches proper consistency and coats the spoon. You should have about 1½ cups of sauce left. Season with salt and pepper if needed and finally swirl in the remaining butter, cut into small pieces. Slice the meat thinly and serve 2 to 3 slices per person with the sauce around the meat and partially covering the slices. The plates should be very warm.

HUNTER CHICKEN (*Poulet Chasseur*)

YIELD: 4 servings

1 tablespoon butter
1 (2¾-pound) chicken, quartered, keep the
    carcass bones for stock
2 tablespoons chopped onion
1 clove garlic, peeled, crushed and chopped fine
½ cup dry white wine
1 large tomato, peeled, seeded and coarsely
    chopped (1 cup)
1 teaspoon tomato paste
1 bay leaf
¼ teaspoon thyme
6 to 8 mushrooms, sliced (1¼ cups, loosely
    packed)
½ cup demi-glace
1 teaspoon salt
¼ teaspoon pepper
½ tablespoon parsley, chopped
½ tablespoon tarragon

Melt the butter in a heavy saucepan and brown the chicken over medium heat for 10 to 12 minutes, starting with the skin side down and turning the chicken after 5 to 6 minutes of browning. Add the chopped onion and sauté for 15 to 20 seconds. Add the garlic, white wine, tomato, tomato paste, bay leaf and thyme. Cover and bring to a boil. Turn the heat down and simmer for 10 minutes. Add the mushrooms. Cover and simmer another 5 minutes. Using a spoon, transfer the chicken and solids to a dish. Add ½ cup *demi-glace* to the drippings, bring to a boil and reduce to 1 cup. Season, add parsley and tarragon, pour on top of the chicken and serve at once.

SAUTÉED VEAL WITH SPINACH (*Veau Sauté aux Epinards*)

YIELD: 4 servings

About 12 veal scallopini, 2 to 3 per person, 1½
    to 2 ounces each, completely trimmed (tech-
    nique 81)
2 10-ounces packages leaf spinach
⅓ stick butter, plus 2 tablespoons
Salt and freshly ground pepper to taste
¾ cup demi-glace

Prepare spinach (technique 40) and brown in 2 tablespoons of "brown butter." (Bring the butter to a dark stage to obtain a nutty taste.) Arrange your spinach on individual serving plates. Melt the ⅓ stick butter in one or two large saucepans and sauté the scallopini in foaming butter for approximately 40 seconds on each side. Be careful that the butter is not too hot because veal dries out very fast. Arrange the veal on top of the spinach. Deglaze the drippings in your saucepan with the *demi-glace*. Stir to melt all the juices and reduce to about ¾ of a cup. Season and pour about 2 tablespoons of the sauce on the scallopini and around the spinach on each plate. Serve immediately.

7. White Stock *(Fond Blanc)*

THE WHITE STOCKS (whether they be beef, chicken, fish, etc.) are cooked in the same way as brown stock (technique 6). They are either reduced or thickened with a *roux* although the use of flour is always a subject of controversy among cooks. The *beurre manié* is used, with excellent results, to correct and adjust sauces in some of the greatest kitchens in France as well as in private homes. When the stocks are thickened with a *roux* they are called *veloutés* (mother sauces). With the addition of cream, a *velouté* becomes a cream sauce and the cream sauce, in turn, takes on different names depending on the garnish. For example, a fish stock becomes a *velouté* of fish after it is thickened with a *roux,* then a cream sauce with the addition of cream, then a *sauce Dugléré* with the addition of sliced mushrooms and tomatoes.

In a first-class restaurant, where portions are cooked individually, the white stocks are often reduced to a *glace,* cream is added and the mixture boiled down until it reaches the proper consistency without the addition of flour. It makes a richer and more expensive sauce than a sauce made from a *velouté.* However, for economy as well as health, home cooks, except on special occasions, do not adhere to the criteria of a starred restaurant and a *velouté* is more the norm than the exception. Both methods have their own place and can be enjoyed at different times. A sauce should be light and if it looks and tastes like glue, the culprit is the cook, not the flour.

10 *pounds beef bones (knuckles, shin and marrow bones are good), or chicken bones or half beef, half chicken*
2 *large onions*
2 to 3 *cloves*
2 *stalks celery*
2 *white leeks, washed*
4 *carrots, peeled*
2 *bay leaves*
½ *teaspoon thyme*
½ *teaspoon peppercorns*
4 to 5 *cloves garlic, unpeeled*
½ *bunch parsley (1 cup loose)*

Cover the bones with cold water. Bring slowly to a boil and skim the solidified blood and albumin that rises to the surface of the water. Boil for 2 hours, skimming regularly. Most of the scum will rise to the top during these first 2 hours.

1. Stick one of the onions with the cloves. Add to the pot along with the celery, leeks, carrots, garlic, seasoning and herbs.

2. To give an amber golden color to the stock (if a *consommé* or aspic is to be made from the stock), cut an unpeeled onion in half and brown in a skillet on medium heat on top of the stove until the cut side turns quite dark. Add to the stock. Boil slowly for 6 hours, or 2 hours if you use only chicken bones. Evaporation will reduce the liquid. Add water periodically to compensate. Strain and reduce to 3 quarts. Refrigerate overnight then discard the fat which will have solidified on top of the stock. Pack in small containers and freeze if not needed.

8. FISH STOCK *(Fond de Poisson)*

YIELD: Approximately 1½ quarts of stock

IN OUR DISCUSSION OF STOCKS (techniques 6 and 7) we have explained that long cooking and reductions enrich and intensify taste. The function of a stock, moreover, is to emphasize and enhance the food it is served with, not conceal it. Paradoxically, the same dish which will improve in taste through long cooking may be destroyed in texture by that same cooking. The way to reconcile these facts is to handle each component of the dish in a different manner. Take a fish for example: The head and bones will be separated from the fillets and cooked into a stock then reduced to obtain an essence of strong reduction. On the other hand, the fillets will be barely cooked and when combined with a sauce made from the reduced stock you will have achieved the perfect balance. The same theory and technique applies to our Crayfish Tails au Gratin (technique 31) where the meat of the tail is cooked very briefly and set aside while a sauce is slowly extracted from the cooking of the carcass, and later combined and served with the tails. It works the same way with meat. Take a *salmis* of pheasant: The bird will be roasted briefly at high temperature and the meat of the breast and thighs set aside, since it is the best and most tender part of the bird. The rest of the pheasant is browned further, seasoned, deglazed with wine and stock, reduced, degreased and reduced again to intensify the taste and obtain a shiny concentrated sauce. This sauce finally gets served with the juicy, lightly cooked meat. The cycle is completed and each part of the pheasant has been utilized to the utmost and to obtain the best possible results. Contrary to other types of stocks, a fish stock cooks fast—35 to 40 minutes will be sufficient to get the nutrients and taste from the bones. A fish-court bouillon is usually done with fish bones, vegetables and water. A *fumet de poisson* consists of the bones stewed in butter, first, with the addition of vegetables, white wine, water and seasoning, and becomes the base of *veloutés* and sauces.

2½ *pounds fish bones (use preferably the bones of flat fish such as sole, flounder, fluke, etc.). If fish heads are used, be sure to remove the gills and wash the bones carefully under cold water or the fish stock will be bitter.*
2 *tablespoons sweet butter*
1 *medium onion, peeled and sliced*
2 to 3 *stalks celery, coarsely chopped*
¼ *cup parsley stems*
1 *leek, cleaned and sliced*
2 *bay leaves*
¼ *teaspoon thyme*

½ *teaspoon black peppercorns, crushed (mignonnette)*
1 *teaspoon salt*
1½ *cups dry white wine*
3 *quarts water*

---

1. Place the butter in a large skillet or kettle and add the fish bones. Steam on medium to high heat for 3 to 4 minutes, stirring with a wooden spatula.

2. When the bones begin to fall apart, add the onion, celery, parsley stems and leek, and mix well. Steam for another 3 to 4 minutes, stirring. Add all the other ingredients to bring to a boil. Boil on high heat for 35 to 40 minutes.

3. Strain through a fine sieve. You can freeze the fish stock and use it for soups, or thicken it with a *roux* so it becomes a *velouté*, as well as reducing it to a glaze and finishing it with cream and butter.

9. Skimming Technique *(Technique de Dégraissage des Fonds)*

1. With the stock boiling gently, remove the scum with a tight, "net-like" skimmer.

2. For an alternate method use a ladle. "Push" the fat to one side of the pot by sliding the round back of the ladle on top of the liquid. Then, using the front of the ladle, scoop the fat off. A third alternative is to let the stock cool refrigerated overnight, then remove the fat which will have solidified on top of the liquid.

10. How to Strain Sauces *(Passage des Sauces au Chinois)*

THERE ARE TWO WAYS to strain stocks or sauces. If it is a clear stock or *demi-glace* or any of its derivatives, care should be taken to not crush the solids into liquid or it would make it cloudy.

If you are straining a thickened sauce such as a *velouté* or *béchamel* or hollandaise, you don't have to worry about "dirtying" the mixture and can rub as much through the mesh as possible. In the photographs that follow we are straining through a fine-meshed chinois (strainer) that is the equivalent of a double or triple layer of cheesecloth or kitchen towel.

To strain a stock very finely you should put it through a colander with larger holes first to remove the larger solids and then when the volume is reduced, work it through a finer-meshed chinois. It is particularly important to put *demi-glace* through a fine strainer to get the glossiness that's possible only when all the impurities have been removed.

If you are buying a chinois, be sure to get one with a guard to protect the mesh from getting dented or crushed.

Any sauce that has to do with eggs and has a tendency to curdle—from the sabayon of the hollandaise to a *crème anglaise*—can be strained through this type of fine mesh to conceal or minimize a problem.

1. To remove solids from a sauce or stock, when it's important to keep the liquid clear, bang the side of the strainer either with the palm of your hand or a wooden spatula to encourage the clear stock to strain through. If you crush the solids into the strained liquid the stock or sauce will become cloudy.

2. For thickened sauces, where clarity is not an issue, use the ladle in a plungerlike, push-lift-push motion, forcing the liquid through the mesh.

11. White Butter Sauce *(Beurre Blanc)*

YIELD: About 2 cups

T HE *beurre blanc* (white butter sauce) is an emulsion of butter with wine and/or vinegar which holds together because it is whipped at a proper temperature. Furthermore the whipping beats air into the mixture, which makes it light and increases its volume. In cooking, the word "emulsion" refers to a fat and liquid or other ingredient bound together into a creamy mixture. Mayonnaise is an example of a cold emulsion and hollandaise an example of a hot emulsion. Other types of emulsions appear throughout this book—in the brill recipe (technique 34), the bass with puff paste (technique 36), the mousseline of scallops (technique 28), the cauliflower with lemon butter (technique 45), as well as the asparagus stew (technique 39). In the latter recipe, butter and water are brought to a strong boil and it is the boiling that causes the mixture to bind. This is somewhat confusing as on the one hand boiling may be necessary to get some sauces into emulsion while on the other hand sauces like hollandaise or *beurre blanc* separate if they're brought near the boil. The explanation for this paradox lies in the proportions of fat to liquid.

If a small quantity of butter is mixed and boiled with a large quantity of liquid, the butter will most likely separate and rise to the surface of the liquid. If the proportion of butter and liquid are more or less equal, a strong boil will bind the ingredients together and make a creamy sauce that will hold together for some time depending on temperature (see technique 39). If there's a lot more butter than liquid (as there is in the *beurre blanc*) too much heat will make the mixture separate. This is an important point to grasp because when understood it allows you to bind liquids into fat or to separate fat from liquid at will. For example, in the roast chicken in aspic (technique 62), the natural juices are boiled down to evaporate the moisture and reduce the mixture to solidified juices and clear fat. As the moisture boils off, the proportion of fat becomes greater and this is why it breaks down and separates from the solidified juices. Once the fat is separated, it can be easily poured off and the solidified juices dissolved with water, then strained and reduced to proper consistency. To reverse the process, let's say that you don't want to remove the fat from your natural juices but the mixture has over-reduced and already separated. If you want to bind the liquid and fat back together again, you just replace some of the evaporated moisture (water), bring to a strong boil and it will bind together again. In the case of a *beurre blanc* or hollandaise which, again, is almost all fat, if the sauce starts to separate, remove from the heat, add a bit of cold water and beat with a whisk to bind together again.

The *beurre blanc* can replace a hollandaise on top of any kind of vegetable and is especially good with shellfish and fish.

1 *cup water*
⅓ *cup finely sliced shallots (3 to 5 according to size)*
½ *teaspoon freshly ground white pepper*
¾ *teaspoon salt*
½ *cup good white wine vinegar*
2 *tablespoons heavy cream*
2½ *to 3 sticks sweet butter at room temperature*

1. In a saucepan, preferably stainless steel, combine the water, shallots, pepper, salt and vinegar. Bring to a boil and simmer slowly for 25 to 30 minutes. If the mixture reduces too much during the cooking, add some water. Push the mixture into a sieve, pushing with a spoon to force the shallots through. You should have approximately ⅓ cup of mixture left. If you have too much, reduce it. If you don't have enough, adjust with a bit of water.

2. Add the cream to the mixture and place on very low heat. The mixture should be lukewarm. Add the butter piece by piece, beating rapidly and strongly with a wire whisk after each addition. Do not worry too much about temperature. Up to one stick of butter can be added to the saucepan and the whole mixture boiled without it breaking down. As the quantity of butter increases, reduce the heat to low. Keep adding the butter and beating until all of it is used.

3. You should have a warm, creamy, smooth-textured sauce. Keep lukewarm in a double boiler or on the side of your stove. As long as it doesn't cool enough to solidify, it can keep. At serving time, place back on the stove and heat while beating with the whisk until hot. Serve immediately.

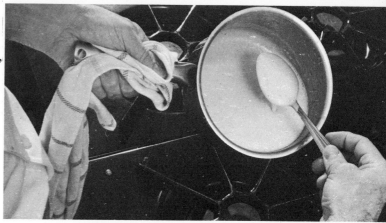

12. Hollandaise Sauce *(Sauce Hollandaise)*

YIELD: About 2 cups

Generally a hollandaise sauce is made with 6 to 7 yolks per pound of butter, but the proportion of eggs to butter can be altered in either direction. If your hollandaise is high in egg yolks it will be less likely to separate but it may become too yolky in taste. If it is high in butter it will be very delicate in taste but very fragile.

Though a hollandaise sauce is usually made with clarified butter (see note), we prefer to use unclarified butter. Because unclarified butter is whole—it has not been separated into its oil and liquid components and the liquid component discarded—it is more watery, and therefore it makes a slightly thinner sauce. However, it gives the sauce a creamier taste and the extra moisture permits it to withstand higher heats than the conventional hollandaise. (The importance of the ratio of liquid to fat in emulsions such as a hollandaise is discussed in the introduction to technique 11.)

Our last modification is that we make the sauce with a base of water, not lemon juice, although lemon juice can certainly be added if desired.

A hollandaise is a base or mother sauce. With the addition of white wine vinegar, shallots and tarragon it becomes a *béarnaise* sauce. If you add tomatoes to the *béarnaise* it becomes a sauce *choron.* If you add *glace de viande* to the *béarnaise* it becomes a *sauce Foyot,* etc. Hollandaise sauce can be made with a browned butter, which gives it a very nutty taste (sauce *Noisette*), or perfumed with orange rind and orange juice to make a sauce *Maltaise,* which is excellent with broccoli, etc.

(*Note:* To clarify butter, place butter in a 180-degree oven until completely melted. Let it rest a few minutes and it will separate into two layers: a milky residue at the bottom and a transparent oily layer at the top. Clarified butter is the oily part. The milky residue is discarded.)

4 *egg yolks*
2 *tablespoons water*
2 *sticks (8 ounces) sweet butter*
Dash of cayenne
Dash of pepper (about ¼ teaspoon)
Salt to taste (about ½ teaspoon)

1. Place the yolks and the water in a saucepan. Beat over low heat for approximately 5 minutes.

2. The mixture should get hot, but if it comes too close to a boil the eggs will scramble. On the other hand, if the mixture is not hot enough it will get foamy, increase in volume, without acquiring much in the way of consistency, stay too thin and separate into foam and liquid. Make sure you "drive" the whisk with the palm of your hand in the corner of the saucepan, since this is where the eggs will have a tendency to scramble.

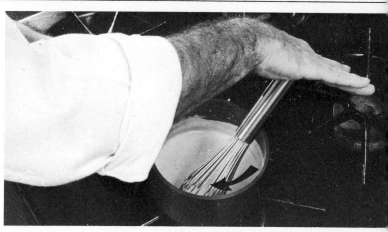

3. When the consistency of the egg yolk mixture is like a *sabayon*, you will notice that between the strokes of the whisk you can see the bottom of the saucepan. This is an indication that it is cooked enough.

4. Start adding the butter, piece by piece, beating between each addition. Keep the hollandaise on a very low heat during the addition of butter. Finally, add a dash of cayenne, a dash of pepper and the salt.

5. The sauce should be creamy, smooth and thick enough to coat eggs, fish or any other food.

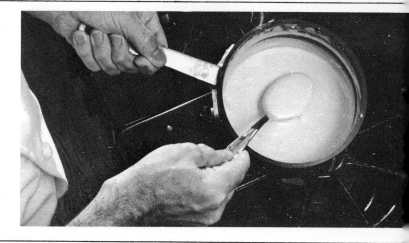

6. If the sauce gets too hot, it will break down. You will recognize this sign if the sauce starts getting oily around the edges. Add 1 tablespoon of cold water or a piece of ice and beat well. The sauce will reconstitute. However, if it completely separates put it together as follows.

7. Place the sauce over heat and stir, so it separates entirely. Incline the pan to one side and let it rest 4 to 5 minutes so that all the oily part comes to the top. Scoop out the oily part and set aside.

8. Place 2 teaspoons of warm water in a clean saucepan or bowl. Take about 1 tablespoon of the thick part of the sauce and add to the water, whisking it in bit by bit. Add more, whisk until smooth, and more again, continuing the process until you have reclaimed all of the thick part.

9. When all the thick part is back together, start adding the oily part, beating as if you were making the sauce again from the start. If the sauce has gotten very hot and some parts have scrambled a bit, put through a fine strainer to eliminate (as best you can) the "scrambled" appearance.

13. How to Prepare Marrow
(Préparation de la Moëlle)

Beef marrow is often used in French cooking. It is removed from the bone, poached and served on toast or served with a sauce, as we will here. It is sometimes used in place of butter in dumplings or quenelles. When the marrow is removed from the bone it is reddish and bloody. It should be placed in cold water in the refrigerator for at least a day and the water should be changed a couple of times to get rid of the bloody part of the marrow and make it white and firm. If the marrow is not soaked in water it will turn dark during cooking instead of being white.

1. Order a large marrow bone from your butcher and have it cut with a saw above or under the knuckles so as to have just the part in between, where most of the marrow lies. Use a hammer to break the bone. Be sure to do it on a butcher block or other heavy sturdy surface or else the vibration will cause the hammer to bounce.

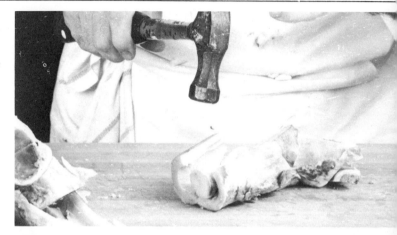

2. When the bone is broken open, use a small knife to remove the marrow, keeping the pieces as large as possible. Be careful not to cut yourself on the the very sharp pieces of bone. Place the marrow under cold water for about an hour, then in a bowl in water in the refrigerator, if possible overnight.

3. Slice the marrow in approximately ⅜-inch-thick pieces. Bring a pot of salted water to a boil and drop the marrow in it. Reduce the heat and simmer very gently for 4 to 5 minutes until the marrow becomes opaque, which indicates that it has been cooked throughout.

4. Using a slotted spoon, remove the pieces of marrow from the pot (they will be floating on top), and place in warm, cooked, artichoke bottoms.

5. Cover the artichokes and the marrow with the red wine sauce made from the recipe on page 23.

14. Eggs with Black Butter (Oeufs au Beurre Noir)

YIELD: 1 serving

HERE ARE a few different ways of preparing eggs. The egg may well be the most versatile of foods. It can be prepared at least one hundred different ways. Eggs in aspic, for example (page 97 in *La Technique*), make a very nice first course for an elegant dinner. The skillet eggs pictured below are served with a black butter that adds a special nuttiness to the eggs. Black butter is also served with poached brains, poached fish, etc.

1 *teaspoon sweet butter, plus 1 tablespoon*
2 *large fresh eggs*
Dash of salt
Dash of freshly ground white pepper
1 *teaspoon drained capers*
About 1 teaspoon red or white wine vinegar

1. A clever way to control the flow of vinegar or soy sauce or other liquid seasoning and to allow you quick access without screwing bottle tops on and off all the time is to store the seasoning in a wine bottle topped with a cork "pour spout." To make the spout, remove a strip on each side of the cork and then replace the cork on the bottle. To use the liquid (we are using vinegar here to make the black butter), shake the bottle directly over the bowl or skillet.

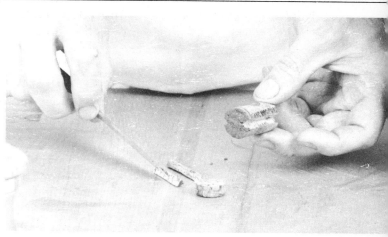

2. Break the eggs in a saucer. Melt 1 teaspoon of butter in a skillet and when it is foaming lightly, slide the eggs into the skillet. Cook for approximately 1 minute on very low heat. The edges of the whites should not curl. At the last moment you can cover the eggs with a lid for 10 to 15 seconds, to cook the top slightly and give them a shine. (Eggs cooked this way are often called "mirror eggs.") Slide the eggs onto a plate and sprinkle them lightly with salt, pepper and the capers.

3. Add the 1 tablespoon of butter to the skillet and cook until it turns dark brown and is smoking. Pour directly on top of the eggs. Add the vinegar to the hot skillet, swirl around to warm it up and pour the few drops left on top of the eggs. Serve immediately.

15. Eggs "Cocotte" with Cream (Oeufs Cocotte Bressane)

YIELD: 6 servings

THESE EGGS are very easy to make. Unfortunately they are not served too often. The eggs are cooked in small soufflé molds or ramekins and eaten as a first course for dinner or for a light breakfast or brunch.

6 large eggs, very fresh
Salt
Pepper
6 tablespoons heavy cream

1. Use small ramekins or soufflé molds, no more than ½ cup in size. Butter the molds and sprinkle salt and pepper in the bottom.

2. Break an egg into each ramekin.

3. Place the ramekins in a skillet with tepid water around (a *bain-marie*) and cover. Place on top of the stove and let the water boil for approximately 1 to 1½ minutes. Uncover. The eggs should be barely set and still soft in the center.

4. Note that the eggs are shiny and glazed on top. Remove from the *bain-marie* and serve garnished or plain. With a bit of heavy cream on top, they are called eggs Bressane; with peas, they will become eggs Clamard, etc.

5. Sometimes the garnish is placed in the bottom of the mold and the egg is broken directly on top. In our case, put 1 tablespoon of heavy cream in the bottom of the mold, break the egg on top and cook, covered, as indicated above. The time of cooking will have to be increased by at least 30 seconds to a minute.

16. Scrambled Eggs *(Oeufs Brouillés)*

YIELD: 2 to 3 servings

IN CLASSIC FRENCH COOKING, the scrambled eggs are whisked into a very smooth purée and finished with cream and butter. They can be cooked in a double boiler using a wooden spatula, or on a low to medium heat using a whisk. Use a heavy, sturdy saucepan to obtain even heat. The eggs can be garnished with a bit of brown sauce or with a sauce *Périgueux* (a brown sauce with chopped truffles) as we have done here, or a fresh purée of tomatoes and grated Parmesan cheese, or peas, or sautéed chicken livers, etc. They can also be served plain. The eggs acquire a different name with each different garnish. They can be served as a first course, as well as for breakfast or lunch.

5 *large eggs, very fresh*
1 *tablespoon, plus ½ tablespoon sweet butter*
Salt and freshly ground white pepper to taste
1 *tablespoon heavy cream*

1. Break the eggs in a bowl and beat with a whisk. (Reserve the nicest half shells if you will be using them in your presentation.) Add the salt and pepper. Melt 1 tablespoon of butter in a large saucepan and add the eggs.

2. Cook on low heat, stirring all the time to mix well. Be sure to move the whisk in the corners of the saucepan where the eggs tend to set first. As soon as they begin to hold together but are still creamy, remove from the heat. Keep mixing. Remember that the eggs will continue to cook for a while after they are removed from the heat. Beat in 1 tablespoon of heavy cream and ½ tablespoon of sweet butter in pieces until smooth. Taste for seasonings and add salt and pepper if needed.

3. Spoon eggs onto individual plates, reserving enough to fill the egg shells. Fill the shells, embed in the center and garnish with a sauce *Périgueux*.

17. Deep-Fried Eggs *(Oeufs Frits Américaine)*

YIELD: 3 servings

THIS IS ANOTHER UNCOMMON WAY to prepare eggs. Instead of poaching them in water, we poach them in oil. The center comes out runny and soft, just like regular poached eggs. Only one egg can be done at a time, and it must be cooked very fast so that the white is wrapped around the yolk and nicely browned. Deep-fried eggs are usually served with bacon and fried tomatoes for lunch.

2½ to 3 cups vegetable oil
6 large eggs, very fresh

1. Place the oil in a 2-inch-deep non-stick skillet. (There should be at least 1½ inches of oil so the eggs can be immersed.) Heat to 360 degrees and warm two wooden spatulas in it (to prevent the eggs from sticking to the spatulas). Break one egg at a time into the oil, or break in a cup and slide it into the oil if you are afraid of being splashed with hot oil. Then, use the two spatulas to gather the egg white around the yolk.

2. "Squeeze" the egg slightly (between the spatulas, against the side of the skillet) for a few seconds to keep the egg white contained—so it doesn't spread as it cooks. If the egg sticks to one spatula, scrape it off with the other spatula. Turn the egg in the oil and cook it approximately 1 to 1½ minutes altogether.

3. Remove the egg with a slotted spoon, drain on paper towels and serve immediately. When the egg is taken out of the oil it will be nicely puffed. If kept a few minutes, it will deflate slightly.

4. Serve on toast with a slice of fried tomato and one or two slices of bacon. Like the preceding egg recipes (technique 15), this dish can be served with a variety of garnishes and with each different garnish, it changes its name.

18. Hard-Boiled Eggs Clown-style
(Oeufs Durs en Clown)

YIELD: 6 servings

BEFORE YOU HARD-BOIL EGGS, make sure they are not cracked. Take two eggs and tap them gently close to your ear. The sound should be crystal clear. If one of the shells is slightly broken, even if the crack is invisible, it will sound cracked, and if placed in hot water this way, the egg white will seep out.

Place the eggs in a sieve and lower into boiling water or place the eggs in a saucepan and pour boiling water on top. Bring to a boil and simmer for 11 to 12 minutes. Immediately run the eggs under cold water until cold. Crack the shells on the side of the sink and "roll" gently on a hard surface so the shell gets cracked all around. Peel under cold water so the water runs between the egg and the membrane (between the egg and the shell). If the eggs are not cooled immediately, the yolk becomes greenish and acidic.

This plain hard-boiled egg preparation is nice for children's parties, easy to prepare in advance and fun. It can be served with the peppery dressing we describe, or with a simple mayonnaise or oil and vinegar dressing.

Eggs

6 *to* 8 *hard-boiled eggs*
1 *cucumber*
1 *slice boiled ham*
A few black olives
1 *tomato*

Dressing

1 *can (2 ounces) flat anchovy fillets with oil, cut into small pieces*
2 *tablespoons capers*

1 *hard-boiled egg, diced, and the trimmings of the other eggs*
¾ *cup finely diced boiled ham*
⅓ *cup coarsely chopped black olives, preferably the oiled, cured type*
¾ *cup olive oil, preferably virgin*
About ⅓ *cup lemon juice*
¾ *teaspoon salt*
½ *teaspoon freshly ground black pepper*
⅓ *cup diced red peppers*

Combine all the dressing ingredients and arrange in a flat serving dish.

1. Trim the eggs on both sides.

2. Cut a "nose" in the middle of the egg by outlining a "triangle" and lifting it from the egg on one side. Make two little holes on each side of the nose for eyes, and place a piece of black olive in them.

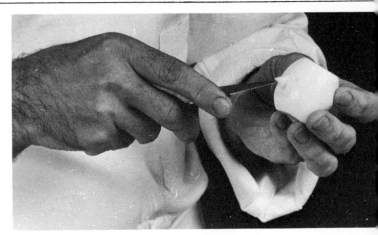

3. Make an opening to simulate the mouth and slide a piece of boiled ham in it, for the tongue. Cut the cucumber in thin slices and place on top to simulate the brim of a hat.

4. Slice a tomato in 6 to 8 ¼-inch slices. Place the tomato slices on top of the dressing as a base for the eggs. Top with the eggs and finish the hat with olive halves. Serve.

19. Mushroom Fish *(Champignon Sculpté en Poissons)*

1. Start with a large mushroom that's very firm and very white. Cut the top of the cap off the mushroom. The newly formed surface will become the background for the fish. Starting at the center of the mushroom, make 3 curved cuts at spaced intervals. These will be one side of the fish.

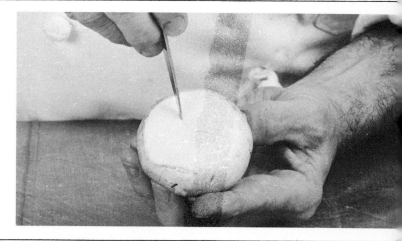

2. Then, starting at the edge of the mushroom, make 3 corresponding cuts to form 3 ovals. Each oval represents the body of a fish, minus the tail.

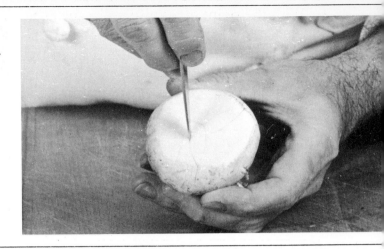

3. Pretending that the fish are interwoven, "draw" a tail at the end of each body.

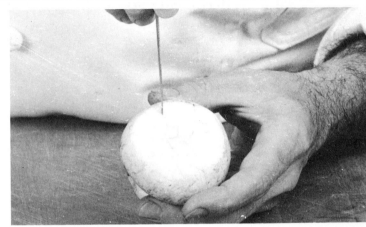

4. To set the fish in relief—to make them raised—you have to remove a thin layer (⅛ inch or less deep) of mushroom all around them. Slide your knife into the mushroom, in between each cut, and gently lift out the pieces of mushroom. Work slowly all around the mushroom until the fish are in relief.

5. If you want to make a more elaborate carving, cut a small triangle between each fish and remove the piece of mushroom. Within that triangle, cut another triangle and remove the piece of mushroom. Then, within the second triangle, make a third one and so forth, making a sort of triangular steps which form designs in all the free spaces around the fish.

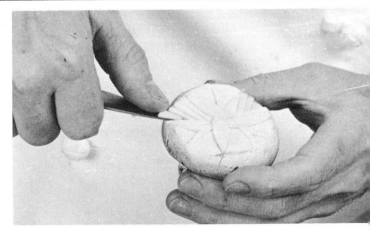

6. With the point of a knife make the eyes, the gills and the scales, then trim the mushroom around.

7. Slice the decorated part off the cap, coat with lemon juice to keep it white or poach in a mixture of lemon juice and water for a few seconds, and use to garnish the top of a fish dish or a cold salad.

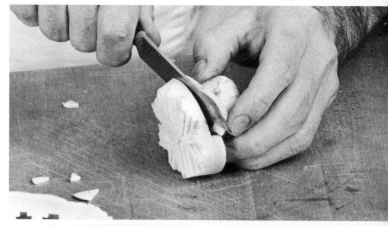

20. Cucumber Turtles *(Tortues en Concombre)*

CUCUMBER TURTLES ARE A FUN garnish for cold fish, cold salads, cold roasts, etc. Slice the cucumber lengthwise on both sides, discarding the center part with the seeds. Use only the fleshy part of the skin. Cut into chunks about 3 inches long.

1. With the point of a knife, start outlining a turtle on the green part of the cucumber.

2. Carve the turtle out; the head like a lozenge, the four legs and the small tail.

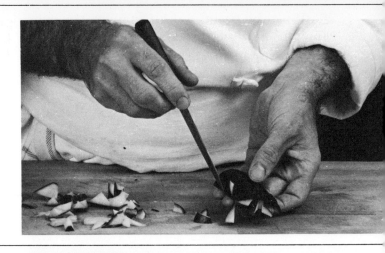

3. Mark the eyes on the head, score a crisscross design on the back and carve out the toes.

21. Apple Swans *(Cygnes en Pommes)*

APPLE SWANS ARE EASY to make and lovely to decorate a buffet, or a cold aspic dish or simply as a centerpiece, by arranging several of them in the center of a table.

1. Take a large apple (greening, red delicious, etc.) and cut about a ½-inch slice off one side of the apple.

2. Place the slice flat side down and, using a small pointed knife, "draw" a head and neck in one piece the full length of the apple slice. Carve it out and set it aside.

3. The head piece can be done in a multitude of ways, with the head looking down or up. Use your imagination and try to make the most out of the shape and thickness of the apple slice.

4. With the point of a knife, "drill" a small hole on one side of the apple to hold the neck in place. Insert the neck and adjust until the neck fits snugly. Then set the neck aside, so it does not get in the way while you work on the wings and tail.

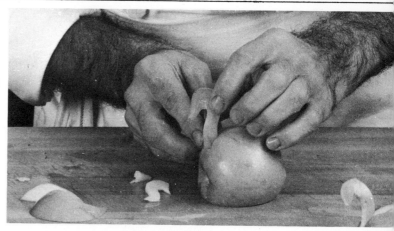

5. On one side of the apple cut wedges by first holding the knife vertically and slicing down and then holding it horizontally and slicing across.

6. You should remove approximately 5 wedges for each wing, keeping them as thin as possible (as the wedges get larger they become more difficult to cut out). Repeat the same procedure on the other side of the apple to make the other wing.

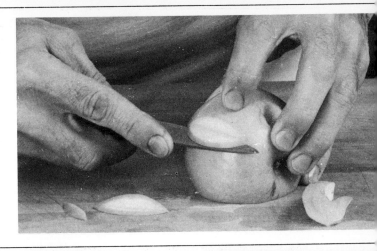

7. After the two sides have been carved for the wings, cut the back of the "swan" to make the tail. Four wedges are enough for the tail.

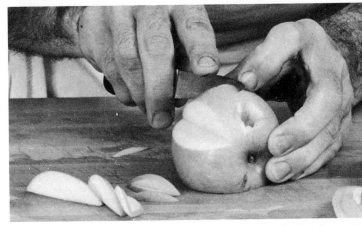

8. Now that all the cutting is done, the wedges are put back together to simulate the tail and the wings. Stagger the wedges at spaced intervals so it fans out. You will notice that the wedges stick to one another nicely.

9. Repeat the process with both wings and place the head on the swan. Sprinkle the whole apple with lemon juice to keep it from discoloring.

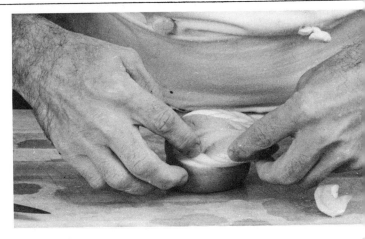

10. The "swans" are delicate and make an elegant decoration. Alternate green, yellow and red apples.

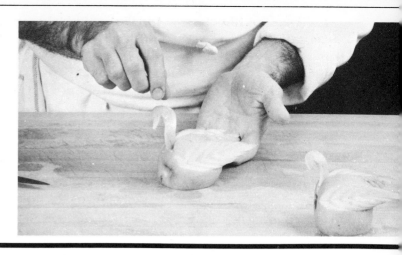

22. Vegetable Flowers *(Fleurs en Légumes)*

To dress up a buffet, there is nothing as colorful and festive as a bunch of flowers made of vegetables. They are fun to make and rewarding—follow the instructions below, but extend the idea and create on your own. Use your imagination since the possibilities of shape and color are practically endless. In the next technique we will show how to make vegetable vases to hold such flowers.

1. Peel a carrot. With this carrot, we will first make several flowers similar to a daisy. With the point of a knife, cut petals from the tip of the carrot. Cut into the carrot on an angle but don't cut through as you want the petals attached. Rotate the carrot as you carve so the tip of the carrot comes to a point as you cut. Be sure not to separate each petal.

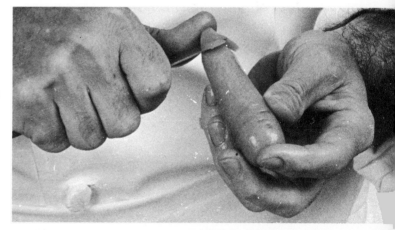

2. Rock the "flower" back and forth to gently separate it from the carrot in one piece.

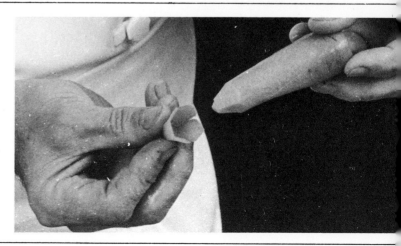

3. Place the flowers in a bowl of cold water to keep them crisp and bright until ready to use. Then finish with a little piece of black olive in the center of one flower, a caper in the center of another one and a piece of pimiento in the center of a third.

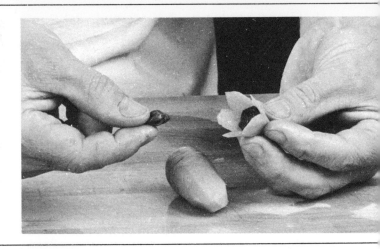

4. Proceed the same way with radishes. Choose oval radishes, if possible, and start cutting the petals.

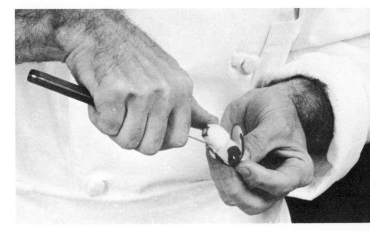

5. Place half a small olive upside down in the center of the radish. (A piece of red tomato or pimiento or green pepper can replace the olive for a different flower.)

6. Slice a piece of peeled carrot very thinly, without separating the slices. Turn the carrot so that all the slices are stacked one on top of the other. Cut into thin strips, which are still held by the core.

7. The carrot is now cut into thin strips held together at one end. Place in cold water overnight or for a few hours—the strips of carrot will curl and the "flower" will open up. Proceed as shown in the picture.

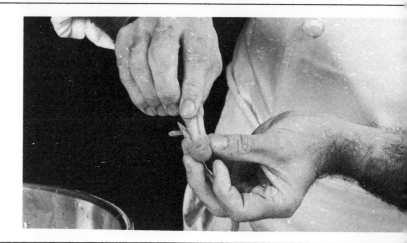

8. Peel a white onion but leave the root on. Start cutting it into slices held together by the root end.

9. Slice the onion across so all the slices are cut into strips held together by the root. Place in ice water.

10. On the right you have an onion that's completely cut and ready for immersion in ice water. On the left is an onion which has been soaked in ice water for a few hours.

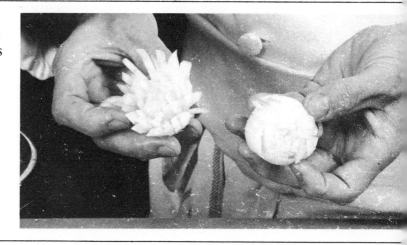

11. Here is a variety of flowers made with radishes. The one being worked on is made the same way as the carrot and the onion in steps 7 to 9.

12. Taking an olive, green or black with the pit in it, insert your knife through the skin and cut around the pit to loosen. Remove the pit so you have a hollow receptacle.

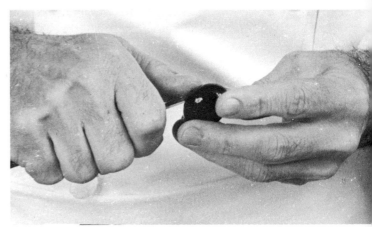

13. Cut the root of a scallion. Trim away the green. Insert your knife three quarters of the way down through the stem of the scallion and split it open. Turn it around. Keep pushing your knife through and pulling it up to split the scallion into fine strips.

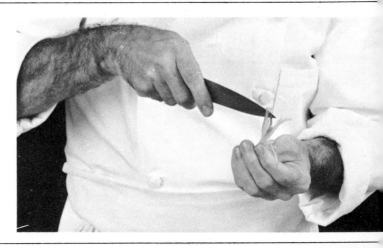

14. Scallions after having been crisped in ice water for a few hours.

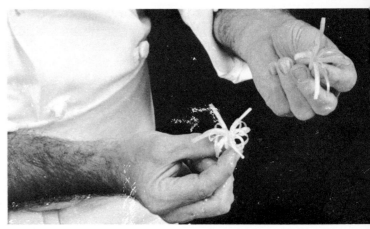

15. Place the crisped scallion into the cavity of an olive to make another flower.

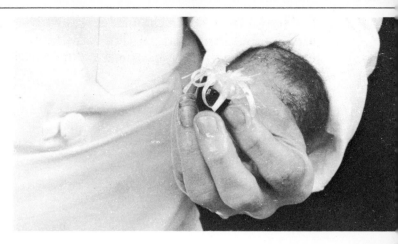

16. Slice a yellow turnip into very thin strips; roll a slice and fold it in half.

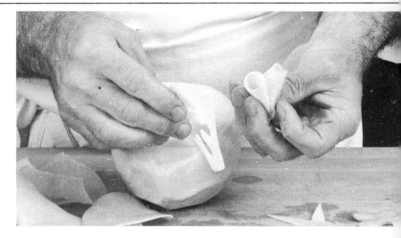

17. Hold the folded slice of turnip with a toothpick and insert a piece of feathered red pimiento, carrot or radish in the two holes. This forms another flower.

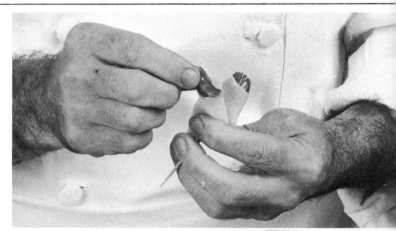

18. Using a vegetable peeler, make thin carrot slices. Stack them together and shred both ends.

19. Overlap several slices to form a large, shaggy, open flower. Stick half a radish, a piece of cherry tomato or a piece of olive in the center.

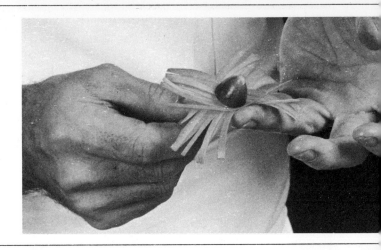

20. To form stems for your flowers, use thin pieces of wood such as long matches or pieces of wire cut from coat hangers. Use the green of scallions to shield and dress the wires. Insert the wire in the hollow of the scallion.

21. Once the wire is dressed, stick a cut radish on top or another flower. The green of the scallion should be longer than the metal stem so it can be turned under and around the bottom of the flower to form the chalice. Remember that these are only a few examples of the flowers that can be made with vegetables. Use your imagination to create new flowers—try working with lemon peel, pimiento, leeks, asparagus, etc. It is important that the flowers be kept in ice water for a few hours so they crisp into the right shape.

23. Flower Vases with Squash
(Vases de Fleurs en Courges)

DIFFERENT TYPES OF VASES can be made from different kinds of squash. Simply hollow them out and decorate by feel. These hollowed squash can be used not just for vases, but to serve fruit salads in, vegetable salads, ice cream, etc. They can even be used as goblets to serve punch.

1. Cut out a duck from a piece of paper. Using the duck as a pattern, sketch its shape all the way around the squash with the point of a knife.

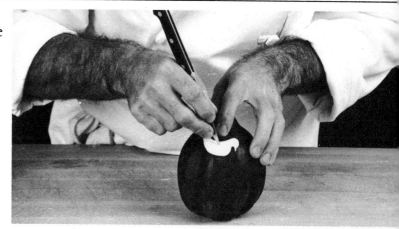

2. Cut out strips to outline the ducks. Carve out thin lines at the tail of the duck to simulate the feathers. Draw lines under the duck to imitate water. Cut a hat off the squash and outline a couple of lines to form a design near the opening. Hollow the squash and set it aside until ready to use (cover it lightly with plastic wrap and refrigerate it to prevent it from drying out).

3. For another vase, use a butternut squash. Cut the cap off and with the point of your knife, outline long stems, flowers and leaves. Decorate all around the squash. Empty the squash if it is to be used as a receptacle. Leave the inside flesh if it is to be used as a vase.

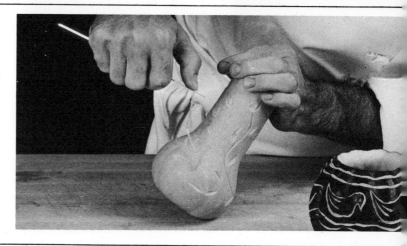

4. With another acorn squash, make a basket. Cut away one side. Now cut away the other side in the same manner to form a center handle.

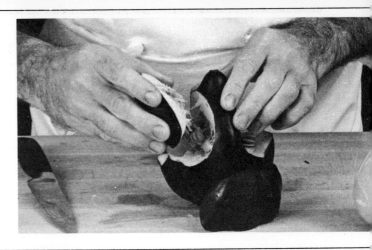

5. Using a spoon, remove the seeds from the inside of the squash. With a small, sharp knife, cut the flesh off the handle to make it very thin. Cut the flesh from the inside of the basket in the same manner so the squash is hollowed and thin all around.

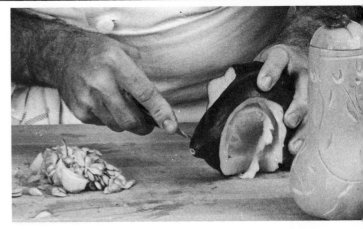

6. Cut away a decorative strip next to the edge of the basket to outline it. You can leave it plain or continue decorating.

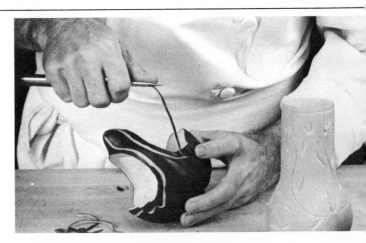

7. Three types of baskets which can be used to hold vegetables.

Fish and Shellfish

24. How to Prepare Shrimp
(Préparation des Crevettes)

SHRIMP (in the United States this refers usually to shrimp tails) are available in different sizes and prices. The large ones are very expensive. The smaller the shrimp, the less expensive they usually are. They always have the best flavor bought fresh, unshelled. For a shrimp cocktail, simply poach the shrimp with their shells in a vegetable stock (boiled water, carrots, onions, thyme, bay leaf, parsley, celery and black peppercorns) for about 10 minutes. Drop the shrimp into the boiling stock. Cover, barely bring back to a boil, then remove from the heat. Allow the shrimp to cool in the liquid where they will take on the flavor of the stock. The stock can be re-used to make a *consommé* of shrimp or a soup. To peel shrimp, hold from underneath, grab the appendage on one side of the tail, break it and pull it out. The shell should come out in sections, uncurling from around the flesh. Remove all the shell and keep only the tail part attached—if you want to present them this way for decorative purposes. What follows are a few different ways of preparing shrimp.

TO BUTTERFLY SHRIMP

1. To butterfly shrimp, put it flat on the table and cut the thick part of it with a knife to split it open. Do not cut through completely. At that point you may notice the intestinal tract which runs like a vein along the back of the shrimp. Its presence is not too important in a small shrimp, but in large ones it imparts a bitter taste and therefore should be removed. Sometimes shrimp have almost no intestinal tract and are very clean.

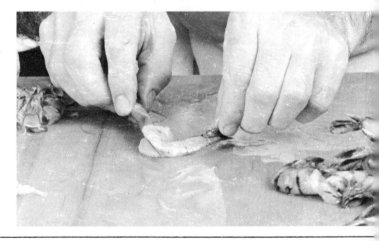

SHRIMP WITH GARLIC *(Crevettes à l'Aïl)*

2. One attractive way to serve shrimp is to arrange them in a gratin dish alongside one another with their tails sticking up. During cooking the shrimp stiffen and retain that position. They can be sprinkled lightly with salt and pepper and covered with snail butter (see technique 25). They can also be sprinkled with a few drops of lemon juice, butter, salt and pepper and cooked in a 425-degree oven for 4 to 6 minutes. Serve as a first course or main course for lunch.

SHRIMP SALAD (Salade de Crevettes)

1 pound fresh shrimp, shelled (25 to 30 to the pound)
½ pound onions, peeled and very thinly sliced (about 2 cups loose)
2 tablespoons good red wine vinegar
1½ teaspoons salt
1 teaspoon freshly ground white pepper

½ teaspoon grated orange rind
1 cup Italian parsley, coarsely chopped
½ cup good olive oil, preferably virgin

3. Place all the ingredients for the shrimp salad, except the orange rind, parsley and oil, into a large skillet. Cook for 2 to 3 minutes on medium heat, stirring with a wooden spatula. The mixture should not even reach a complete boil. As soon as the shrimp stiffen and whiten, remove from the heat and pour the whole mixture into a bowl. Add the rest of the ingredients, toss all together and let it cool and marinate for at least 1 hour before serving. The shrimp should be served at room temperature as a first course with toast or regular bread.

25. Shrimp Bread (Pain aux Crevettes)

YIELD: 6 to 8 servings

THE COMBINATION of bread, butter, shellfish, garlic and parsley is so good, why not put them all together—which is what we do here—for an attractive and unusual first course. We used a 1-pound *pain de ménage* type bread (technique 84), but other types of bread can certainly be used. In fact, individual rolls can be stuffed with 6 to 8 shrimp and served one per person. Scallops, crabmeat, snails, etc., can be substituted for the shrimp.

1 pound round bread (see technique 84)
3 large cloves garlic, peeled
½ cup loose parsley leaves
1 stick (4 ounces) sweet butter, softened
2 teaspoons Ricard or Pernod or any other anise-flavored apéritif
1 teaspoon salt
½ teaspoon finely ground black pepper

½ pound fresh shrimp, peeled, about 25 to 30 to the pound (see technique 24)
Extra salt and pepper to taste

1. Remove the top of the bread and hollow it out. Chop the inside pieces in a food processor until finely ground. Set aside. Crush the garlic and chop it finely by hand or in the food processor along with the parsley. Add the butter, Ricard, salt and pepper and blend again until smooth.

2. Arrange a layer of shrimp in the bottom of the bread. Sprinkle lightly with salt and pepper. Spread one third of the butter mixture on top, then a layer of bread crumbs. Arrange what is left of the shrimp, salt and pepper, another third of the butter and the remaining bread crumbs. Dot the top with the remaining butter and bake in a 400-degree oven for 25 to 30 minutes, without the lid. It should be nicely brown on the top, cooked and very hot inside. The juice from the shrimp will be absorbed by the bread crumbs and the bread shell. Place the lid on the bread for the last 5 minutes to heat it up. Serve at the table cut into wedges.

26. Stuffed Squid *(Calamars Farcis)*

YIELD: 4 servings

SQUID IS INEXPENSIVE, high in protein, low in calories and easily obtainable in the United States. Like a lot of other shellfish it is tough only if over-cooked. It should be either cooked very briefly or braised a long time in order to be tender. It's the in-between cooking that makes it as hard as rubber. The Basques as well as the Spaniards prepare calamari or squid using the ink that is contained in a bag inside the tentacles. The ink is not needed in our recipe. In fact, in the United States the small saclike appendage full of ink is sometimes removed before the squid reaches the marketplace. For our recipe, we used small tender squid about 6 inches long. After being cleaned as explained in the technique below, squid can be sliced, breaded and deep-fried or sautéed briefly, or blanched and marinated in oil, lemon or lime juice and served partially raw as a *seviche*.

Stuffing	**Sauce**
8 *squid (about 1¾ to 2 pounds, not trimmed or cleaned)*	2 *small ripe tomatoes, peeled, seeded and coarsely chopped (¾ cup)*
2 *tablespoons sweet butter*	½ *cup finely chopped onions*
⅓ *cup finely chopped onion*	3 to 4 *cloves garlic, peeled, crushed and chopped (1 teaspoon)*
2 *cloves garlic, peeled, crushed and chopped fine (½ teaspoon)*	1 *cup dry white wine*
1 *cup finely chopped mushrooms*	½ *teaspoon dried saffron pistils (optional)*
1 *teaspoon salt*	
¼ *teaspoon pepper*	
1 *cup fresh bread crumbs*	

1. Separate the head and the tentacles from the body of the squid by pulling. Remove the purplish skin and fins from the central body—also by pulling. They should come off easily. Turn the saclike body inside out to wash it. You will notice that there is a soft bone or plasticlike piece, called the "pan," which you should also discard. Wash well and turn the body back into its original shape.

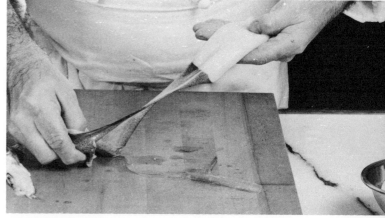

2. Cut the beak and head from the tentacles (the beak will pop out when you apply pressure to the head). Keep only the tentacles.

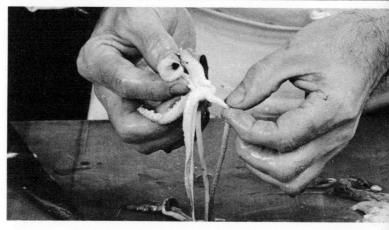

3. Coarsely chop the tentacles. To prepare the stuffing, sauté the onions in butter for about 1 minute. Add garlic, mushrooms and chopped tentacles and fins. Continue cooking for 2 to 3 minutes until the mixture of squid stiffens and the juices are reduced almost completely. Add the salt and pepper and allow to cool slightly. Add bread crumbs and toss lightly.

4. Place the stuffing into a pastry bag without any tube and stuff the bodies of the squid. Sprinkle the tomatoes, onion and garlic in the bottom of a large saucepan and arrange the stuffed squid on top. Place the stuffed squid one against the other so that the closed end or side of a squid is pushed against the open side of the next squid to block the opening and keep the stuffing from falling out while the squid cooks. Sprinkle with the white wine and saffron. Cover the squid with a piece of buttered parchment paper, place a cover on top and bring to barely a simmer on top of the stove (about 180 degrees). If the temperature is too high the squid will burst. It must not boil. Cook in this manner for approximately 15 to 20 minutes.

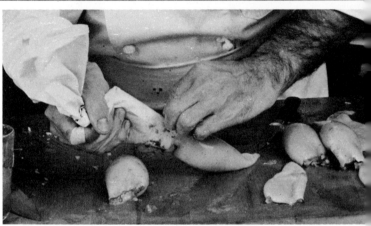

5. Remove the squid and arrange on a gratin dish or serving platter. Cover with the piece of parchment paper and set aside. Reduce the juices in the pan on top of the stove to about 1¼ cups. Taste and add salt and pepper if needed. Be sure to pour the juices that have accumulated in the gratin dish back into your sauce otherwise your sauce will be too thick.

6. Pour the reduced sauce on top of the stuffed squid, sprinkle with parsley and serve immediately.

27. Frog's Legs *(Cuisses de Grenouilles)*

YIELD: 2 to 3 servings

I N FRANCE, the green frog is commonly used and is about half the size of the bull frog that we use in the United States. The bull frogs are quite large and tender when young. The meat is usually pale beige and plump. If you come across darker-colored meat or stringy-looking flesh, it is likely that the frog is older and will be tough. Frog's legs are usually served as a first course for a dinner or as a main course at lunch. Two pairs of legs should be enough for a first course and 3 to 4 for a main course, depending on their size. Serve with plain boiled potatoes. Photographs 1 and 2 explain how to sauté frog's legs. Picture 3 illustrates two ways—one with *demi-glace* and the other with stewed tomatoes—to serve frog's legs once they have been sautéed. Notice that both recipes are finished with a garlic butter, photograph 3.

6 *pairs of frog's legs (approximately 1 pound), washed and dried*
1 *teaspoon salt*
¼ *teaspoon freshly ground white pepper*
½ *cup milk*
½ *cup flour*
1 *tablespoon vegetable oil*
2 *tablespoons sweet butter*
¾ *cup stewed tomatoes (make half of the sauce recipe in technique 66, omit the olive) or ½ cup demi-glace (technique 6)*
½ *stick sweet butter*

2 *tablespoons finely chopped parsley*
2 to 3 *cloves garlic, peeled, crushed and finely chopped (1 teaspoon)*

1. Cross the frog's legs by inserting one leg through the calf muscle of the other. Sometimes the hole is there, sometimes it isn't. You may have to cut between the muscle and the bone of one leg to be able to insert the other one. Put the legs in a dish, and add the salt, pepper and milk and let sit for ½ hour if possible.

2. Place about ½ cup flour in a plastic bag. Drain the frog's legs from the milk, place them in the bag and shake vigorously. Pat the frog's legs gently to remove excess flour. For 6 pairs of frog's legs, place the oil and the 2 tablespoons of butter in a large skillet. Heat until the mixture is foaming and place the frog's legs flat in the skillet. They should not overlap. Cook over medium to low heat approximately 6 minutes on each side for large legs and a bit less for smaller legs. They should be browned on each side. Arrange on a serving dish.

3. Put the stewed tomatoes in the center of the serving dish (round platter in photograph) or pour ½ cup hot *demi-glace* around the legs (gratin dish in photograph). Melt ½ stick butter in a clean skillet and when it foams add the parsley and garlic. Cook for 5 to 10 seconds, shaking the pan. Spoon over the frog's legs.

28. Mousseline of Scallops with White Butter *(Mousseline de Coquilles Saint-Jacques au Beurre Blanc)*

YIELD: 6 to 8 servings

THE *mousseline* or "zéphyr" (named after the sweet, light wind of Greek mythology) is the lightest of those mousse-type concoctions made with fish, shellfish or meat. The *mousseline* is made with scallops and whipped cream, only. The ingredients have to be fresh and of good quality for the dish to work. Even though it is a sophisticated dish it is economical because ¾ pound of scallops will feed 8 people as a main course and approximately 12 people for a first course. The *mousseline* cooks in a water bath in an oven at fairly low temperature so the mixture doesn't expand while cooking and keeps a tight texture. (The same *mousseline,* cooked on a cookie sheet in the oven, puffs up like a soufflé and can be served as such.) It can also be cooked ahead, cooled off and reheated gently in hot water. In fact, pre-poached *mousseline* can be placed cold in a 400-degree oven and will puff like a soufflé in a few minutes. The *mousseline* can be made in a large soufflé mold as well as a savarin mold, or, as in our recipe, in small baba molds about ¾ cup each. If the scallops have been frozen, thaw slowly under refrigeration to lose the least possible amount of moisture.

The *mousseline* is served as a first course for an elegant dinner or as a main course for brunch or a light dinner accompanied by poached cucumbers or a purée of mushrooms.

Mousseline

¾ pound cleaned sea scallops
½ teaspoon salt
¼ teaspoon freshly ground white pepper
Pinch of curry powder
½ cup heavy cream
1 cup heavy cream, softly beaten

1. In Europe scallops usually have a roe or tongue left on top, which is bright orange (coral) and considered a great delicacy. In the United States, only the large center muscle is served. On that large center muscle there is a small sinew on one side which should be removed when they are to be sautéed briefly or eaten raw in a seviche. In our particular recipe, since the scallops are ground, the piece of sinew is left on.

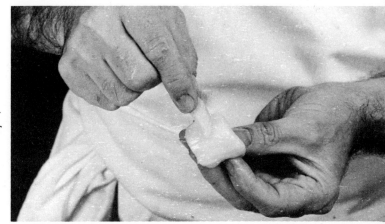

2. Butter the molds heavily and decorate as shown with blanched green of leek. (You can also use carrots, sliced thin and blanched, or a slice of truffle. Both the mousseline and the sauce are white so the addition of a touch of color makes the dish attractive.) Place the scallops in a food processor with the salt, pepper and curry powder. Purée the scallops for 10 to 15 seconds. Stop the motor and scrape the pieces that stick to the sides of the bowl back into the purée. Purée again for 5 to 10 seconds. Add the ½ cup heavy cream, and blend for another 10 to 15 seconds until smooth. Beat the 1 cup of heavy cream until it holds a soft peak. Do not overwhip the cream or the *mousseline* will bleed and may break down. Gently whisk the scallop purée into the whipped cream.

3. If you have a lot of molds, fill them up with a pastry bag. Otherwise, place a heaping tablespoon in each mold and bang the bottom of the mold on a pot holder or folded towel so the mixture packs well and air pockets are removed.

4. Finish filling the molds, banging them again on the table. Smooth off the top with a spatula. Arrange the molds in a roasting pan.

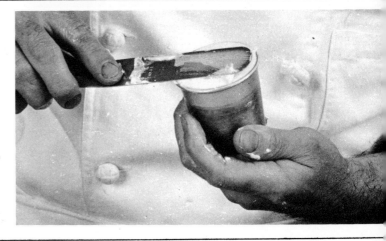

5. Cut a rectangular piece of parchment paper to fit the top of the pan. Butter half of the piece, fold the other half on top and open so the whole piece of paper is coated.

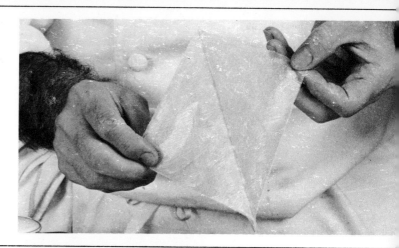

6. Place the paper on top of your molds. Fill the roasting pan with tepid water and place in a 350-degree oven for 15 to 20 minutes. If the *mousselines* raise about ¼ inch above the mold and are firm and springy to the touch, they are cooked. If you use a larger mold, you will have to increase the cooking time.

White butter sauce (Read about emulsions on pages 15–17.)

1 *cup dry white wine*
½ *cup water*
¼ *cup finely chopped shallots*
1 *tablespoon good wine vinegar*
½ *teaspoon freshly ground white pepper*
½ *teaspoon salt*

2 *tablespoons heavy cream*
2 *sticks (8 ounces) sweet butter, softened*

7. Place all ingredients for the sauce—except the butter—in a sturdy saucepan and place on medium heat. Bring to a boil and reduce until you have about ⅓ cup left. Force through a metal strainer, to purée the shallots, or purée in a food processor. Add the cream and place on low heat. (If possible, use an asbestos pad to diffuse the heat slowly.) Start adding the butter, beating with a wire whisk between additions. Add the butter slowly (it should take about 3 to 4 minutes to incorporate the two sticks of butter) and beat steadily to emulsify and add

air to the mixture. The sauce should never boil. Keep warm on the side and reheat at the last moment before serving.

8. Unmold the *mousseline* on your hand, allowing any cooking liquids to drain through your fingers. Arrange the *mousselines* on individual warmed plates. If some of the design sticks to the bottom of the mold, pull it out and replace gently on the *mousseline*.

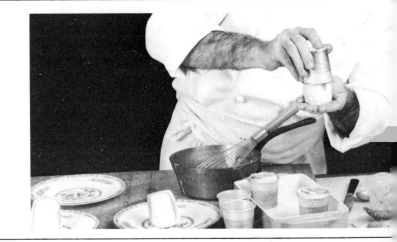

9. Heat the sauce just before serving and place about 2 tablespoons on top of each *mousseline*. Serve immediately.

29. Lobster Soufflé Plaza-Athénée

(Soufflé de Homard Plaza-Athénée)

YIELD: 8 main course servings or 12 first course servings

ONE OF THE BEST WAYS to enjoy lobster is simply broiled. However, a 2-pound lobster serves only one person whereas if you stuff it and glaze it with a sauce, it can serve two. In the soufflé Plaza-Athénée, a specialty of that famous hôtel-restaurant in Paris, the same lobster serves 4 people (and two lobsters, 8) as a main course for a lunch or 5 people as a first course for a dinner. The soufflé may be more complicated and sophisticated than a plain broiled or boiled lobster but it is far less expensive. Other fish or shellfish can be substituted for the lobster, such as scallops, shrimp, leftover fish, or other fillers can be added such as mushrooms. Dungeness crab, as well as spiny lobster and crayfish, also make an excellent soufflé. By following just steps 1 to 6 of the recipe you can make a *Homard Américaine* (or *Armoricaine*), a stewed lobster with wine, tomatoes and garlic, which can be served as is without the soufflé mixture on top. You can also make a lobster *consommé* from the carcass, claws, etc. (Add a carrot, onion and celery, and water or water and chicken stock, boiled for 1½ hours and strained, and use it as is, or with the addition of vermicelli or other pasta.) For the first part you will need:

2 *live lobsters, approximately 2 pounds each*	1 *sprig fresh tarragon or a small dash of dried tarragon leaves*
⅓ *cup dry white wine*	
1 *tablespoon flour*	2 *medium to large ripe tomatoes, coarsely chopped*
1 *tablespoon sweet butter*	2 *bay leaves*
1 *tablespoon olive oil*	1 *cup dry white wine*
3 *cloves garlic, crushed, with skin left on*	2 *tablespoons tomato paste*
½ *cup coarsely chopped parsley*	½ *teaspoon freshly ground black pepper*
¾ *cup finely chopped onion*	1 *teaspoon salt*
1 *or 2 stalks celery, finely chopped (½ cup)*	3 *cups light fish stock, or chicken stock or water*
½ *teaspoon thyme*	
2 *tablespoons good Cognac*	
1 *carrot, peeled and coarsely chopped (¾ cup)*	

To finish the sauce

1 *cup heavy cream*
1 *tablespoon Cognac*
1 *tablespoon sweet butter, cut into pieces*

Soufflé mixture (Read about soufflés on pages 318–319.)

2½ *tablespoons sweet butter*
3 *tablespoons flour*
1 *cup milk*
½ *teaspoon salt*
¼ *teaspoon freshly ground white pepper*
3 *eggs, separated, plus 3 egg whites*
2 *tablespoons grated Parmesan*

1. When choosing a lobster, pick one that is very active, an indication that it was recently caught. If the lobster is almost dead the meat in the tail and claws will have shrunk and the yield will be smaller. Like other shellfish, lobster spoils rapidly once dead, which is why it should be bought alive. (If you don't want to cut up the live lobster yourself, ask the fishmonger to do it for you, but insist that he save the liquid from the body as it is an essential ingredient for the sauce.) Hold the lobster and break off

the large claws where they meet the body. It shouldn't take more than a split second. Using a meat pounder crack the claws so the meat will be easy to remove after cooking.

2. Separate the tail from the body by jerking the tail back and forth until it loosens enough to pull out.

3. With a heavy knife split the body in half along the middle of back and crack it open (See page 112 in *La Technique* for more details about cutting up lobster.) Discard the stomach (a bag usually full of gravel) which is near the eyes at the pointed end of the body.

4. Place all the liquid from the lobster plus the tomalley or the liver (the pale green part) and the roe—if it is a female—(the dark green part) into a bowl. Add ⅓ cup dry white wine and 1 tablespoon flour. Mix well with a whisk and set aside. This will be the thickening and flavoring agent for the sauce. Put the oil and butter in one extra-large or two medium-size saucepans and heat until very hot. Place all the lobster pieces in the saucepan and sauté for 1 to 2 minutes on very high heat until they begin to turn red. Add the Cognac and ignite.

5. When the flames die, add the onion, carrot, celery, thyme, bay leaf, tomatoes, tomato paste, white wine, stock, pepper and salt. Cover, bring to a boil and boil for 3 to 4 minutes. Remove the claws and tail from the stock (the meat won't be thoroughly cooked but gets cooked again later on) and continue cooking the rest of the mixture for 25 minutes more. When the claws and tail are at room temperature, remove the meat from the shells.

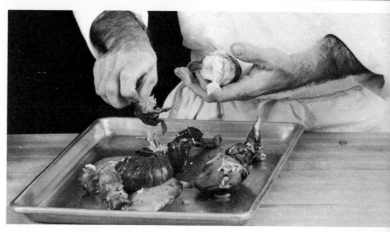

6. Butter a 4- to 5-cup baking dish, cut the meat into 1- to 2-inch pieces, and arrange in the baking dish. Return the shells to the stock for a few minutes or the remainder of its cooking time. When the sauce is cooked, strain through a food mill with large holes or through a colander into a clean saucepan. Press all of the solids to extrude as much of the liquid as possible. Add the flour/wine mixture and, stirring with a whisk, bring to a boil. Boil for 3 to 4 minutes and strain into another bowl through a fine strainer. You should have approximately 2 cups of sauce. Place 1¼ cups of sauce on top of the lobster meat. To the reserved sauce, add the cream, bring to a boil and reduce by half. Add the Cognac. Sprinkle the butter on top of the sauce to keep it from forming a skin. At serving time you will stir the butter into the sauce.

7. Melt 2½ tablespoons butter in a saucepan, add 3 tablespoons flour and cook, stirring, for 1 minute on medium heat. Add 1 cup milk and bring to a boil while stirring with a whisk. It will thicken. Let boil for about 10 seconds. Add ½ teaspoon salt and ¼ teaspoon white pepper and remove from heat. After 1 to 2 minutes, whisk in 3 egg yolks and 1½ tablespoons of Parmesan cheese. Beat 6 egg whites. Quickly whisk one-third of the beaten white into the mixture; fold in the remaining whites carefully. Spread on top of the lobster.

8. Even the mixture out with a spatula and sprinkle with the reserved ½ tablespoon of Parmesan. Score with a spatula to form a design and place on a cookie sheet in a preheated 375-degree oven for approximately 25 minutes.

9. This is what the soufflé looks like coming out of the oven. Serve immediately with the extra sauce on the side. This is a "double decker" soufflé—one layer of lobster meat with the sauce and one of cheese soufflé on top.

10. For a decoration, the legs, antenna and tail shells can be made into a butterfly. Take a thin leg and push the antenna into the hollow part of it to make a long tail.

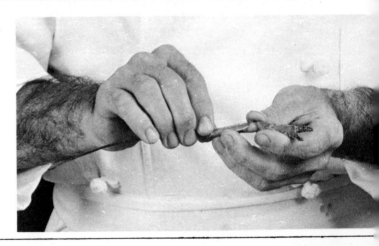

11. Remove the two pieces on either side of the lobster tail. These will be the wings of the butterfly.

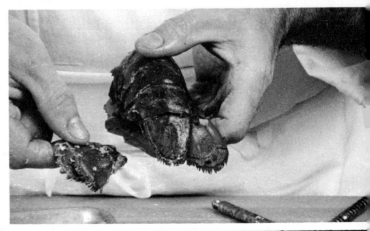

12. Force a toothpick through the joints of the butterfly "tail" and position a butterfly "wing" on either side.

13. Place on top of the soufflé. (Remember these butterflies when you make a lobster or cold seafood salad—anytime you're cooking lobster.)

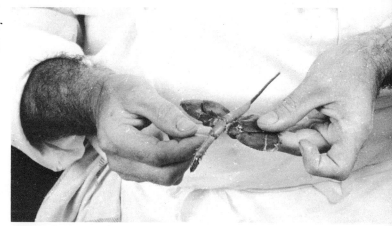

30. Shellfish Sausage *(Boudins de Fruits de Mer)*

YIELD: 8 to 10 servings

As its name implies, this is a purée of shellfish formed into the elongated shape of a sausage. The sausage can be small or it can be large—one sausage to serve one person or one sausage for 2 or 3. Sausage casings—whether small or large from lamb or hog or beef in size order—are often hard to come by and are delicate to work with. We chose not to use regular sausage casings and mold our sausage in foil. The foil allows you to choose the size and shape of your sausage, and because the sausage are skinless they are easier to manage on the plate. The sausage can be prepared ahead of time, kept in foil until ready to serve, then reheated in hot water in the foil. Serve with boiled salted cucumbers or tiny boiled potatoes.

Sausage

1 *pound fillet of sole, preferably gray or lemon*
  sole, trimmed and cut into ½-inch pieces.
  Ask your fishmonger for a cup worth of
  trimmings. (See note.)
½ *pound raw shrimp, with the shells*
½ *pound scallops*
1½ *cups heavy cream*
1 *teaspoon salt*
¼ *teaspoon freshly ground white pepper*
1 *tablespoon fresh herbs, chopped finely, a mix-*
  ture of tarragon, parsley, chives, chervil, etc.

(Note: The fish should be as fresh as possible so it has texture and albumin to hold the cream. If the fillets are burnt by ice or defrosted, the mixture will lack albumin and will bleed or separate.)

Sauce

2 *tablespoons butter*
½ *cup celery leaves*
¾ *cup onion, sliced thin*
1 *bay leaf*
¼ *teaspoon thyme leaves*
½ *teaspoon salt*
½ *teaspoon crushed peppercorns*

½ *cup dry Sherry*
3 *cups fish stock or water*
1¼ *sticks sweet butter*

1. Cut scallops into ¼-inch pieces. Peel the shrimp and cut into ½-inch pieces. Keep the shells to flavor the sauce. Purée the fish in the food processor for a few seconds. Push pieces of fish back into the purée with a rubber spatula, and blend again for a few seconds until you have a smooth mixture. Add ½ cup of cream and blend for a few seconds more. Whip the remaining cream until it holds a soft peak. (Do not overwhip.) Whisk the fish purée into the lightly whipped cream. Fold in the scallops, shrimp, salt, pepper and herbs.

2. Cut 3 large pieces of aluminum foil (about 14 inches long) and butter. Place one-third of the mixture in each.

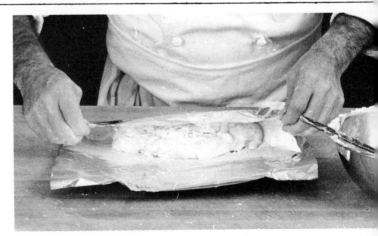

3. Roll the mixture to enclose it and twist the ends to tighten.

4. Place the "sausages" in a large skillet. Cover with cold water and use a small lid as a weight to hold the sausages down and keep them immersed. Cover with a normal lid, bring to 180 degrees, and cook for about 15 to 20 minutes. (If you are making smaller sausages, cook for less time.) Don't let the water boil or even simmer. Remove from heat and let the sausages sit in the water for about 10 minutes.

5. Remove the sausages from the water and unwrap carefully. Transfer to a buttered dish, cover with wax paper and keep warm in a 160-degree oven while you make the sauce. (Discard any liquid that accumulated in the foil.)

6. Put the trimmings from the fish in a saucepan. Place the shrimp shells in the food processor and purée for a few seconds. Add to the trimmings with the celery leaves, onion, bay leaf, thyme, salt, peppercorns, Sherry and fish stock. Bring to a boil. Boil gently for 20 to 25 minutes. Strain, then reduce the liquid to ½ cup. Place on low heat and add the sweet butter, piece by piece, beating between each addition (read about emulsions on pages 15–17). Add salt and pepper if needed. Coat the sausages and serve immediately.

31. Crayfish *(Écrevisses)*

THESE TINY SWEET WATER LOBSTERLIKE CRUSTACEANS are native to just about every part of the world except Africa. In the United States they come from Louisiana, well known for its crayfish, and California. The Pacific crayfish is usually quite clean, while crayfish from Louisiana sometimes require scrubbing to rid them of mud. There are many different species of crayfish, some too small to be eaten. To be edible they should be at least 4 to 5 inches from tail to head. Only the tail meat gets eaten (the body can be used to make soups, sauces and seasoned butter). Count on a dozen tails per person as a main course. Like all shellfish, crayfish should be handled live. Two different, classic ways of preparing crayfish follow—one in a hot broth, the other a crayfish au gratin—both are usually served as a first course. Crayfish can also be substituted for lobster in the Lobster Soufflé Plaza-Athénée (technique 29).

CRAYFISH IN BROTH *(Écrevisses à la Nage)*

YIELD: 2 servings

2 dozen crayfish (about 2 pounds)
1 large leek (white part only), cut into julienne
    (see technique 3) (1 cup)
1 large onion, peeled, cut in half and thinly sliced
    (2 cups)
2 small celery ribs, peeled and cut in julienne (½
    cup)
2 carrots, peeled and thinly sliced (1 cup)
2 cups dry white wine

1 cup water
½ teaspoon thyme
3 bay leaves
4 strips lemon rind (use a vegetable peeler)
1½ teaspoons salt
½ teaspoon freshly ground black pepper
½ teaspoon red pepper flakes or a good dash
    cayenne pepper (optional)
1 small bunch Italian parsley, stems removed,
    very coarsely cut (1 cup)
2 tablespoons sweet butter

1. The central intestinal tract has to be removed or the crayfish will taste bitter. Hold the crayfish down as shown, grab the center flap of the tail and twist gently back and forth to loosen it.

2. Pull and the intestinal tract attached to it should come out. (If it breaks, try to pull it out with the point of a knife, but don't worry if you can't get it. The crayfish is still edible.)

3. Melt the butter in a large frying pan. Add the leek, onions, celery and carrots. Sauté on medium heat for 1 minute. Add the wine and water, thyme, bay leaves, lemon, salt, pepper and optional pepper flakes. Bring to a boil and boil on high heat for 2 minutes. Add the crayfish and parsley, stir to mix, cover and bring to a boil. Simmer gently for 2 minutes. Remove from the heat and let the crayfish cool in the broth.

4. When cooled, arrange the crayfish on a platter with all of the vegetable garnish on top. *Trousse* a few crayfish to decorate the top of the dish. To *trousse* take one of the front claws, turn it upside down being careful not to break the claw at the joint, and gently push the smaller "pincer" part into the shell of the tail to hold the claw in place.

5. Repeat with the other claw. The crayfish are ready to be "seated." To enjoy the crayfish, you have to use your fingers, which means this is not a dish for a formal dinner party.

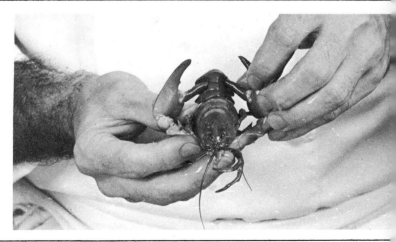

CRAYFISH TAILS AU GRATIN *(Gratin de Queues d'Écrevisses)*

YIELD: 2 servings

This expensive dish is served in some of the best restaurants of France. It is a time-consuming dish, very elegant and very rich. To make the crayfish go a bit further, you can reuse the shells to make a *bisque* of crayfish. (After you strain the crayfish in step 3, cover the shells and strained solids with water and boil for 2 hours, then strain. Adjust to 2 quarts and use as a base for sauces, *consommés* or thicken with tomatoes and cream for the bisque.)

2 dozen crayfish (about 2 pounds), gutted (see steps 1 and 2, pages 92–93)	*1 teaspoon salt*
2 tablespoons sweet butter	*½ teaspoon freshly ground pepper*
2 tablespoons good Cognac	*1 tablespoon tomato paste*
3 tablespoons chopped shallots	*1 cup heavy cream*
½ cup coarsely chopped leek	
1 tablespoon chopped celery	
3 tablespoons coarsely chopped carrots	
1 large tomato, peeled and chopped	
1 cup dry white wine	
2 cups light fish stock	
½ teaspoon thyme leaves	

1. Separate the body from the tail of the crayfish. Melt the butter in an extra large skillet or saucepan, until very hot. Add the crayfish tails and sauté for about 1 minute, until they turn red. Remove from the heat and let cool.

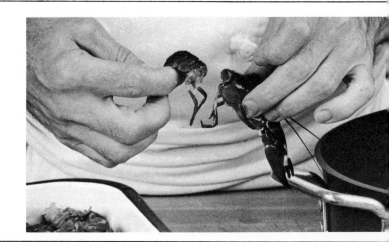

2. Remove the meat from the tails and set aside.

3. Chop the bodies coarsely. Place, with the tail shells, in the butter and continue sautéing on high heat for 2 to 3 minutes until the bodies turn red. Add the Cognac and ignite. When the flame subsides, add the shallots, leek, celery, carrots, tomato, white wine, fish stock, thyme, salt, pepper and tomato paste. Cover and bring to a boil. Lower the heat and simmer for 30 minutes. Remove from heat and strain through a food mill fitted with a large-holed disk. Press all the solids to extrude as much of the liquid as possible, then strain the juices again through a finer sieve. You should have approximately 1½ cups of liquid left. If not, reduce to right amount, or add water to adjust. Add the cream, bring to a boil and reduce by half. Arrange the tails in two small baking dishes (about 1 dozen per person) and heat in a hot oven for 1 or 2 minutes. Pour the hot sauce on top and serve immediately.

32. Goujonnettes of Sole *(Goujonnettes de Sole)*

GOUJON IS A SMALL fresh water fish that's called gudgeon in English. In France it is deep fried and eaten like French fries. *Goujonnette* is made from larger fillets of fish and cut into small *goujon*like strips and deep fried.

Fried fish is usually coated with flour or bread crumbs and either pan fried or deep fried. Deep-fried fish is usually soaked in beer and then flour or bread crumbs. Pan-fried fish is usually soaked in milk and then flour.

Fillet of sole is often used for *goujonnettes*. Serve with a hollandaise, *béarnaise, beurre blanc* or a lemon butter.

1. Cut the fillets in long strips about ¼-inch wide by 4 to 5 inches long.

2. Place the fish strips in a small bowl and cover with beer. Lift the pieces of fish from the beer and dip them into flour. Shake well.

3. Place the flour-coated strips of fish into a colander and shake well to eliminate excess flour. Heat vegetable oil to approximately 375 to 400 degrees and dip the *goujonnettes*, a handful at the time, into the fat. Fry for 6 to 8 minutes on high heat, until nicely browned all around.

4. Lift the *goujonnettes* from the oil with a slotted spoon and drain in a pan lined with paper towels. Sprinkle lightly with salt and arrange on a platter or in a folded towel. Serve with lemon wedges, lemon butter or a sauce.

33. Fillets of Sole in Lettuce Leaves

(Filets de Sole Claudine)

YIELD: 4 servings

THE FILLETS are topped with a purée of mushrooms, wrapped in lettuce leaves and then poached. Because of the salad wrapping, they stay quite moist, which makes them ideal for a party and the dish can sit for a while where normally fillet of sole would dry out. We generally use gray or lemon sole, though fillet of trout, striped bass and other fish will do as well.

This dish is served with a light *velouté*, rather than with a reduction of cream and fish juices. The sauce for the Stuffed Brill (technique 34) as well as for the Mousseline of Scallops (technique 28) or the Shellfish Sausage (technique 30) could be substituted.

1 *pound fillet of sole (about 4 ounces per person), split in half lengthwise with the small piece of bone between the halves removed*
1 *extra-large head iceberg lettuce, the leafy type*
1 *large carrot, peeled, sliced thin and cut into julienne (1 generous cup loose)*
1 *leek, white and light green parts only, cut into julienne (1 cup loose)*
6 *ounces mushrooms, finely chopped (about 2 cups loose)*
½ *teaspoon freshly ground white pepper*
1½ *teaspoons salt*

1 *cup dry white wine*
1 *tablespoon sweet butter*

Sauce

2 *tablespoons sweet butter*
1 *tablespoon flour*
1 *cup heavy cream*
2 *tablespoons chopped parsley*

1. Core the lettuce, then insert the tips of your fingers in the hole and spread the lettuce apart. This helps loosen the large outside leaves. Separate the leaves and pick out 6 to 8 of the largest ones. (Reserve the rest of the lettuce for another use.) Drop the large leaves in boiling water and as they wilt push them down gently into the water. Bring the water back to almost a boil, at which point the leaves will be soft. Place the whole kettle under cold running water until the leaves are cold. Gently lift the leaves out of the cold water and drain on paper towels.

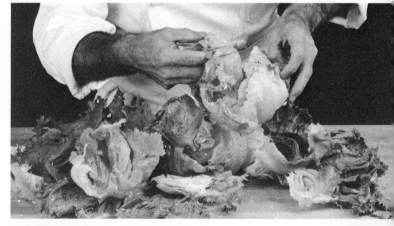

2. Place the chopped mushrooms in a skillet over medium heat and cook until all of the liquid expelled from the mushrooms evaporates. This will take about 5 to 6 minutes depending on the freshness of the mushrooms and how much liquid they exude while cooking. Season with ¼ teaspoon salt and put an equal amount of the purée of mushrooms on top of each lettuce leaf.

3. Butter a large skillet and sprinkle with ½ teaspoon salt and ¼ teaspoon freshly ground pepper. Cover with the julienne of carrots and leek. Fold 2 single fillets and place over the mushroom mixture on each leaf. The white fleshy side of the fish should be on the outside or the fillets will unfold during cooking.

4. Fold the leaves over the fillets and place each package, seam side down, on the julienne of vegetables. (The purée of mushrooms is now on top of the fish.)

5. Pour the wine over the fillets, cover with a piece of buttered parchment paper and then with a lid. Bring to a boil and simmer gently for about 8 minutes, depending on how tightly the fillets are packed together. They can also be brought to a boil, then cooked in a preheated 425-degree oven for 8 to 10 minutes.

6. To make the sauce, melt 1 tablespoon of butter in a heavy saucepan and add the flour. Cook over medium heat about 1 minute stirring with a whisk. Holding the fillets in place with the lid, pour the cooking liquid from the fish into the *roux*. Mix carefully with a whisk. Bring to a boil and continue whisking until it thickens. The mixture is now called a *velouté*. Let simmer gently for about 5 minutes. You should have approximately ¾ cup of *velouté* left. Add the cream, bring to a boil and allow to boil for 2 to 3 minutes, until the mixture is

reduced to about 1¼ cups. Taste for seasonings and add salt and pepper if needed. Break the remaining tablespoon of butter into small pieces and place on top of the sauce; it will melt and form a film which will prevent any "skin" from forming on top of the sauce.

7. Remove the packages from the saucepan and arrange the julienne of vegetables on a serving platter.

8. Place the packages on top of the julienne, cover with the piece of parchment paper used during the cooking, and set in a 160-degree oven until ready to serve.

9. At serving time make sure you pour out or blot with paper towels the juices which have accumulated around the fillets of sole. If left, they will thin down the sauce.

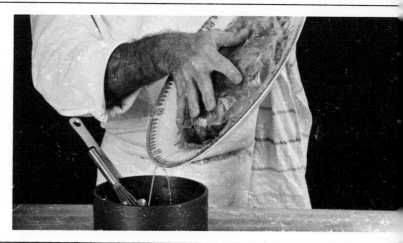

10. Heat the sauce, stirring in the butter; add a few drops of lemon juice if desired and pour over the fillets. Dot with chopped parsley.

11. Cut in half, note how the sole is white and moist and has a light cover of mushrooms on top. Serve immediately with stewed cucumbers, zucchini or tiny boiled potatoes tossed with butter and parsley. Excellent as a main course for a light dinner, or in a smaller package as a first course for a dinner or as lunch.

34. Stuffed Brill *(Barbue Farcie)*

YIELD: 4 to 6 main course servings or 8 to 10 first course servings

THE BRILL is a type of small turbot from the flat fish family. It is similar to an extra large sole which is what we used in this technique because brill, unfortunately, is not always available. Other kinds of flat fish can also be boned and stuffed in the same manner.

1 *brill or lemon sole, approximately 3 pounds, neither gutted nor trimmed*

Stuffing

½ *stick (2 ounces) sweet butter*
1¼ *cups fresh bread crumbs (3 to 4 slices white bread)*
2 *tablespoons freshly chopped parsley*
6 *shallots, peeled and finely chopped (⅓ cup)*
¾ *cup coarsely chopped shrimp, peeled, deveined and briefly cooked*
½ *teaspoon salt*

¼ *teaspoon freshly ground white pepper*

To cook the fish

¾ *stick (3 ounces) sweet butter*
1 *small leek, finely chopped (½ cup)*
2 *cups sliced mushrooms*
1 *cup dry white wine*
¼ *teaspoon freshly ground white pepper*
½ *teaspoon salt*

To finish the sauce

¼ *cup heavy cream*
½ *stick sweet butter (2 ounces)*
1 *tablespoon chopped fresh herbs (parsley, tar-*
    ragon, chives, etc.)
Salt and freshly ground pepper to taste

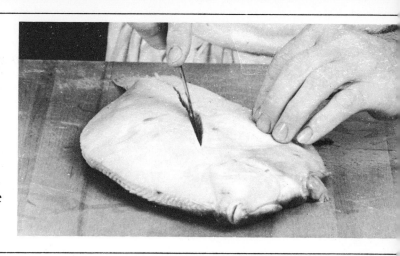

1. Trim away the outside bones of the fish and place it flat on a chopping board, white side up. With a sharp knife, cut along the central line.

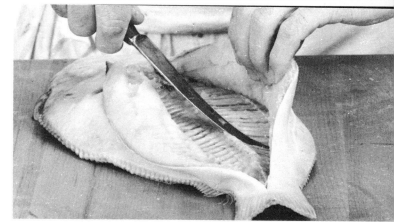

2. Using a flexible bladed fish knife (in France this knife is actually called a *filet de sole*), separate the flesh from the bone by sliding the blade along the central bone. Repeat on the other side. Do not cut through the skin. You will notice that the flesh stops near another layer of bone.

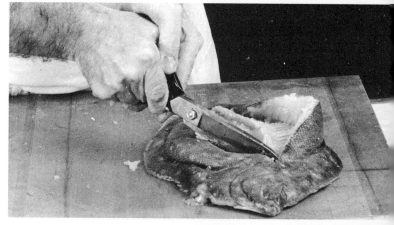

3. Turn the fish black side up and repeat the same procedure on this side. Using a large pair of shears, cut the bone away from the fish on both sides.

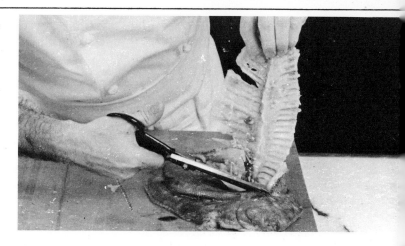

4. Cut the central bone as close as you can from the tail and from the head. It should come out in one piece.

5. The fillets are now completely loose, but still held together by the head and the tail. To prepare the stuffing, melt the butter in a skillet and add the bread crumbs. Cook, stirring, until the crumbs are nicely browned. Place in a bowl and add the parsley, shallots, shrimp, salt and pepper.

6. Butter a roasting pan with 1 tablespoon of butter. Line the pan with the mushrooms and leek. Place the fish over this mixture, arranging the bottom fillets so they touch. Place the stuffing inside and cover with the two top fillets. Sprinkle with salt and pepper and pour the white wine on top.

7. Cover with a piece of butter parchment paper and place the roasting pan on top of the stove. Bring to a boil and place in a preheated 425-degree oven for 20 minutes. Remove from the oven and, using a knife, remove the black skin and discard. Remove the solids around the fish and place in a bowl.

8. Using a small knife, pull away the layer of bones next to the fillets. It slides out easily. Discard the bones.

9. Holding the fish in place with the lid, pour the cooking liquid into a saucepan and set aside for the sauce. You should have about ½ cup of liquid.

10. Place a serving platter on top of the fish and turn upside down. Arrange the solids around the fish.

11. Pull off the skin on the white side and discard. Cover the cleaned fish with parchment paper and keep warm in a 160-degree oven while you make the sauce. Add ¼ cup heavy cream to the reserved cooking liquid and bring to a boil. Reduce, if necessary, to ¾ of a cup. Add the ½ stick of butter, piece by piece, whisking between each addition as you would for a *beurre blanc* (technique 11). Taste for seasonings and add salt and pepper if necessary. Remove the fish from the oven. Blot off any juices that may have accumulated around the fish.

12. Pour the sauce over the fish. Sprinkle with fresh herbs and serve immediately.

35. Whiting Breaded "En Colère"

(Merlan "en Colère")

WHITING is unfortunately looked down upon in most households in this country. It is a very good, inexpensive fish. It has only a large central bone and no small bones, which means it is easy to eat. It is extremely delicate provided it is well cleaned. Whiting can be served plain, poached or sautéed in butter, as well as deep-fat fried.

In our recipe, it is twisted into a crown shape called "en colère," "angry-style," so-called because its tail is secured in its mouth.

2 to 3 whiting

Breading

2 tablespoons flour
2 cups fresh bread crumbs

Batter (enough for 2 to 3 whiting)

1 egg, slightly beaten
1 teaspoon vegetable oil
1 tablespoon water
¼ teaspoon salt
Dash of freshly ground white pepper
Vegetable oil for frying

1. Each whiting should weigh approximately 1 pound before gutting. Make sure you remove the gill as well as the thin black skin inside the cavity on both sides of the wall of the abdomen. If the black veil is left in, it will make the fish bitter. Trim the fins, and wash under running water. Dry the whiting with paper towels.

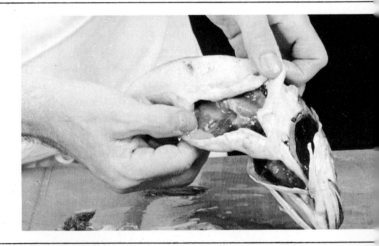

2. To prepare the batter, mix all the ingredients together. Coat the whiting lightly with flour and pat all over to shake off the excess. Dip into the egg batter to coat well and push off the excess with your fingers.

3. Roll the egg-coated whiting in the bread-crumbs. Pat gently so the crumbs stick to the fish. Twist the fish to place the tail between the jaws and squeeze them out to close and hold the tail in place.

4. Heat at least 2 inches of oil to about 350 degrees. Lower the fish into the oil and cook for 8 to 10 minutes. It should be well browned outside. To check if the fish is done, insert a fork or knife along the back bone of the thickest part of the fish—the flesh should separate from the bone easily. Drain the fish on paper towels and serve on a platter with fried parsley in the center (technique 43), lemon wedges and, if you wish, a piece of *maître d'hôtel* butter on top (butter seasoned with parsley, lemon juice and salt).

36. Sea Trout or Bass in Puff Paste
(Bar en Feuilletage)

YIELD: 8 to 10 servings

WHEN YOU BAKE *en croûte*, pick a large fish rather than a small one. You need a certain amount of time to cook the dough regardless of the size of the fish. With a large fish the dough will have enough time to cook without the fish getting overdone. Small fish tend to overcook by the time the dough is ready. Other crusts can be used instead of puff paste. In addition, the fish can be cooked boned or not boned, with or without a stuffing.

1 5-pound sea trout, whole, gutted with fin on, or 2 large fillets about 1½ pounds each
½ pound loose flesh of fish (use trimmings from the sea trout)
½ cup heavy cream
½ teaspoon salt
½ teaspoon freshly ground white pepper
½ cup finely chopped parsley
1 tablespoon minced fresh chives
1 tablespoon chopped fresh tarragon
1 teaspoon salt to sprinkle fillets
1½ to 2 pounds puff paste (technique 91)

1 egg with 1 egg yolk thoroughly beaten for glaze

Herb butter sauce

1 cup dry white wine
½ of the chopped herbs (⅓ cup) left from the mousse
2 sticks (8 ounces) sweet butter, softened and cut into small pieces
2 egg yolks
½ teaspoon freshly ground white pepper
½ teaspoon salt

To make the sauce: Bring the wine to a boil and boil for 1 minute. Add the herbs left-over from the mousse and bring again to a boil. Remove from the heat and pour the mixture in a food processor. Add the egg yolks, pepper, salt and about one quarter of the butter. Blend for about 15 seconds. (The boiling wine will cook the egg yolks enough.) Add remaining butter and blend for another 15 to 20 seconds to homogenize. This makes a very light foamy sauce, which should be served as soon as possible.

If it cannot be served right away, keep warm in a double boiler and whip a few seconds before serving.

1. Fillet the fish and remove the skin and sinews from both fillets and trim. Scrape any loose fish off the bone (you will need about ½ pound to make the mousse). Keep the bones to make a stock for a sauce or fish soup. To make the mousse: Purée the loose flesh in a food processor, add the cream, salt and pepper and blend again until smooth. Do not overblend or the cream may turn into butter.

2. Roll the puff paste ⅛ inch thick into two rectangles at least 2 inches wider and longer than the fish. Place a piece of parchment paper on a large cookie sheet and unroll a rectangle of puff paste on top. Place 1 fillet on the dough and sprinkle lightly with salt. Spread the fish mousse on the fillet and sprinkle half the herbs on top.

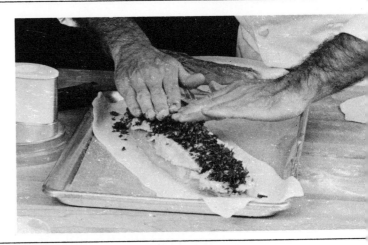

3. Lay the second fillet over the mousse. (A fish fillet is thicker at the head end than at the tail. When you position the second fillet over the first reverse direction so that you have thick over thin on one side and then thin over thick on the other.) Sprinkle lightly with salt. Brush the dough around the fillets with the egg glaze.

4. Unroll the second layer of puff paste on top of the fish and press all around the fish to make sure both layers adhere.

5. Trim around the fillets, trying to make the package look like a fish. Decorate with strips of dough and a round for the eyes. Brush with egg wash.

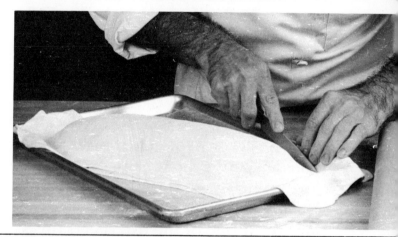

6. Using the tines of a fork, mark strips on the tail.

7. With the large end of a pastry tube (or the back of a spoon), make "scales" on the fish, cutting halfway through the dough, but not completely through. Place the fish in the freezer for 20 minutes or in the refrigerator for 1 to 2 hours.

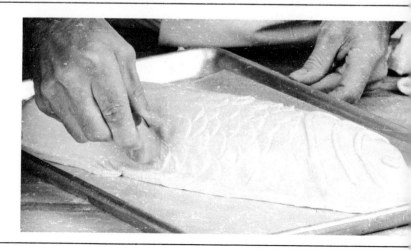

8. Bake in a preheated 350-degree oven for 50 to 60 minutes. Let rest 5 minutes and with a large spatula, remove to a serving platter. Keep warm in a 180-degree oven while making the sauce or until serving time. Cut the fish into 1-inch slices and serve on hot plates with the sauce all around.

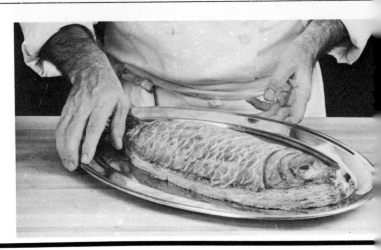

37. Pâté of Fish Tricolor

(Pâté de Poisson Trois Couleurs)

YIELD: 12 to 14 servings

THIS *pâté* of fish is particularly suited for a dinner party or a cold buffet. The contrast of colors makes it very attractive: the white of the whiting mousse against the green herb mousse; the orange salmon and the pale pink sauce. The *pâté* and the sauce—made with oil, tomato, cayenne and pepper—should be served cool but not too cold. We use three types of fish in this mousse. If one of the fish called for is not available, substitute another. The *pâté* can also be served hot with one of the hot fish sauces served with the brill, the bass in puff paste or the *mousseline* of scallops (techniques 34, 36, 28), etc.

Mousse

3½ pounds whiting, whole but gutted
2 egg whites
1 teaspoon salt
½ teaspoon freshly ground white pepper
2 cups heavy cream

Garnishes

¾ pound salmon
2 large fillets of sole (about 10 to 12 ounces each), separated into single fillets and each pounded to ¼ inch thick

Herb mousse

4 to 5 shallots, peeled and coarsely chopped (about ¼ cup)
1 cup dry white wine
¼ teaspoon freshly ground white pepper
½ teaspoon salt
1 small bunch watercress leaves (about 1 cup lightly packed)
1 small bunch cleaned spinach leaves (about 1 cup)
½ tablespoon fresh chopped tarragon or chives or any other herb
2 tablespoons chopped fresh parsley

Sauce

1 *large tomato, peeled, seeded and coarsely chopped (approximately 1 cup)*
½ *teaspoon good paprika*
Dash of cayenne pepper
1 *teaspoon salt*
¼ *teaspoon freshly ground white pepper*
1 *tablespoon good red wine vinegar*
1 *egg yolk*
1 *cup good olive oil, preferably virgin, at room temperature*

To prepare whiting mousse: Clean the whiting (technique 35), bone out, remove the skin as well as the black membrane in the inside cavity. You should have approximately 1½ pounds of flesh after the cleaning. Place the flesh in the bowl of a food processor and purée for approximately 40 to 50 seconds. Push through the fine screen of a food mill to remove any sinews left (*optional*). Put the mixture back into the bowl of a food processor with the egg whites, salt and pepper, and with the machine on, slowly add 1 cup of cream—it should take 10 to 15 seconds. Beat the other cup of cream to a soft peak and whisk the fish mixture into the cream.

To prepare the sauce: Combine all the sauce ingredients, except the oil, in the container of the food processor and blend for 30 to 40 seconds until smooth. With the motor still on add the oil slowly (it should take about 10 to 15 seconds), taste for seasonings and set the mixture aside. If it is too thick, which happens, thin down to a creamy consistency with 1 to 2 tablespoons of lukewarm water.

To prepare the herb mousse: Place the shallots, white wine, pepper and salt in a saucepan (preferably not aluminum because of discoloration). Bring to a boil, then reduce until there is approximately ⅓ cup left (about 5 minutes). Add the watercress and spinach, stirring. Cook covered for ½ minute, until the greens wilt. Uncover and keep boiling down until there is only about 1 tablespoon of liquid left. Set aside to cool. When cold, blend with the parsley and tarragon in the bowl of a food processor until smooth. Then combine with about 1 cup of the whiting mousse.

1. Line an 8-cup mold with approximately ½ inch of fish mousse on the bottom and the sides.

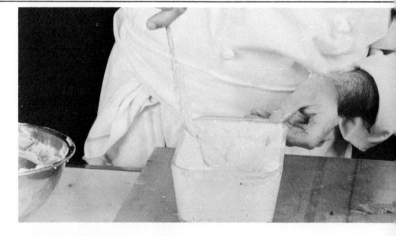

2. Cut the fresh salmon into thin, ¼-inch slices and line the fish mousse with a layer of salmon slices.

3. Sprinkle the salmon with salt and pepper and line the top and sides of the salmon with a thin layer of fish mousse and then the pounded fillet of sole.

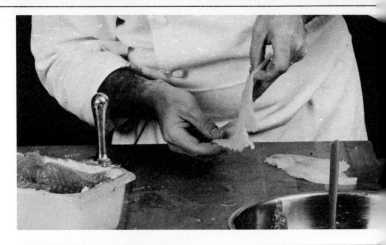

4. Place the green herb mousse in the center.

5. Cover the green herb mousse with more fillet of sole and slices of salmon. Finally, cover the top of the salmon with a layer of the whiting mousse. Smooth the top with a spatula, cover with buttered parchment paper, then with aluminum foil. Place the mold into a pan of tepid water that comes approximately three-quarters of the way up the sides of the mold. Place in a preheated 275-degree oven for 1½ hours. At the slow temperature, the texture will be smooth. Cooked too fast, the *pâté* will develop tiny holes and the texture will be too airy.

6. Remove from the oven and let cool at room temperature for a few hours, Refrigerate overnight. Unmold and slice into ¼-inch slices. Place approximately 2 tablespoons of sauce in the bottom of each individual plate with a slice of *pâté* on top.

POACHED SCALLOPS WITH A GREEN SAUCE *(Coquille Judie)*

YIELD: 6 servings

For another easy, tasty and decorative shellfish dish, make this poached scallops with a green sauce.

1½ *pounds scallops (bay or sea scallops which should be very fresh)*
1 *cup dry white wine*
1½ *teaspoons salt*
2 *cups mushrooms, cleaned and cut into large chunks*
1 *cup watercress leaves*
2 *cups spinach leaves*

Remove the small muscle or nerve on the scallops. If you use sea scallops, slice into halves or three slices if they are large. Place the scallops, mushrooms, wine and salt in a large saucepan (not aluminum because of discoloration) and heat on a medium heat until it almost comes to a boil. Stir once in a while. You will notice that the scallops whiten and stiffen as they cook. They should just barely cook through and they do not even need to come to a full boil. Strain the mixture in a colander and cover to prevent too much drying. Place the juices back into a saucepan and add the watercress and spinach. Bring to a boil stirring; the greens should be wilted. Remove with a slotted spoon and place in the container of a food processor. Reduce the juices to ½ cup and add to the greens. Blend for a few seconds until smooth.

Sauce

1 *egg yolk*
2 *tablespoons heavy cream*
1 *cup good oil (preferably virgin olive oil or a mixture of olive and peanut oil)*
¼ *teaspoon freshly ground white peppercorns*
Small strips of tomato skin for garnish

Add the egg yolks and the cream to the greens and blend for a few seconds until smooth. Add the pepper and the oil with blender on as you would make a mayonnaise. It should have the consistency of a salad dressing. Place some sauce in each individual plate with a few scallops in the center. Decorate with the tomato skin. The sauce should be cool but the scallops should be at room temperature.

38. Smoking Fish *(Fumage des Poissons)*

COMMERCIALLY SMOKED FISH is very expensive and often not as good as fish smoked at home. The commercial product is usually more salted and more smoked than the homemade product because the manufacturers want the fish to have the longest "shelf-life" possible.

Smoking your own fish is fun and rewarding. There are only a few smoked fish available on the market—such as white fish, sturgeon, trout and salmon—but you can smoke practically any type of fish at home. We have had great results with mullets, porgie, eel, pike, etc. There are two basic ways of smoking: the hot and cold methods. The hot method partially cooks the fish as it smokes. The cold method smokes the fish but leaves it raw.

If you have one of the small home smokers, often sold at camping equipment outfitters, you will be able to hot smoke but not cold smoke. If you have no smoker, you can make one yourself from an old refrigerator or metal locker. It can be used for both the hot and cold methods. Hot smoking is done at temperatures between 140 and 160 degrees. Cold smoking temperatures shouldn't go above 90 degrees.

Before you smoke—whichever way you choose—you have to cure the fish with salt. Here, too, there are two different methods: You can cure it in a liquid brine (salt and water), or with dry salt. The salt leeches all the moisture out of the fish thereby depriving the bacteria of the medium necessary for its survival. It is in this way that salting preserves. Use the kosher-type coarse salt which is a sweeter, better, more natural salt—without the additives put in regular salt to prevent caking.

Both meat and fish are smoked by being exposed to the smoke given off by smouldering wood chips. Different types of woods can be used—hickory, maple, alder, juniper and most woods from fruit trees. Resinous woods such as pine, spruce, etc., should be avoided. Herbs such as bay leaves or thyme can be added to the wood chips to flavor the smoke.

In the first technique we are hot smoking trout in a little home smoker. In the second, we will cold smoke salmon in a converted ice box smoker. Hot smoking is necessary with a tight, firm fleshed fish such as sturgeon, eel and even trout. The tougher the flesh, the higher the temperature should go; 120 degrees will be sufficient for trout but it should go up to 180 degrees for eel. Because of its particular texture salmon is cold smoked. If subjected to temperatures above 90 degrees, it will cook through. The proteins coagulate around 120 degrees and force the moisture of the fish out (it is visible as a white custard-like sediment), the flesh will flake and the salmon cook.

SMOKED TROUT (*Truites Fumées*)

YIELD: 12 first course lunch or brunch servings

6 *trout, 12 ounces each, gutted and cleaned*
4 *cups water*
2 *cups kosher salt*
1 *tablespoon sugar*
Hickory or alder chips

1. Bring the water to a boil and add the salt and sugar. Mix to dissolve and let cool. (The saltiness of the brine can be checked with an hydrometer—the specific gravity should be 1155 at 60 degrees Fahrenheit—or by floating an egg on top of the brine; a bit of eggshell the size of a 50 cent coin should emerge from the water.) Place the trout in the brine for 2 hours. Remove, wipe dry with paper towels inside and out, and rub lightly with vegetable oil.

2. Skewer the trout, three at a time, through the gills and mouths. (We used sticks of wood as skewers.)

3. Hang the trout in the smoker. Plug in the hot plate, fill up the little tray with the wood chips, return to the smoker and put the cover back on the smoker. Leave the trout in the smoker approximately 2 hours. (It will take about 30 minutes before the chips are hot enough to produce smoke.)

4. After about an hour, replenish the tray with more wood chips. The temperature at this point will be between 140 and 160 degrees. After 2 hours, unplug the smoker and leave the trout in for another hour to cool and set.

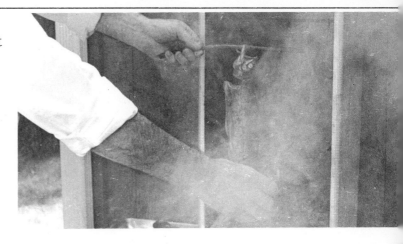

5. Take the trout out. They will have a nice yellowish color, be slightly warm to the touch and a little soft. Sometimes the weight of the trout causes it to break at the side of the head and fall.

6. Refrigerate for at least 1 day to allow the trout to set and the taste to develop. Then remove the skin: Start at the belly and "unwrap" to the back.

7. Continue unwrapping to the other side. The skin will come off in one piece.

8. Remove the head and split the top fillet in half following the line down the center of the trout.

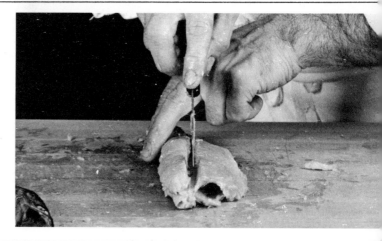

9. Pull out the back fillet, which is the thickest and the nicest. It should slide off the bone easily. Then push away on the other side to separate the belly fillet from the bone.

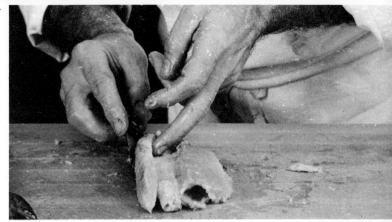

10. Remove the central bone which should come out in one piece. The trout is now ready and is usually served with toast and butter. For an elegant first course serve *La Truite Fumée Gloria*, which is a lukewarm, boned-out fillet of trout rolled and filled with scrambled eggs (see technique 16).

SMOKED SALMON (*Saumon Fumé*)

Use a large thick salmon. Ours weighed 10 pounds (gutted, head on) but a 15 pounder would have been even better. If you don't want to smoke a whole fillet, you can smoke half a fillet as long as the flesh is thick. Take your piece in the thickest part of the fillet. The instructions that follow are for one side of salmon, 3½ pounds with skin on but boned, and head and tail removed.

½ of a 10-pound salmon, scaled, washed and
  filleted
2 cups kosher-type salt mixed with 1 tablespoon
  sugar
⅓ cup vegetable oil

1. Clean and fillet the salmon. Your fishmonger can do this for you or you can do it yourself following the instructions on pages 133–135 of *La Technique*.

2. Using a pair of tweezers or small pliers, pull out the tiny bones which run down the center of the fillet. The bones can also be removed after smoking, but if left they make carving difficult.

3. Spread some of the salt mixture on a large rectangular piece of aluminum foil and place the salmon, skin-side down, on top. Spread the rest of the salt mixture on top, sprinkling just a little on the tail because it is thin and shouldn't absorb too much salt. There should be about ⅛ inch of salt mixture on top of the fillet except for the tail end.

4. Pack the salmon tightly in the aluminum foil and refrigerate for 5 hours during which time the salmon will cure. Adjust the curing time for larger or smaller slabs of salmon. (If the salmon has been frozen, it will be more mushy and absorb more salt faster.) Remove from the aluminum foil, wash under cold water and dry carefully with paper towels.

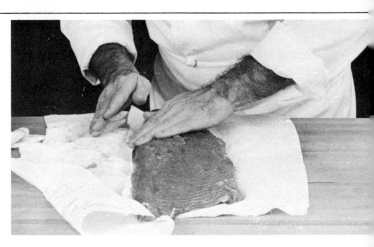

5. Place the salmon on a wire rack and let it dry for approximately 6 hours or overnight in front of a fan. A thin veil will form on top of the skin which should be dry to the touch. Rub the fillet generously all around with vegetable oil, place on a tray and let marinate in the refrigerator for 2 to 3 hours. Then place in the smoker.

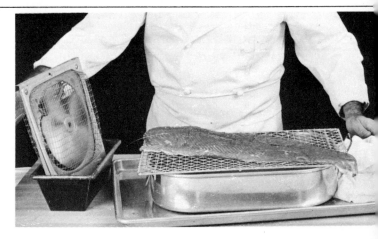

6. We use an electric barbecue starter to get the wood chips smoking. Note that an aluminum gutter elbow was fitted to go through the refrigerator. This leaves the source of heat on the outside so that only the smoke enters the refrigerator. With this method the temperature will not exceed 90 degrees inside the box. For hot smoke, place the barbecue starter and sawdust directly inside the refrigerator so that the temperature goes up to between 160 and 180 degrees.

7. Embed the barbecue starter into the wood chips. Wrap the opening of the aluminum elbow and the top of the flower pot with aluminum foil to contain the smoke and force it through the pipe into the refrigerator. Plug the starter in for 3 minutes. The chips will start smoking after about 1 minute. After 3 minutes of smoke, unplug. The chips will continue to smoke for a few minutes. Let the salmon "rest" (without opening the door) for 1 hour.

8. Repeat the same procedure twice more. This gives a total of 9 minutes of intense smoke and about 3½ hours in the smoker.

9. Let the slab dry and settle under refrigeration for at least 1 day before using. Slice thin on a slant and serve plain with a dash of lemon juice and thin, buttered slices of black bread. The salmon can also be seasoned with capers, olive oil and ground black pepper. If the salmon is frozen after smoking, the texture will be mushier after defrosting and will not cut into thin, transparent and elastic slices.

Vegetables

39. Asparagus Stew *(Râgout d'Asperges)*

YIELD: 4 servings

THIS IS A VERY SIMPLE, elegant and delicious dish. It can be served as a first course or as an accompaniment to broiled lamb chops, pan-fried veal steaks or to any sauceless meat.

2 *dozen green asparagus*
⅓ *cup water*
½ *teaspoon salt*
½ *stick (2 ounces) sweet butter, cut into pieces*
¼ *cup finely chopped parsley*

1. Peel the asparagus, then cut on the diagonal into 1-inch lengths. (Peeling asparagus makes them edible from head to stem. See pages 175–177 of *La Technique* for more about preparing asparagus.)

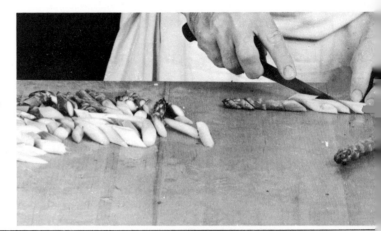

2. Place the asparagus in a skillet with the water and salt, cover and bring to a strong boil. Boil for 1½ minutes, uncover and add the butter and the parsley.

3. Return to a strong boil, shaking the pan to bind the ingredients together. Boil for 20 to 30 seconds until the sauce thickens and becomes foamy. The mixture will rise like milk ready to boil over. (To understand how and why the butter and water bind together, read the discussion on emulsion on pages 15–17.)

4. As soon as it foams, remove from the heat (further cooking will reduce the amount of moisture in the sauce and make the butter and water separate). Pour onto a serving dish and serve immediately.

40. How to Prepare Spinach
(Equeutage des Epinards)

THERE ARE TWO BASIC WAYS of preparing spinach: in *purée*, when both leaf and stem are finely ground, and *en branches* (whole leaf), when the leaf is left whole and the stem removed. A *purée* of spinach is usually made with a light cream sauce, seasoned with nutmeg, salt and pepper and served with fried *croûtons* and hard-boiled eggs. It is a very good accompaniment to a roast of veal or a roasted chicken. Spinach prepared *en branches* is used in *timbale* or as a bed for poached eggs, fish, oysters or veal (called *à la florentine*).

LEAF SPINACH *(Epinards en Branches)*

1 *pound fresh spinach*
¼ *inch water in a large saucepan (not aluminum) with a cover*
½ *teaspoon salt*

1. Note how the long stem runs along the underside of the spinach leaf.

2. Take hold of the leaf on both sides of the stem and pull the stem out. The stems can be used in soups or mixed with other whole leaf spinach if the whole mixture is to be used for a *purée*. Wash the spinach carefully.

3. Bring the water and salt to a strong boil and pile the spinach on top. Cover and cook on high heat for 2 to 3 minutes. The spinach will wilt but will still remain green.

4. Drain in a colander and run under cold water until cool enough to handle. Press into a ball, squeezing out the water, then cover with plastic wrap and keep in the refrigerator until needed.

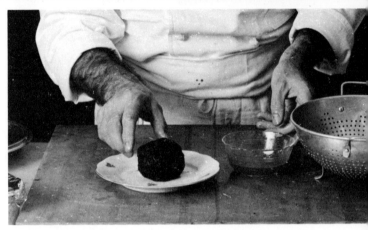

SPINACH MOLD (*Timbale d'Epinards*)

YIELD: 6 servings

6 to 8 ½-cup soufflé molds, buttered
1 pound fresh spinach (prepared as above)
1 teaspoon salt
½ teaspoon freshly ground pepper
⅛ teaspoon freshly grated nutmeg
3 tablespoons sweet butter
2 teaspoons flour
¾ cup milk
½ cup heavy cream
3 large eggs
6 slices firm white bread, cut into 2½-inch
    rounds and fried in a skillet with butter and
    vegetable oil until golden brown

Cook spinach as explained in steps 3 and 4 and chop coarsely. Sprinkle with the salt, pepper and nutmeg. Melt the butter in a heavy saucepan and let it cook until it is dark brown. Add the spinach and mix with a fork. The dark brown butter gives the spinach a very nutty taste. Sprinkle the spinach with the flour, mix it in well, add the milk and bring to a boil, stirring constantly. Let it boil for ½ minute, take off the heat and let it cool off on the side for 10 to 15 minutes. Beat the eggs, mix in the heavy cream and stir the whole mixture into the spinach.

5. Fill the prepared molds with the mixture, dividing the solids and liquids equally, and place in a pan of tepid water. Bake in a preheated 350-degree oven for 25 to 30 minutes, or until set. The water should not boil. The timbale should rest for at least 15 to 20 minutes before being unmolded. To serve, run a knife around the inside of the mold to loosen the timbale. Unmold each timbale on a piece of bread and arrange around a roast, or serve, plain or with a light cream sauce.

41. How to Prepare Endives
(Cuisson des Endives)

YIELD: 6 to 8 servings

BELGIAN ENDIVES, which are the best in the world, make a great salad. (Separate the leaves, pile them together, cut into a fine julienne, then put in ice cold water to curl.) Endive are also good cooked. They can be served plain or in their broth or with a white sauce. (Wrap a slice of ham around each head or half a head, cover with a white sauce, sprinkle with cheese, and brown under the broiler.) Cooked endives can also be sautéed in butter, or covered with melted butter and chopped parsley *(meunière)* as well as puréed and finished with cream and seasonings. The basic way to cook endive follows.

3 pounds endive (medium size), approximately 12 to 15 pieces
½ tablespoon sugar
1 teaspoon salt
¼ stick (1 ounce) sweet butter
Juice of 1 lemon (approximately ¼ cup)
⅓ cup water

1. Wash and clean the root of the endive very lightly if brown and discolored. Do not cut enough to separate the leaves. Trim any discolored leaves. Rinse carefully under cold water and arrange in layers in a sturdy stainless or enameled pan.

2. Add the sugar, salt, lemon juice and water and cover the endive with a round of parchment paper. Place a plate on top of the paper and then the regular lid on top. The paper helps the endive steam better and the weight gently presses them down into their own juices. The top lid prevents the steam from escaping during cooking which would make the endive dry. Notice that the recipe has just a bit of liquid; the endive will render liquid of its own cooking.

3. Bring to a boil on top of the stove and either simmer on top of the stove or place in a preheated 400-degree oven for 25 to 30 minutes. The endives should still be firm when cooked. Let cool in the broth. When cool enough to handle, remove, arrange in a terrine or bowl, pour the juices on top, cover and keep in the refrigerator until ready to use.

42. How to Peel and Prepare Green Peppers *(Poivrons Epluchés et Farcis)*

PEPPERS CAN BE SLICED thin and eaten raw in a salad. They can be chopped, sautéed and served with eggs or fried with onions as a garnish, or served with hamburgers or steaks. However, if you are going to stuff them, the skin should be removed. Peeling them greatly improves their taste and texture. We have used the long tapered Italian pepper in the photographs that follow; they are sweeter, thinner and more tender than the ordinary ones.

TO PEEL AND SEED PEPPERS

1. Place the peppers on a rack under the broiler approximately 1 inch away from the heat. The Italian peppers will take approximately 10 to 12 minutes of browning and the regular type approximately 14 minutes. Turn them after 5 to 6 minutes of browning.

2. When they are charred all around, re-move from the oven and place them in a plastic bag. Close the bag and let them steam and soften in the bag for about 10 minutes.

3. Steaming the peppers in a plastic bag makes the skin very easy to remove. Hold by the stem and pull the skin, which should come off easily.

4. Pull the stem and with it will come most of the seeds. Remove the seeds left inside with a teaspoon.

5. Another method is to open the pepper and spread it flat out on the table, scraping out all the seeds.

GARLIC PEPPERS (*Poivrons à l'Aïl*)

8 *peppers, roasted, with skin and seeds removed*
6 *to 8 garlic cloves, peeled, chopped and crushed*
(1 tablespoon)
1 *teaspoon salt*
½ *teaspoon freshly ground white pepper*
½ *teaspoon red wine vinegar*
4 *tablespoons virgin olive oil*

6. Cut the peppers into ½-inch-wide strips. Combine with the other ingredients and let the whole mixture marinate for at least 2 hours before serving. Serve at room temperature with crunchy bread, or as a side dish or mix into a salad. The garlic peppers will keep in the refrigerator for at least 2 weeks.

STUFFED GREEN PEPPERS (*Poivrons Verts Farcis*)

8 *to* 10 *medium Italian-type peppers (peeled, seeded and opened*
½ *cup long grain rice (2 cups cooked)*
1 *tablespoon olive oil*
⅓ *cup chopped onions*
2 *cloves garlic peeled, crushed and chopped fine (about ½ teaspoon)*
½ *teaspoon freshly ground black pepper*
½ *teaspoon salt*

Pinch of thyme leaves
1¼ *cups finely diced boiled ham*
2 *tablespoons chopped parsley*
2 *tablespoons olive oil (for sprinkling on top)*

Boil the rice in 3 cups of salted water for 30 minutes and drain.

7. Heat the oil in a skillet, add the onions and sizzle for 1 to 2 minutes. Add the garlic, pepper, salt and thyme. (If you are going to serve the peppers cold, overseason the stuffing.) Remove from the stove and add the ham, parsley and cooked rice. Place 2 to 3 tablespoons of stuffing on each open pepper, fold and turn upside down so the seam side is underneath.

8. Place them side by side in an au gratin dish, sprinkle with the 2 tablespoons of olive oil and additional salt and pepper. Cover and place in a preheated 400-degree oven for ½ hour.

9. The stuffed peppers are also made with the regular, thicker-type pepper. Peel as explained previously and pull out the stem. You will notice that this pepper holds its shape better. With a spoon, remove the seeds without opening the pepper.

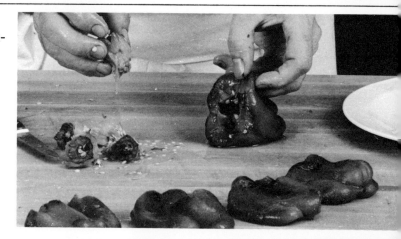

10. Use a pastry bag without any tube to stuff the pepper.

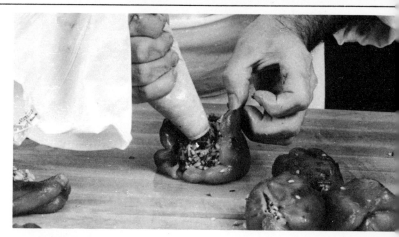

11. If the pepper opens, fold back on the stuffing and place seam side down in the au gratin dish. Cook in a preheated 400-degree oven for ½ hour. The stuffed peppers can be served warm as a vegetable, as well as a main course for lunch or as a first course for dinner. They can also be eaten cool, sprinkled with olive oil.

43. Fried Parsley *(Persil Frit)*

PARSLEY SHOULD BE FRIED in hot, clean fat, and there should be enough fat to cover the parsley completely. It should be fried fast or it will become dark and bitter. In classic French cooking fried parsley is served with fried fish, fried eggs or fried croquettes.

2 cups curly parsley, washed and well dried
2 cups vegetable oil
Dash of salt

1. Bring the oil to 375 degrees and drop a handful of parsley at a time into the hot oil. Mix with your skimmer.

2. Fry for 10 to 12 seconds at the most. Lift out and dry on a paper towel. Sprinkle lightly with salt and serve immediately.

44. Patti Pan Squash with Tomatoes
(Patisson Blanc à la Tomate)

YIELD: 6 servings

THE SMALL PATTI PAN SQUASH has a beautiful scalloped shape that lends itself to some very attractive dishes. The young ones (washed, cut in half, seeded and sliced very thin) are excellent used raw in salads. They can also be cooked in water, made into a purée and finished with butter, salt and pepper. That same purée, with the addition of eggs, milk, salt, pepper and Swiss cheese, can be turned into a lovely gratin of squash. Served our way, it is a nice garnish for a roast of beef, a chicken or other roasted meats. The young squash don't have many seeds. The older the squash, the more seeds it will have. Seeds should be removed.

6 *small young patti pan squash*
2 *to 3 ripe tomatoes, skin and seeds removed and diced (about 2 cups)*
1 *teaspoon chopped onion*
2 *tablespoons sweet butter*
½ *teaspoon salt*
¼ *teaspoon freshly ground white pepper*

To make the tomato stew, heat the butter in a saucepan. Add the onions and sauté for ½ minute. Add the tomatoes, salt and pepper. Cover and cook 2 minutes. Uncover and

cook an additional 2 to 3 minutes on high heat to reduce some of the moisture and thicken the mixture.

1. Cut a "lid" off the patti pan, preferably on the stem side.

2. Using a small coffee spoon, scoop out the inside seeds. Be careful not to go into the flesh itself.

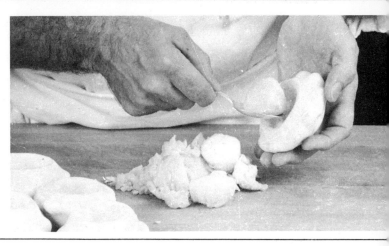

3. Place ½ inch of water and ½ teaspoon salt in a saucepan and bring to a boil. Place the squash with their lids in the water, cover and bring to a strong boil. Boil for 3 minutes. Using a slotted spoon or a fork, remove the squash and set aside. Let cool until ready to use.

4. Sprinkle the inside of the squash slightly with salt and brush with melted butter if desired. Heat in the oven 1 to 2 minutes until warm. Fill the squash with the hot tomato stew, place the lids back on top and serve as an accompaniment or on its own with a poached egg.

45. Broccoli and Cauliflower with Lemon Butter *(Choux Panachés au Beurre de Citron)*

YIELD: 10 servings

WHEN YOU SHOP FOR BROCCOLI, look for a head that's a beautiful deep green with tiny flowerets tightly packed together—a young broccoli, tender and very flavorful. In older broccoli, the flowerets start to open up, and the vegetable becomes softer, stronger in taste and is no longer crisp and tender. This versatile vegetable can be steamed briefly and served plain with lemon and salt or with melted butter and lemon, as well as with a white sauce. It can also be made into a purée or served crunchy in small pieces mixed with filets of anchovies, garlic and olive oil as a first course or part of hors d'oeuvre. Cauliflower can also be prepared many ways. The whole head can be cooked in one piece, as in our recipe, or in flowerets. It can be served with a cream sauce, or au gratin. It can be puréed or fried in butter "Polonaise style" with hard chopped eggs. Choose very tight, white, firm heads which are indications of youth and freshness. Older cauliflower is fibrous, slightly yellowish, softer and has a much stronger odor. Cauliflower and broccoli belong to the same family and are mixed together and served with a lemon butter sauce in the recipe below.

2–3 bunches broccoli (about 4 pounds)
1 large cauliflower (2 to 3 pounds)

Foaming lemon butter

1½ tablespoons water
1 tablespoon lemon juice
Dash of salt
Dash of white pepper
⅔ stick sweet butter, softened

1. Cut the broccoli into flowerets. Trim the stems. Peel away any fibrous skin.

2. Peel the pieces of stem.

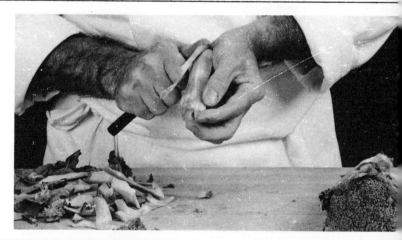

3. Cut the peeled stems into pieces and combine them with the flowerets.

4. Place ½ cup water and ½ teaspoon salt in a large stainless steel pan and bring to a strong boil. The water should cover only the bottom of the pan. Add the broccoli in one layer. Pieces should not overlap. Cover and bring to a strong boil. Boil for approximately 4 minutes, covered. Remove the broccoli with a slotted spoon and place it on a tray. It should be green and crunchy. Set aside to cool until ready to use.

5. The cauliflower can be cooked whole after the green leaves and any bruised parts are removed.

6. Place 1 inch of water and ½ teaspoon salt in the bottom of a stainless steel saucepan. Bring to a strong boil and place the cauliflower in one piece in the boiling water. Cover and boil about 10 minutes. The cauliflower should be tender but still quite crunchy. (It could be served as is with a piece of fresh butter on top.)

7. For our recipe, separate the flowerets from the core. Heavily butter a large Pyrex or stainless steel bowl and sprinkle with salt. Line the dish with cauliflower, then broccoli, then cauliflower again, pressing the vegetables down slightly as you layer them.

8. Keep layering until the bowl is full. Sprinkle the top with salt and cover with a piece of buttered parchment paper. At serving time, heat the bowl in a *bain-marie* on top of the stove, or place it in a preheated 300-degree oven for 10 to 15 minutes, just long enough to warm the vegetables through.

9. Unmold on a serving platter and make a lemon butter.

10. Bring the water, lemon juice, salt and pepper to a strong boil and drop pieces of butter in the boiling mixture, bit by bit, shaking the pan with one hand and adding the butter with the other. After all the butter has been added, the mixture will start foaming and will rise like milk about to boil over. As soon as it does, remove it from the heat. (If the mixture continues to boil it will separate.) Pour on top of the unmolded vegetables and serve right away. This dish can be served by itself or as a garnish to meat, chicken or poached fish.

46. Eggplant Custards *(Papetons d'Aubergines)*

YIELD: 8 servings

LONG, NARROW EGGPLANTS are usually more meaty and have fewer seeds than the large ones. Often large eggplants are baked in the oven, then the center is mashed with cooked onions, olive oil and seasonings and served as a dip that's known as "poor man's caviar." Slices of eggplant fried with skin on are used to line a mold filled with ground cooked lamb in the famous *moussaka* served with a tomato sauce. Eggplant is also good cut into little strips, dipped into a batter of beer or egg whites and deep fried. It is an essential ingredient of the famous *ratatouille* of Provence: a stew of eggplant, zucchini, onions, garlic, olive oil, etc., served hot or cold.

This dish is thought to have been created for the Popes when they lived in Avignon. It is from them that it gets the name *papetons*. It is a delicate dish, which can be made in large or small molds and is excellent by itself as well as with a roasted saddle of lamb or roast of veal. You will need 8 small baba molds, approximately ¾ cup each.

Eggplant custards

2 *pounds small, firm eggplant*
2 *teaspoons salt*
1 *cup peanut oil*
2 *medium-size cloves garlic, peeled and crushed*
6 *large eggs*
1 *cup heavy cream*
1½ *teaspoons salt*

Tomato sauce

2½ *pounds ripe tomatoes, cut into large chunks*
3 *tablespoons good olive oil*
1 *cup finely chopped onions*
3 *cloves garlic, peeled, crushed and chopped*
1½ *teaspoons salt*
½ *teaspoon freshly ground white pepper*
¼ *teaspoon sugar*
1 *tablespoon sweet butter*

Heat the oil in a heavy saucepan and add the onions. Sauté for 2 minutes on medium heat and add the garlic. Stir for a few seconds and add the tomatoes. Cover and cook for about 10 minutes on medium heat. Add the salt, pepper and sugar, stir well and remove from heat. Push the mixture through a food mill fitted with the fine screen. Add the butter bit by bit to the sauce, until well blended. Taste for seasonings and add salt and pepper if needed.

1. Peel the eggplant with a vegetable peeler keeping the skin as thin as possible. Blanch a few strips of skin for 1 minute in boiling water, then drain and cool under cold water. These will be used to decorate the molds. Slice the peeled eggplant into ½-inch slices. With the point of a knife, score both sides of the slice to form diamonds. Sprinkle with 2 teaspoons salt and spread the slices on a cookie sheet. Place another cookie sheet on top of the eggplant slices, and weigh it down with cans or other heavy objects. Keep pressed for ½ hour. The salt-

ing and pressing remove some of the bitter juices from the eggplant and prevent the slices from absorbing too much oil during cooking.

2. Blot the slices with paper towels. Heat about 3 tablespoons of oil in a skillet, and fry a few slices at a time on both sides until nicely browned. Set the slices in a colander after they are browned to allow some of the oil to drain. Place the fried eggplant in a food processor with the garlic and process until very smooth. (If the eggplant are very seedy, push the mixture through a food mill fitted with the fine screen.) Add the eggs and blend well. Stir in the cream and the 1½ teaspoons salt.

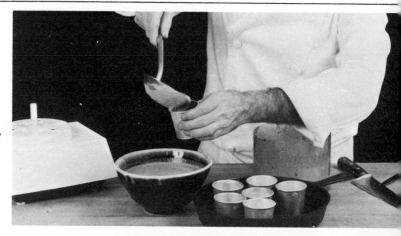

3. Butter several small molds or a large mold. Cut the strips of skin into flowers or different patterns.

4. Decorate the bottoms and sides of mold (the skin will stick to the butter). Fill with the eggplant mixture and place a piece of buttered parchment paper on top. Place the molds in a skillet with water around; cook in a preheated 375-degree oven for 25 to 30 minutes, until set. Remove and let sit for 10 to 15 minutes. If the decoration sticks to the mold when unmolding, remove and rearrange on top of the eggplant. *Papetons* are often decorated after unmolding rather than before. Cover with the tomato sauce and serve.

47. Zucchini Puff Paste *(Feuilletés de Courgettes)*

YIELD: 4 servings

Zucchini is a very good and very handy vegetable. It can be served in salad (see technique 56) as well as au gratin or just plain stewed or stewed in butter. With the addition of puff paste and a light butter sauce it can be made into a very elegant dish.

About ⅓ pound puff paste (technique 91)
¾ pound small zucchini, sliced into thin strips or
*   wedges*
½ cup water
4 tablespoons sweet butter, cut into pieces
1 teaspoon fresh lemon juice
Pepper and salt to taste

1. Roll out a strip of puff paste approximately ¼ inch thick. Cut 4 strips about 5 inches long by 1½ inches wide. Line a cookie sheet with parchment paper and place the strips of puff paste on it. Brush with egg wash, and score the top in a crisscross pattern, for decoration. Place the tray in the freezer for 15 to 20 minutes, then in a preheated 375-degree oven for approximately 30 minutes, until well puffed, browned and crunchy. Set aside until ready to use.

2. Place the zucchini with the water and a dash of salt in a skillet, bring to a boil, cover and boil on high heat for 1 minute. Add the butter, the lemon juice and a little extra salt and pepper and bring back to a boil, shaking the pan so that the butter binds with the liquid. Warm the puff paste strips in the oven for a few minutes and cut into halves. Arrange some zucchini strips across the bottom part of the puff paste, moisten with the butter sauce, cover with the second part of the puff paste and serve, hot, immediately.

48. Swiss Chard au Gratin *(Côte de Bettes au Gratin)*

YIELD: 6 to 8 servings

ALTHOUGH COMMON IN EUROPE, particularly in Italy and France, the Swiss chard as well as the cardon are not often served in the United States. Cardon stalks are peeled the same way as are the Swiss chard. The pieces of stalks are cooked in water or in a *blanc* (a mixture of water and flour) and sometimes served with marrow, in gratins or with cream sauce or red wine sauce. Swiss chard can be steamed and sautéed in butter or cooked in the juice of a roast. The green of the Swiss chard can be eaten and cooked like spinach. When the green is very tender it can be used in salads. The Swiss chard is often prepared with a *persillade* (parsley and garlic added at the last moment with butter and sautéed) and at other times in a gratin to serve with a roast chicken or broiled steaks—which is what we will make below.

3 pounds Swiss chard as purchased
1 tablespoon sweet butter
1 tablespoon flour
1½ cups milk
1 cup heavy cream
½ teaspoon salt
¼ teaspoon freshly ground white pepper
½ cup grated Swiss cheese

1. Cut the leaves off on each side of the stalk. The 3 pounds of Swiss chard cleaned yield approximately 1¾ pounds of stalks.

2. As you get toward the end of the stem, remove the green with the end of the stem. Keep the greens for soups or cook as you would spinach.

3. The stems are sometimes very wide and often not flat. Cut the stem in strips so the stalks are more manageable and easier to peel. To peel, cut a piece approximately 2 inches long from the stem. Do not cut completely through.

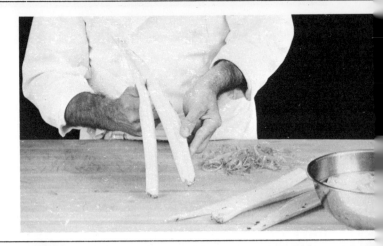

4. Break the "cut" piece and pull off. Note the fibers that hang from the large part of the stem.

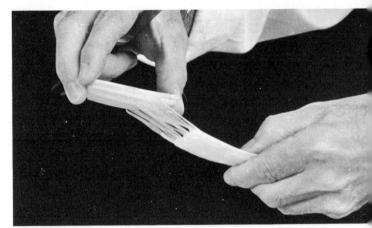

5. Take the fibers and pull them off so that a complete side of the stem is clean. Repeat the same procedure on the underside of the stem. Removing the fibers makes the chard much more tender and is especially necessary when the vegetable is large and a bit old. As they are peeled, drop in cold water to prevent discoloration.

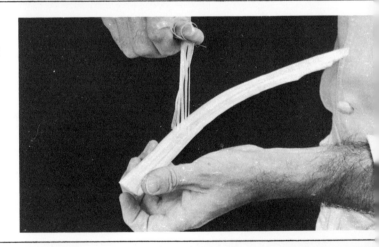

6. Drop the white stems into salted boiling water. Bring to a boil and boil for approximately 6 minutes. Drain in a colander. The pieces should be tender but still firm. For our white sauce, melt the butter in a saucepan over medium heat and add the flour. Whisk and cook for about 1 minute, then add the milk and, still whisking, bring to a boil. Boil for about ½ minute. Remove from the heat and add the cream, salt and pepper. Mix well. Butter a 6-cup au gratin dish and arrange the chard in it. Sprinkle with the grated cheese and pour the sauce on top.

7. Place on a cookie sheet in a preheated 375-degree oven for a generous 40 minutes. If not brown enough after this time, place briefly under the broiler. Let the gratin rest at least 10 minutes before serving.

49. Braised Stuffed Cabbages *(Choux Farcis)*

YIELD: 6 servings

THE CABBAGE is excellent left raw and sliced very thin in salad. It is a great winter vegetable which blends well in soups or boiled with different types of sausages or pork or other meats. The cabbage can be stuffed whole (the stuffing is placed between the leaves) as well as made into small stuffed cabbage balls. To make 12 small stuffed cabbage balls, use one 3-pound cabbage, preferably Savoy, the leafy, curly type.

Stuffing

1 tablespoon sweet butter
1 large onion, finely chopped (1 cup)
3 cloves garlic, finely chopped and crushed
1 pound reserved cabbage from the heart
1 cup water
1 pound ground pork (preferably from the shoulder or butt)
1 pound ground beef, not too lean
3 large eggs

2 teaspoons salt
1 teaspoon freshly ground white pepper
⅓ cup chopped parsley

Braising

2 medium carrots, peeled and coarsely chopped (1 cup)
1¼ cups coarsely chopped onions
5 cloves garlic, finely chopped (1 teaspoon)
2 cups good chicken stock

1. Cut off the core of the cabbage and spread out the leaves so they detach from the center. Try not to break the large leaves that are needed as wrappers for the stuffing.

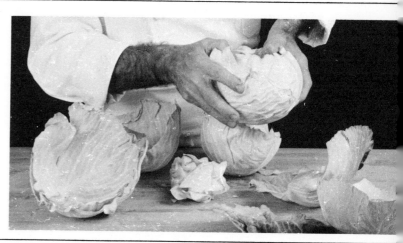

2. The central part of the cabbage should be chopped finely and used in the stuffing. It will make approximately 1 pound.

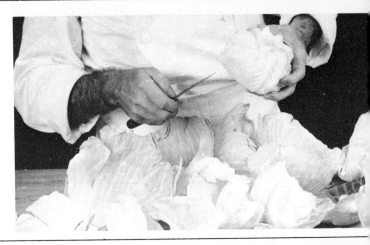

3. Plunge the leaves into a large pot of boiling water, pushing them down gently as they get wilted. When they are all immersed, let the water come to a boil and boil gently for 5 minutes. Then place the kettle under cold running water. When cold, drain the leaves in a colander, place them flat on the table and remove approximately 2 inches of the toughest part of the stem. You should have about 15 to 20 leaves.

4. Make the stuffing: Melt the butter in a large skillet. Add the onions and sauté gently for 1 to 2 minutes. Add the garlic, stir, then add the chopped cabbage and 1 cup of water. Bring to a boil, cover and cook for 5 minutes on high heat. Place the meats in a mixing bowl. Add the eggs, salt, pepper and parsley and mix well with your hands. Combine with the cooked cabbage mixture and mix well again. Place one leaf in a ladle with sides overlapping and fill it up with about ½ cup of the stuffing mixture.

5. Cover the filling with the overlapping cabbage and press down to give the cabbage shape and make sure the stuffing is well packed and wrapped.

6. The cabbage should be well formed and round.

7. Another method of stuffing leaves is to lay a cabbage leaf out on a kitchen towel. If it is broken, add several pieces to form a large leaf. Place the stuffing in the center and bring the cabbage leaves over it.

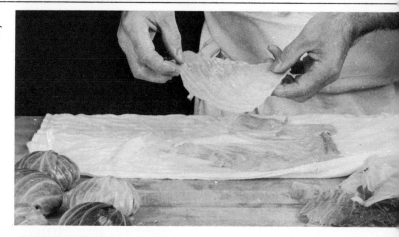

8. Fold the towel into a ball and squeeze tightly to shape the cabbage into a ball. The cabbage can also be molded without the use of the towel, just by hand, but if you use the ladle or the towel, the cabbages will be more uniform in size.

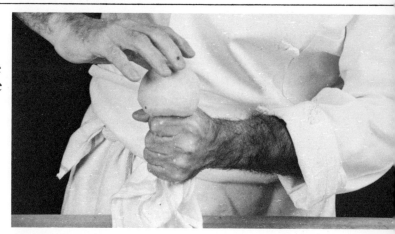

9. Place all of the braising ingredients except the chicken stock in the bottom of a roasting pan. Arrange the stuffed cabbages on top, side by side, with the folded side down, so they touch one another. Pour the chicken stock over. Cover the pan with a cookie sheet or aluminum foil and bring to a boil on top of the stove. Place in a pre-heated 350-degree oven for 2 hours. Remove the cover and arrange the cabbages on a serving platter, draining all the liquid. Place the liquid and vegetable garnish on top of the stove in a saucepan and reduce

on high heat by about two-thirds. You should have approximately 2 cups of liquid left. Pour about 2 tablespoons of the sauce on top of each cabbage and serve. This dish is also excellent reheated.

50. Soap-shaped Potatoes *(Pommes Savonnettes)*

YIELD: 4 to 5 servings

THE *pommes savonnettes* make a very nice garnish for a roast filet of beef, roast chicken and most roasted meats. The slices of potatoes looking like little cakes of soap are placed flat into a saucepan, and cooked with water and butter on very high heat. The potatoes get very moist by absorbing some of the water and when the water evaporates they start to brown in the butter that is left behind. They get beautifully brown on the outside and soft in the center. These are based on the same principle as *pommes fondantes* (melting potatoes), which are cooked with butter and chicken stock and when three-fourths of the way cooked, when almost all of the liquid has been absorbed, the potatoes are cracked with a spoon lightly, so they finish absorbing the rest of the liquid. They are not browned further, but served at that point.

Pommes savonnettes remain at their best for 15 minutes, but they quickly acquire reheated taste, so serve them as quickly as possible. Choose large Idaho potatoes of the same size.

5 large potatoes (about 15 to 18 slices)
2 tablespoons butter
1½ tablespoons vegetable oil
¾ cup water

1. Peel the potatoes and trim into long, even cylinders. Use the trimmings to make soups, potato croquettes, mashed potatoes, etc.

2. Cut the potato cylinders into 1-inch disks.

3. Bevel the edges for a more finished look and to keep them from getting battered during cooking.

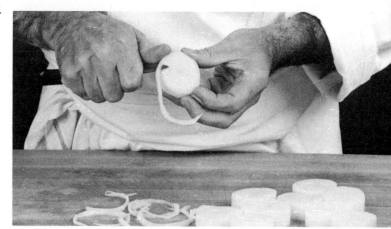

4. Take a heavy non-stick skillet or sauce-pan and arrange the potatoes snugly in the bottom, without overlapping. Place the nicer side of the slices face down in the skillet. Add more potatoes if necessary to fill the skillet. Add the butter, oil and water. The water should come three-fourths of the way up the slices. Bring to a strong boil on top of the stove, then place on the lower shelf of a preheated 475-degree oven or directly on the floor of the oven. The water must continue to boil so it will evaporate. If the water doesn't boil, the potatoes will cook and end up falling apart. If your skillet has a plastic handle, be sure to cover it with several layers of aluminum foil so it doesn't get damaged during cooking. Cook for 35 to 40 minutes, until the potatoes are very tender and brown. After about 25 to 30 minutes, the water should have completely evaporated and the potatoes should have begun to brown. The top will brown only slightly, but the bottom will be a beautiful dark brown in color. Let the potatoes rest for 2 to 3 minutes, then flip each one over.

Arrange them with the nicest side up on a platter, brush with butter and serve immediately.

51. Straw Potato Cake *(Pommes Paillasson)*

YIELD: 4 to 6 servings

POMMES PAILLASSON are made from potatoes that are peeled, washed and then cut into a fine julienne with a *mandoline* (a slicer) or by hand. Once the potatoes have been cut into julienne they have to be cooked right away or kept in water to prevent discoloration. The water bath washes off some of the potato's starch. If the potatoes are not kept in water but are cooked right away, the starch left in the potatoes will make them "cake" or hold better. On the other hand, they will be slightly gooey inside. If they have been washed they will be less starchy in taste but more fragile in construction—the potatoes will be more likely to disentangle. The starch acts like a glue. Whichever method you use, the taste is the same, only the texture is slightly different. Use large Idaho potatoes. One large potato will give you approximately 1 cup. Pommes paillasson should be served immediately as should most fried potatoes or they will take on a reheated taste. These potatoes are known as *rosti* in Switzerland and also *Darphin* potatoes in France.

4 *cups julienned potatoes (use baking potatoes)*
2 *tablespoons sweet butter*
4 *tablespoons vegetable oil*
¼ *teaspoon salt*
Dash of white pepper

1. Peel and wash the potatoes then cut into julienne. Wash the julienne and dry in paper towels or cook right away. In a non-stick skillet, heat the butter and oil. When very hot, add the potatoes, salt and pepper and coat well with fat by stirring. Use a fork to spread the potatoes around.

2. Use a large, flat spoon to press the potatoes down so the strips cohere together into a cake. Cook on medium heat for 4 to 5 minutes at least, pressing down on the cake once in a while. Flip the pancake over and cook another 4 to 5 minutes on medium to low heat. The potato pancake should not be more than ½ inch thick, crunchy on the outside and soft in the middle. If you cannot flip the pancake in one stroke, place a plate on top, turn it upside down and slide back into the skillet. Serve as soon as possible.

52. Straw Potato Nest *(Nid en Pommes Paille)*

THE POTATO NEST is done with julienne potatoes and is usually used as a garnish filled with tiny *pommes soufflés* or potato croquettes. To make the nest you need a special double wire basket available in specialty stores. For each nest you need approximately 2 cups of loose julienne potatoes. Washing the potatoes julienne will give you a nest which won't hold together as well as the one with unwashed potatoes which, however, won't release as well from the metal nest because the starch will stick to the metal wires. However, it works both ways. (See technique 51 for more about washing potatoes.)

1. Using a knife or a *mandoline* (vegetable slicer), slice the potatoes into slices 1/16-inch thick. Pile them together and cut into a thin julienne. Wash and dry, if desired.

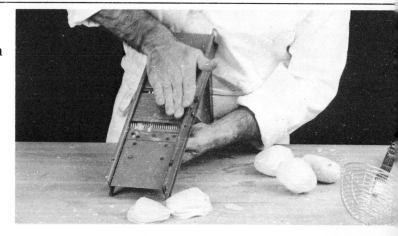

2. Dip the wire basket in the hot oil. Then fill the bottom part of the basket with potato strips. Make a hole in the center and place the smaller part of the nest in the basket.

3. Secure both parts with the clip.

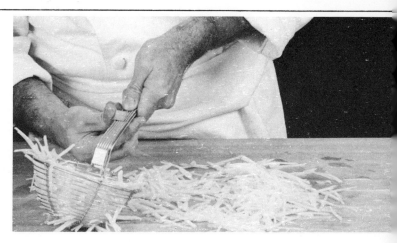

4. Drop the potatoes in 400-degree vegetable oil and cook for 4 to 5 minutes on high heat. Be sure that the potato nest stays completely immersed during cooking by holding it down into the oil.

5. To unmold, remove the clip and trim away the pieces of potato sticking through both the outside and inside of the nest. This makes it easier to release the potatoes from the mold.

6. Jiggle the wire basket and lift it up from the potatoes.

7. The potatoes may still be hard to remove. Turn upside down, and using a towel, press the mesh to bend it and help the potatoes release. Use a small knife to pry it out.

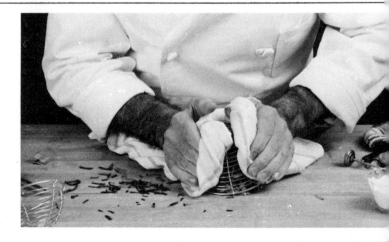

8. The potato nest released, and ready to be served.

53. Waffle Potato Nest *(Nid en Pommes Gaufrettes)*

1. Using the *mandoline,* cut the waffle potatoes. (See page 202 in *La Technique* for more information on how to cut waffle potatoes.) Arrange slices of waffle potatoes in the bottom layer of the wire basket to simulate a tulip. (See the introduction to technique 52 for more about this metal nest.)

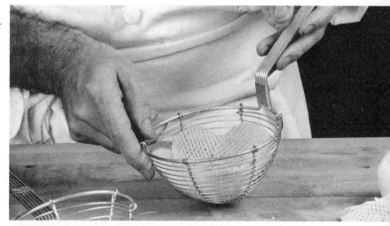

2. Place the smaller nest on top, secure with the clip and dip in 400-degree vegetable oil. Make sure that the whole nest is immersed. It will take approximately 3½ minutes to cook. Remove from the oil, unclip and start jiggling the two parts of the nest to separate them. The nest may remain attached to the top part or may stick to the bottom part. (In our case the nest stuck to the top.)

3. Using a knife, pry all around and trim the inside to release the nest. The waffle nest is even more fragile than the straw potato nest.

4. The potato nest can be filled with straw potatoes or soufflé potatoes and served as a garnish for roasted poultry.

54. Dandelion Salad *(Salade de Pissenlits)*

YIELD: 6 servings

DANDELION SALAD announces the coming of spring and although there is some cultivated dandelion, it does not approach the taste of the wild one. Dandelion should be picked early in the season. Look for plants growing in gravel or soft earth; somewhere where the stem will have been covered half way up, and will have had a chance to get white like endive, with the same tender and slightly bitter and stringent taste. Although dandelions are commonly eaten in the French countryside, our recipe is a specialty of Lyon. The fat of the *lardons* is used instead of oil in the dressing for the salad. The salad is served on lukewarm plates with crusty bread and with a light Beaujolais.

1 *pound cleaned, washed and dried dandelion*
¾ *cup salt pork, cut into small sticks* (lardons)
2 *slices of toast*
1 *garlic clove, peeled*
2 *hard-boiled eggs, shelled*
2 *cloves garlic, peeled, crushed and chopped fine*
1 *small can (2 ounces) anchovies in oil*
1½ *teaspoons good red wine vinegar*
½ *teaspoon salt*

½ *teaspoon freshly ground white pepper*
2 *tablespoons good olive oil, virgin if possible*

1. The dandelion greens should be picked before the flower stage or they will be too tough and bitter. Use your knife to dig into the ground and remove the whole plant along with the root. Scrape the root of any dirt, removing any black parts but preserving as much of it as possible so the dandelion leaves still hold together by the root. Split the large plants in half so they can be washed properly. Wash several times in cold water, drain well and dry.

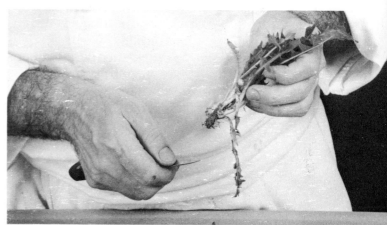

2. The salt pork, also called corned belly and sweet pickle, is cured unsmoked bacon. Cut into ½-inch slices and then cut each slice into small strips (*lardons*). Place the *lardons* in cold water and bring to a boil. Boil for 1 minute, then drain and rinse under cold water. Set aside.

3. Rub the toasted bread with a whole peeled clove of garlic on both sides. In order for the bread to "abrade" the garlic it must be well toasted. Cut each slice of bread into 6 *croûtons*. Cut the 2 hard-boiled eggs into 6 segments each.

4. Place the anchovy fillets on the table and using the blade of a knife, crush and smear them down into a purée. Chop the 2 cloves of garlic very fine and add to the anchovies. Purée until smooth with the blade of a knife. Place the *lardons* in a skillet and fry them on medium heat until crisp. Meanwhile, place the purée of anchovies and garlic into a salad bowl, add the vinegar, salt, pepper and olive oil and mix well. When the *lardons* are ready, add them with their fat to the mixture and stir well.

5. Add the washed and dried greens and mix thoroughly. Sprinkle the *croûtons* and the eggs on top. The salad should be slightly lukewarm. Serve immediately. This is also good made from very thinly sliced red or white cabbage.

55. Spinach Salad with Chicken Livers *(Salade d'Epinards aux Foies de Volaille)*

YIELD: 6 servings

THIS SALAD can be made without the chicken livers and with or without the red peppers. The combination, however, makes it colorful, interesting and tasty.

8 *cups (loosely packed) fresh spinach, stems removed (see technique 40)*
5 to 6 *chicken or duck livers, cooked in fat (see technique 62)*
1 *large sweet red pepper (green if red is not available), sliced*
1 *small clove garlic, crushed and chopped fine*
1 *teaspoon French mustard*

2 *teaspoons good red wine vinegar*
Salt and pepper to taste
¼ *cup good olive oil or peanut oil*

1. Cut the red pepper in half lengthwise, remove the seeds and slice very thin. Wash the spinach and drain carefully in a salad dryer. Mix together the garlic, mustard, red wine vinegar, salt and pepper. Slowly add the oil, mixing carefully. Take 1 tablespoon of the mixture and combine with the sliced pepper. Set aside at room temperature until ready to serve. This can marinate for at least 1 hour.

2. At serving time, slice the chicken or duck livers on a slant into slivers. Mix the spinach with the remaining dressing and arrange in a bowl. Arrange the pepper around the spinach and sprinkle the livers on top. Serve immediately.

56. Vegetable Salads *(Salades de Légumes)*

VEGETABLE COOKERY has progressed considerably in recent years as people have grown more interested in lighter and less caloric cooking. Fortunately, vegetables are now cooked faster and served crunchier. A revived interest in gardening coupled with a widened enthusiasm for Oriental cuisines has also influenced this new trend toward an appreciation of fresh vegetables. Vegetables are cooked differently in restaurants than at home. In a restaurant most green vegetables—asparagus, spinach, string beans, peas, broccoli, etc.—are cooked in a lot of salted boiling water and, when cooked enough, plunged into cold water for a few minutes to stop further cooking and keep them green. This system destroys a certain amount of the vegetable's vitamins, which is why steaming or cooking in a tiny bit of water is preferable. However, it is the only practical way to cook great quantities of vegetables.

A small amount of vegetables will cool fast and retain its color without being plunged in cold water. Just undercook them a little, as they continue to cook for a few minutes after being strained.

Certain vegetables such as string beans and asparagus are excellent steamed and served right away. However, if they are allowed to sit a while exposed to the air they shrivel and begin to look wrinkled. If they are not to be served immediately, it's better to cook the vegetables in a little bit of water (less moisture gets pulled out of the vegetables while cooking) or cover them with a wet towel after cooking to prevent shriveling.

Cooked vegetables, besides being an accompaniment to meat, make very good salads. They usually improve in taste if they marinate in the dressing for 30 minutes before serving. Vegetable salads should not be served too cold and thought should be given to the combination of vegetables for the taste as well as color. Recipes for a few vegetable salads follow.

STRING BEANS AND TOMATO SALAD
(Salade de Haricots Verts et Tomates)

YIELD: 4 servings

Choose the thinnest string beans you can find. They should be firm, green and long. Remove both ends taking with them the string, if any. Wash the beans in cold water.

1 *pound string beans*
1 *tablespoon good red wine vinegar*
3 *tablespoons good peanut or grape-seed oil*
Salt and pepper to taste
3 *large tomatoes with or without the skin*

1 *tablespoon red wine vinegar*
⅓ *cup virgin olive oil*
⅓ *cup thinly sliced onions for garnish*
15 *to* 20 *basil leaves*

1. Place approximately ½ inch of water in a wide stainless steel saucepan and add ½ teaspoon salt. Bring to a strong boil. Add 1 pound cleaned string beans. They should cover the bottom of the pan in one layer. Cover and bring to a strong boil. Keep boiling, covered, over high heat for 3 to 5 minutes, depending on the size of the beans and how fresh they are.

2. Using a skimmer, lift the beans from the pan and spread them on a large plate to cool off. They should be crunchy and a beautiful green in color. Toss the beans with the wine vinegar and oil. Season and set aside.

3. Peel the tomatoes if desired and slice crosswise very thinly. Place the seasoned string beans in the center of a large platter and arrange the slices of tomatoes around. Sprinkle generously with salt and pepper. Tomatoes require a lot of salt. Then sprinkle with the vinegar and the oil.

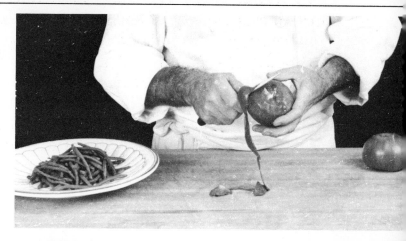

4. Wash the fresh basil and separate the leaves. Pile the largest leaves together.

5. Roll the leaves into a tight bundle and cut them into a very thin julienne.

6. Cut the onion into very thin slices and separate the slices into individual rings.

7. Sprinkle the onions on top and border with the julienned basil leaves.

BEET SALAD *(Salade de Betteraves)*

YIELD: 6 servings

4 to 5 fresh beets
1 teaspoon French mustard
2 tablespoons heavy cream
Freshly ground white pepper to taste
Salt to taste (beets require a lot of salt)

1. Cover beets with cold water and add salt. Bring to a boil and cook covered approximately 1¼ hours, or until tender when pricked with the point of a knife. Remove from water and allow to cool. Peel.

2. Slice in ¼-inch slices, stack slices together, a few at à time and cut into ¼-inch strips. Add dressing, toss and let sit until ready to serve.

ZUCCHINI SALAD *(Salade de Courgettes)*

YIELD: 4 to 6 servings

2 to 3 small zucchini, washed
1 tablespoon good peanut or olive oil
1 teaspoon good red wine vinegar
¼ teaspoon ground black pepper

1. Trim both ends of each zucchini. Cut into 2-inch chunks. Split each section lengthwise in four. Remove the piece in the center where the seeds are. Slice all the pieces in 2 to 3 sticks, depending on size.

2. Spread on a cookie sheet, sprinkle lightly with salt and place in a preheated 425-degree oven for 3 to 4 minutes until the zucchini starts to "sweat." Remove from oven and allow to cool. Add the dressing ingredients, mix well and serve at room temperature.

CARROT SALAD (*Salade de Carottes*)

2 *large carrots, peeled and cut into 1½-inch chunks*
¼ *cup slivered almonds*
1 *tablespoon olive oil, preferably virgin*
Dash of salt and pepper

Cut each carrot chunk into slices. Stack the slices together to cut into strips about ⅛ inch thick. Place in cold water. Add a dash of salt, bring to a boil and boil for 2 minutes.

Drain. Combine with other ingredients. Serve at room temperature.

MUSHROOM SALAD (*Salade de Champignons*)

1 *cup sliced mushroom caps*
1½ *teaspoons lemon juice*
1 *tablespoon good peanut or grape-seed oil*
Salt and freshly ground pepper to taste

Combine all ingredients, mix well and serve immediately.

57. Roman-style Gnocchi (*Gnocchi Romaine*)

YIELD: 6 to 8 servings

THERE ARE TWO TYPES of gnocchi—*gnocchi Parisienne* and *gnocchi Romaine*. The Parisian gnocchi is made from cream puff dough seasoned with Parmesan cheese, formed into small dumplings, poached in water, then usually baked in a white sauce and served au gratin all puffed up like little quenelles. The Roman gnocchi is made into a polenta from semolina and milk, cooled, cut into shapes and either fried or baked with butter, cream and cheese.

3 *cups milk*
2 *tablespoons sweet butter*
2 *teaspoons salt*
½ *teaspoon freshly ground white pepper*
⅛ *teaspoon freshly grated nutmeg*
1 *cup semolina or farina (granulated hard durum wheat flour)*
3 *large eggs*
1 *cup heavy cream*
1 *teaspoon vegetable oil*

¼ *stick (1 ounce) sweet butter, melted*
¾ *cup grated Swiss cheese*
1½ *cups heavy cream*

1. Place the milk, butter, salt, pepper and nutmeg in a large, heavy kettle, and bring to a boil. Pour in the semolina, mixing vigorously with a whisk. Reduce the heat and cook for 2 to 3 minutes, stirring with a wooden spatula until the mixture becomes very thick and lifts up from the sides of the pan. Set aside for 15 minutes until it cools slightly.

2. Beat the eggs in a bowl until well homogenized, then add the cream and combine. Add the egg and cream mixture to the semolina in one stroke and mix thoroughly with the whisk. Be sure to work fast or the basic mixture will lump. Place the mixture back on medium heat and bring to a boil, mixing constantly with the whisk. Remove from the heat as soon as it boils and thickens more.

3. Oil a cookie sheet (about 12 by 16 inches) and pour the mixture on it.

4. Spread the mixture out with a spatula that's been wetted in water. The mixture should be about ½ inch thick. Cover with plastic wrap and refrigerate until cold and set, at least 2 to 3 hours.

5. Using a round cookie cutter about 3 inches in diameter, cut rounds from the cold semolina mixture. Butter an au gratin dish and arrange the pieces overlapping slightly.

6. Pour the melted butter on top of the rounds. Sprinkle with cheese and place the dish on a tray in a preheated 425-degree oven for about 15 minutes or until slightly browned.

7. Meanwhile, gather all the trimmings into a solid flat piece so that more rounds can be cut out of it.

8. When the gratin is slightly brown, pour the cream on top and place back in the oven for about 10 to 12 minutes, until glazed and beautifully browned. If not brown enough, place the tray under the broiler for a few minutes. Let the dish rest for 5 to 6 minutes before serving.

58. Onion Soup *(Soupe à L'Oignon)*

YIELD: 6 servings

ONION SOUP is widely served all over France, sometimes *gratinée*, that is with a crust on top, sometimes just as a broth. It can be served in a large terrine, as well as in individual crock pots. After an evening at the theater, it is usually served *gratinée*. The onions are sometimes sautéed lightly and left in the soup, as in our recipe; other times they are browned to a dark stage then slightly singed with flour, cooked, then pushed through a food mill as in the Lyonnaise version which is made with water rather than stock.

4 *cups thinly sliced Bermuda onions (3 to 5 onions, depending on size)*
1 *pound good Swiss cheese, grated (Emmenthaler or Gruyère)*
3 *tablespoons sweet butter*
10 *cups chicken stock, or a mixture of chicken and beef stock, or a mixture of water and stock*
1 *clove garlic, crushed, peeled and chopped very fine*

1 *teaspoon salt (to taste)*
1 *teaspoon black pepper (to taste)*
2 *dozen slices of French bread, cut very thin and toasted under the broiler*

1. Use sweet yellow onions, making sure you remove all the skin and the roots. Cut them in half across and slice very thinly. Melt the butter and brown the onions on medium heat in a large saucepan for 5 to 6 minutes, until slightly brown. Stir in the stock, garlic, salt and pepper and boil for 30 minutes.

2. Place 4 to 5 slices of bread in each individual ovenproof bowl (use 12-ounce bowls).

3. Half fill each bowl with the stock. The bread will soften as it absorbs the liquid. Gradually keep adding liquid until the bowls are filled evenly and to the top. This is very important because the cheese crust must not sink into the bowl if it is to brown in the oven.

4. Sprinkle the cheese on top without pushing it into the liquid. You will need at least 2½ ounces of cheese per bowl or a good ½ cup (the drier the cheese the better).

5. Press the cheese around the edges of each bowl so that when it melts it sticks to the sides and forms a crust that will stay put instead of sinking into the liquid.

6. Place the bowls on a cookie sheet and bake in a preheated 400-degree oven for approximately 35 minutes, until nicely browned all around. Serve right away, one bowl per guest.

Poultry and Meat

59. Goose Liver Pâté in Aspic

(Foie Gras Truffé en Gelée)

YIELD: 8 to 10 servings

FRESH FATTENED GOOSE liver *pâté* is not available in this country where the forced feeding of geese or ducks is forbidden by law. The canned "pure foie gras," studded with truffles, costs a small fortune but is a real delicacy. It is the fattened, overfed liver of the goose, or duck, poached with Cognac, stock and different spices, cooked slowly in the fat of the goose, or simply just sterilized in tin cans. There are many ersatz, so-called *pâté de foie,* which are made with trimmings of goose liver, pork and different seasonings. The *pâté* featured in this technique is called a "block"—it is a whole goose-liver *pâté,* cooked with seasoning only. It comes in small as well as large cans (ours weighed 1 pound).

Aspic

1 *cup coarsely chopped celery (leafy part)*
⅓ *cup parsley leaves*
½ *cup carrots, peeled and coarsely chopped*
1 *or 2 branches fresh tarragon or a dash of dry if not available fresh*
1 *cup coarsely chopped green of leek*
½ *teaspoon crushed peppercorns*
4 *egg whites*
½ *cup good Port wine*

4 *envelopes unflavored gelatin*
6 *cups good strong chicken or beef (or a mixture of both) stock*
Salt and pepper to taste

1 *canned black truffle for decoration (tomato skin may be substituted)*

1. Mix all vegetables, egg whites, gelatin and Port wine in a stainless steel or enameled saucepan. Add the cold stock and season highly with salt and pepper. Bring to a boil, stirring the mixture almost constantly to avoid scorching. As soon as it boils, a crust will form on top. Reduce the heat and simmer very lightly for about 10 minutes. Do not stir or disturb the stock anymore at that point. Remove from heat, let set for about 10 minutes, then strain through a fine strainer lined with paper towels. Place half of the liquid in a large shallow glass

bowl. You should have about a 2-inch thickness of aspic. Place in the refrigerator to set.

2. Cut the *foie gras* into 1-ounce slices. Slice the whole block or slice only part of it and leave the rest whole. You will need one truffle to decorate the *foie gras*. Peel the rough surface of the truffle and keep the peel in a jar with either Cognac or Madeira. This can be kept for months in the refrigerator and used as needed, for *pâtés,* sauces, etc. Using a knife or a truffle slicer, slice the peeled truffle as thin as possible. Make little cutouts to simulate the flowers or strips to make the stems and push down to embed into the *foie gras* to decorate.

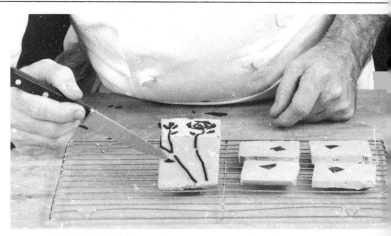

3. If the remaining aspic has set, melt and place on ice. Arrange the slices and the uncut *pâté* on a wire rack over a tray and chill. The *pâté* has to be cold for the aspic to stick to it. Gently stir the aspic with a spoon as it sits in the ice. When it starts looking oily, use a spoon to quickly coat the *pâté*. If the aspic becomes too hard, place the *foie gras* back into the refrigerator, remelt the aspic (including the drippings), and again stir over ice until oily; coat the *foie gras* again. If needed, coat several times to obtain an even color. Keep refrigerated.

4. Arrange the slices on the set aspic with the remaining *pâté* in the center.

5. If there's any set aspic left over, cut it into small strips, then into little cubes. Arrange around the slices. (Aspic should not be put through a pastry bag as is sometimes recommended in recipes.) Keep refrigerated until serving time. Serve very cold, with thin toast and a sweet Sauterne which goes very well with it. It is served as a first course as well as before the salad after the main course in a very elegant dinner.

60. Chicken Liver Custards
(Gâteau de Foies de Volailles)

YIELD: 6 to 8 servings

THE CHICKEN LIVER custard is a specialty of the French area of Bresse, which is known for the superiority of its chicken, and the pale, pink, fatty livers which are considered the best. The custard is a refined dish which is generally served as a first course for an elaborate dinner or as a main course for a brunch or a light dinner. You can make it in individual molds or in a large one with or without the carrots on top. The sauce is a reduction of chicken stock with cream. A tomato sauce with a mushroom garnish is excellent with it, too.

Custard

3 chicken livers, cleaned of filaments and any greenish parts
1 large clove garlic, crushed, or 2 small cloves
1 teaspoon sweet butter
½ teaspoon freshly ground white pepper
1 teaspoon salt
1 teaspoon cornstarch
1 cup milk
6 large eggs
1 cup heavy cream
2 to 3 large carrots, peeled

Sauce

2 cups good chicken stock
1 cup good beef stock
1½ cups heavy cream
1 tablespoon sweet butter
1 tablespoon coarsely minced fresh chives

1. Blend the livers and garlic in a food processor until smooth. In a skillet, melt the butter until hot and add the liver mixture. Using a rubber spatula, stir the livers briefly until they solidify and hold. Place the mixture back in the food processor and blend again with pepper, salt and cornstarch and then add the milk. Blend until smooth and add the eggs and the cream. When well blended, strain into a bowl through a fine sieve.

2. Butter several small soufflé molds or a large 4- to 5-cup mold. Fill the molds with the liver mixture and place in a pan with tepid water. Bake at 350 degrees for about 35 minutes for the small molds, 60 minutes for the large mold. The water around the custard should not boil. If it gets too hot, add some cold water or some ice cubes during the cooking. Remove from heat and let the custard set for at least 20 minutes before unmolding.

3. Slice the carrots very thin either with a vegetable peeler, a *mandoline* or with a knife, as explained in technique 3. Slice some of them into rounds and some of them into long strips. Drop the carrots into boiling water, bring back to a boil and boil for ½ minute until wilted. Lift out into a bowl of cold water to stop cooking and retain color. Drain the carrots and place on a paper towel to dry. Set aside until ready to use. Start decorating the custard. Use the strips around.

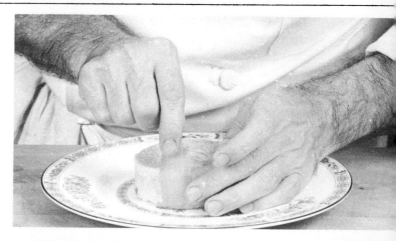

4. Decorate the top of the custard with the carrot rounds and begin the sauce.

5. Place chicken and beef stock in a saucepan and reduce to about ½ cup, to obtain a strong, dark *glace*. Add the heavy cream and bring to a boil and boil on high heat for 2 to 3 minutes until it reduces to about 1½ cups and is slightly syrupy. Add salt and pepper to taste and place the butter, in small pieces, on top of the sauce to prevent skinning. Set aside. At serving time brush the custard with butter to shine the top and heat slightly in the oven. Arrange the sauce around each custard and sprinkle the sauce with the chives. Serve immediately.

61. Braised Chicken Livers
(Foies de Volailles Braisés)

YIELD: About 25 slices

BRAISED CHICKEN LIVERS can be served on *croûtons* (small pieces of toast) for hors d'oeuvre, or sliced thin and added to a salad (see technique 55). They can also be served as a garnish in *vol au vent* or with a brochette. Duck, as well as turkey or goose, livers can be substituted for the chicken livers just as successfully.

8 *ounces large chicken livers, cleaned of large*
   sinews
1½ *teaspoons kosher-type coarse salt*
¼ *teaspoon freshly ground white pepper*
1 *clove garlic, crushed and chopped fine*
½ *teaspoon Cognac*
¼ *teaspoon saltpeter (optional)*
8 *ounces chicken fat, coarsely chopped*

1. Toss the chicken livers with the salt, pepper, garlic, Cognac and saltpeter. Cover with plastic wrap and let macerate in the refrigerator at least 24 hours. This will cure the livers. Chop the chicken fat coarsely (see picture) and place over a medium heat and render slowly for about 15 minutes. Place the livers in a saucepan in one layer and strain the melted fat on top. The livers should be covered with fat. Place the livers in a preheated 275-degree oven for 35 minutes. Remove from the oven and allow the livers to cool in the fat. If the chicken livers are to

be kept for a while, let them cool in the fat overnight. Remove from the fat and place in a jar. You will notice that the fat contains some liquid. Remove the hard fat. Melt. Do not use the juices at the bottom of the pan. Pour the melted fat on top of the livers and let harden in the refrigerator. If the juices are left with the livers for a period of time, they will turn the livers sour. At serving time, remove the livers from the fat, using paper towels to wipe off any fat that clings to the livers. Then cut on a slant in thin slices and serve on toast or in a salad.

62. Cold Glazed Chicken *(Poulet Glacé Arlequin)*

T HIS COLD GLAZED CHICKEN is roasted, then cut into quarters, and the juices reduced to a glaze used to brush the chicken pieces. It is then glazed with a clear aspic and finally presented with a green pea and a red tomato aspic. It can be presented on individual plates or on a larger platter for a buffet. It makes a festive and elegant main course for an after the theater supper. We used a 3-pound chicken.

Aspic

YIELD: about 3½ cups

4 *cups good chicken stock or a mixture of chicken and beef stock*
3 *envelopes unflavored gelatin*
2 *egg whites*
1 *cup leafy part of celery green*
½ *cup coarsely chopped carrots*
¼ *cup coarsely chopped parsley*
1 *to 2 branches fresh tarragon coarsely chopped*
½ *teaspoon crushed black pepper* (mignonnette)
Salt to taste (depending on seasoning of the stock)

Combine all ingredients together in a sturdy saucepan. Bring to a boil, stirring occasionally, and let boil strongly for 4 to 5 seconds, then remove to the side of the stove and let it set 10 minutes. Strain through a fine sieve lined with paper towels. (For more information about aspic, see pages 88–89 in *La Technique*.)

Tomato aspic

YIELD: About ½ cup

1 *large or 2 medium ripe tomatoes*
½ *teaspoon paprika*
¼ *teaspoon salt*
Dash of white pepper
1 *cup melted aspic*

Peel the tomato, cut in half and press the seeds out. Put in a blender with the paprika and blend well. Place in a fine chinois or a paper towel and press most of the liquid out. Combine with remaining ingredients and set aside.

Pea aspic

1 *10-ounce package frozen baby peas (see note)*
2 *cups water*
½ *teaspoon salt*
¼ *stick (1 ounce) sweet butter*

Bring the water and salt to a boil. Add the peas and bring back to a boil. Boil uncovered for 2½ to 3 minutes. Drain immediately and place the peas in a food processor. Blend for 30 seconds. If the peas are allowed to cool or if the peas are not tiny baby peas, the skin will not liquefy properly and the taste will not be as refined or the color as bright. Therefore, it is important to process them immediately after cooking. Add the butter, a dash of salt and blend another 30 seconds. This yields 1 cup of purée. Combine ½ cup of the purée of peas with 1 cup of melted aspic. Set aside. This pea purée is a great vegetable dish by itself—a perfect accompaniment to roasts, poached eggs, etc. In this recipe it is just used incidentally and we only use ½ cup of the mixture.

(*Note:* Fresh peas from the garden are always the best. Unfortunately, so-called fresh peas in the pod bought at the market are often large and starchy. That's why we prefer frozen baby peas.)

1. Truss, salt and pepper the chicken and roast in a preheated 400-degree oven for about 50 minutes, turning it on all sides. When the chicken is cooked, drain it of its juices. You will notice that the juices run nice and clear. Let it mix with the drippings.

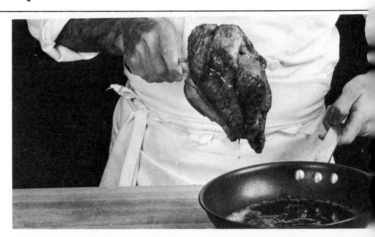

2. Pour out the clear fat—keep it to brown meat or sauté potatoes. (If the drippings are not separated into solidified juices and fat, cook the drippings on top of the stove to evaporate the moisture. When the moisture has evaporated, you will have solidified juice in the bottom and clear fat on top. Cook on medium low heat, being careful not to burn the juices. If the solidified juices are burnt, it will give a bitter taste to the sauce.)

3. When the fat is completely removed, retrieve the solidified juices by adding a little water to the pan and heating until the juices dissolve. Strain through a fine sieve and reduce to 2 tablespoons of *glace*. (To serve a regular roast chicken with juices, reduce less and add 1 or 2 tablespoons of fat back into the juices after stirring to enrich.)

4. Cut the chicken in half.

5. Separate each half into breast and leg. Remove the carcass from the breasts and legs.

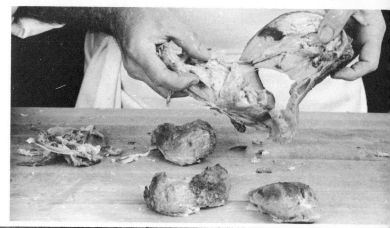

6. Remove the shoulder bone from the breast and cut off the top of the wings. The thigh and drum bones get left in the leg.

7. When the *glace* has reached the concentration of jam (thick and dark without being burnt), place the chicken on a wire rack and brush with the *glace*. The glaze is an extremely concentrated, strong reduction, and is used as a flavoring agent.

8. Place the chicken with the *glace* in the refrigerator to cool it off. Meanwhile, take 2 cups of liquid aspic, place on ice, and stir until almost solidified and syrupy and ready to set. Glaze the chicken, using a spoon. If the aspic solidifies too fast and you don't have enough coating on your chicken, place the tray of chicken back into the refrigerator, remelt the aspic drippings, place on ice again until syrupy and glaze another time. The chicken may have to be glazed several times. Aspic is slow to take on chicken because of the fat in the skin.

9. Cover the plates with a layer of pea aspic. When the aspic is set, cut two triangles and remove from the plates.

10. Clean with a towel so as to have two neat triangles opposing each other.

11. Set the tomato aspic in ice and when it is ready fill the two empty triangles. You now have two green and two red triangles.

12. If you want the dish to be even more decorative, cut two rounds with an upside-down pastry tube.

13. Fill each empty round with aspic of the opposite color. Then place your plates back in the refrigerator. When cold, place your piece of chicken on top and a bit of chopped aspic around. Serve well chilled.

63. Mayonnaise of Chicken
(Mayonnaise de Volaille)

YIELD: 6 to 8 servings

A MAYONNAISE OF CHICKEN is an elegant chicken salad. The word mayonnaise, when associated with poultry, always denotes a cold salad. It could be associated with poached fish, shellfish, lobster, cold meats, etc., and this in turn would be a mayonnaise of fish, shellfish, etc., denoting the same type of technique and the same type of salad. It is delicate and decorative, ideal to serve at a luncheon or a buffet party. The chicken can be poached and the mayonnaise made as well as the ingredients for the decoration. However, the salad cannot be assembled much more than an hour before serving because the shredded lettuce will soften and the mayonnaise will darken and lose its fresh look.

Poaching the chicken

1 3–3½ *pound chicken*
10 *to* 12 *cups cold water*
1 *large carrot, peeled*
1 *leek, cleaned*
1 *stalk celery*
1 *medium onion, peeled and stuck with* 2 *cloves*
1½ *teaspoons salt*
10 *black peppercorns*

Place the chicken and the water in a tall narrow kettle. (If the pot is too wide you will need too much water to cover the chicken and your stock will be weak.) Bring to a boil, skimming off the scum as it rises to the top of the liquid. (See skimming technique 9.) Let simmer for 5 minutes. Add the remaining ingredients, lower the heat and simmer again gently for 45 minutes. Let the chicken cool in the stock.

Mayonnaise

2 *egg yolks*
½ *teaspoon salt*
¼ *teaspoon freshly ground white pepper*
1 *tablespoon good red wine vinegar*
1¼ *cups oil (preferably equal parts of virgin olive and peanut or grape-seed oil)*

Decoration

1 *or* 2 *heads Boston lettuce, cleaned and dried*
1 *tablespoon olive oil*
1 *teaspoon red wine vinegar*
Salt
4 *hard-boiled eggs, shelled and quartered*
1 *tomato, cut in wedges*
1 *tablespoon large capers*
1 *can (2 ounces) anchovy fillets in oil*

1. Remove the cooled chicken from the stock. Strain the stock and freeze it for later use. Pull out the two legs which should separate easily from the carcass, and remove the skin of the breast and the legs.

2. Still using your fingers, remove the bone from the breast as well as from the thigh and drums. Slice the breast meat on a slant to have long, thin slices.

3. Slice then pound the leg meat slightly to extend it and have nice thin slices. Make the mayonnaise. Be sure that the egg yolks and oil are at room temperature or they will separate, especially since there is no mustard in this mayonnaise.

4. Place the yolks, salt, pepper and vinegar in a bowl (not aluminum as it will discolor the mayonnaise) and stir with a whisk. Start adding the oil slowly, while beating with the whisk. As the mayonnaise becomes harder, add the oil a bit faster. The mayonnaise should be a nice spreading consistency. Pile the slices of lettuce together and shred very thinly. Also shred the heart. Season with 1 tablespoon of olive oil, the vinegar, salt, and place in the bottom of a large, open, preferably glass bowl. Use the carrots from the stock in the decoration, or peel a carrot, using a vegetable peeler (see julienne technique 3) and drop in boiling water for approximately 30 seconds to wilt the slices so they can be folded. Refresh under cold water and set aside.

5. Arrange the slices of chicken on top of the lettuce. Be sure to cover all the lettuce. Alternate slices of dark and white meat.

6. Using a spatula, cover the top of the chicken with about ¼ inch of mayonnaise in a dome shape.

7. Arrange the carrot strips as though they were ribbons around a package.

8. Outline the ribbon with anchovy fillets cut in half lengthwise to make thin strips.

9. Take a piece of carrot strip and fold as shown in the picture to make a loop of a bow. Place four loops in the center of the salad.

10. Fold, roll or twist another carrot strip and place in the center of the bow. Decorate salad with hard-boiled eggs, tomato wedges and capers. Serve as soon as possible.

64. Small Ballotine of Chicken
(Ballotines de Volailles Fine Champagne)

YIELD: *4 ballotines*

A BALLOTINE is meat, poultry, game or fish that has been boned, stuffed, tied and roasted. The leg meat is ground and stuffed into the breasts. The ballotines are then braised, and served with a sauce and *glace* of chicken.

Cooking ballotine

¼ stick (1 ounce) sweet butter
½ teaspoon salt
¼ teaspoon pepper
1 cup dry white wine

Ballotine

2 chickens 2½ pounds each
⅓ cup crushed ice
⅔ cup heavy cream
½ teaspoon salt
¼ teaspoon finely ground white pepper

Stock

Carcass, gizzard and neck of chicken
1 large onion, peeled
4 cloves
1 leek, cleaned
3 bay leaves
½ teaspoon thyme

Sauce

Stock (step 5)
1 cup dry white wine
2 teaspoons butter
2 teaspoons flour
1 cup heavy cream
1 teaspoon fine Champagne Cognac

1. Place the chicken on its breast and cut the skin alongside the backbone. Separate the skin from the carcass on one side, following the bones.

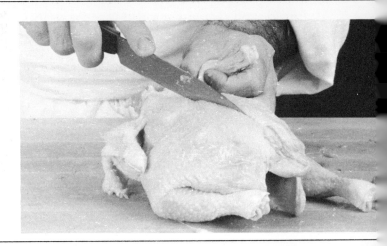

2. After the skin and meat have been separated from the bones, turn the chicken on the other side, remove the wishbone and cut alongside the breastbone.

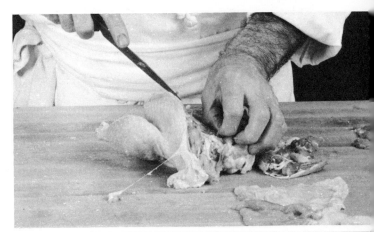

3. Place the chicken on its side and cut through the joint of the shoulder. Start pulling the skin and meat from the central carcass.

4. The meat and skin of the entire half chicken should come off. It will still be attached at the joint of the thigh bone. Cut through the joint of the thigh and pull the chicken half off. The chicken half will still have the bone of the wing and the leg in it.

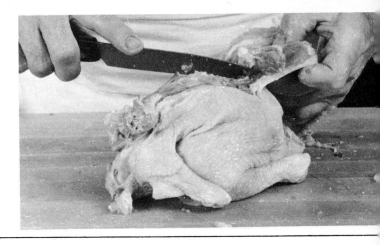

5. Pull out the leg meat and bone from the skin. The object is to keep the breast meat and the skin of the entire half chicken intact to use as a wrapper. Bone out the meat from the leg and set aside (the meat gets chopped later in the food processor). Place the bones, gizzard and neck in water and bring to a boil, then skim the top. Add the onion, cloves, leek, bay leaves and thyme. Bring back to a boil, lower the heat and simmer for 1 hour on medium heat. Strain. You should have approximately 2 cups of liquid. If more, reduce to 2 cups.

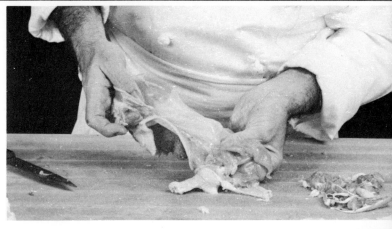

6. To make the stuffing, clean the leg meat of sinew and cut into 1-inch pieces. (You should have approximately 14 ounces of meat left from the 4 legs.) Place in the food processor with ⅓ cup of crushed ice and process for 15 to 20 seconds until smooth. Slowly add the cream, then the salt and white pepper. It should not take longer than a minute to make the mousse. Set aside. Spread out the skin with the breast meat attached.

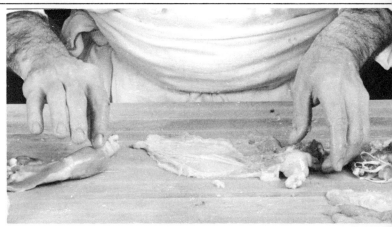

7. Remove the sinew from the small filet of the breast. Lift the meat of the breast from the skin—it will still be attached by the wing bone—and place the filet underneath.

8. Divide the mousse between the four breasts, place directly on the skin and cover with the breast meat.

9. Fold the skin over the meat to encase meat and stuffing together.

10. Tie the little *ballotine* carefully on the top and around with kitchen string. (This is covered in technique 98, pages 258–260, in *La Technique*.) Melt butter in a heavy saucepan, sprinkle the meat with the salt and pepper and brown the pieces gently on medium heat on both sides, for approximately 12 minutes altogether, 5 to 6 minutes on each side. Add white wine to the mixture, cover and simmer very slowly for 15 minutes.

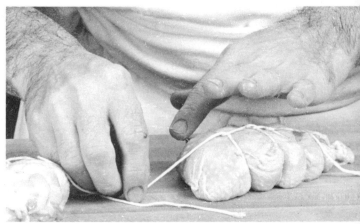

11. Place the *ballotine* on a platter. When cold enough to handle, remove the string and trim off the extra skin. Keep warm uncovered in a 160- to 180-degree oven while you make the *glace* and sauce.

12. Strain the cooking juices into a small saucepan. If there is no juice left, add some water, stir to dissolve all the solidified juices and strain into a clean saucepan. Reduce on low heat to obtain 2 to 3 tablespoons of glaze (see technique 62). At some point during the reduction the sauce may separate into fat and juices. If this happens, pour the fat out, add 1 or 2 tablespoons of water to the mixture left and boil to combine together. You should have approximately 2 to 3 tablespoons of *glace* of chicken.

13. While the *glace* is cooking, make the fine champagne sauce. Take the 2 cups of stock, add the white wine and reduce the whole mixture on high heat to 1 cup. Melt the butter in a saucepan and add the flour. Cook for 30 seconds, stirring with a whisk and add the cup of reduced stock, stirring constantly with the whisk and bring to a boil. Add the cream, bring to a boil again and reduce for 3 to 4 minutes while boiling. You should have approximately 1⅓ cups of leftover sauce. It should be smooth and creamy but not too thick. Season with salt and pepper and finally, add the Cognac. Place ¼ cup of sauce on very warm plates, and using the *glace,* make two circles in the sauce.

14. With the point of a knife, pull through the *glace* and the sauce to make a streaky design. Place the *ballotine* in the center with about 1 tablespoon of sauce on top and some drippings of *glace* on top of that. Serve immediately. The *ballotine* is good served with rice pilaf, or *pommes savonnettes* (technique 50), and a green vegetable.

65. Chicken with Morels *(Poulet aux Morilles)*
YIELD: 4 servings

T HE MORELS are wild mushrooms that can be found along the edges of the woods and on hillsides in early spring. Fresh-picked morels can be toxic eaten raw in salad. They can also be toxic when cooked if you eat large quantities of them at frequent intervals. However, they are perfectly safe after they have been dried which is the way they are usually bought in specialty stores. Dry morels are very expensive but 1 ounce goes quite a long way. Use the tiny, pointed black-headed type which is the best morel.

1 3½-pound chicken
1 ounce dried morel mushrooms
5 to 6 shallots, peeled and finely sliced (2 table-
    spoons)
2 tablespoons sweet butter
½ teaspoon salt
¼ teaspoon freshly ground black pepper
½ cup dry white wine
⅓ cup dry Sherry
1 cup heavy cream

1. One ounce of tiny dried black-headed morels, usually imported from Europe.

2. Soak the morels in water for at least 15 to 20 minutes. If they are whole, split them in half lengthwise to dispose of the sand. The inside is like a very hollow furrow. Cut off the tips of the stem.

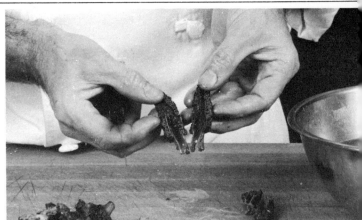

3. Discard the soaking water as there will be sand at the bottom of it. Wash the morels again, several times if necessary, in luke-warm water, until there is no sand left in the bottom of your bowl. Lift the morels gently out of the water so as not to take the sand with them. Drain and press gently to extrude some of the water.

4. Cut the legs from the chicken and sepa-rate into drums and thighs. Pull the skin off the meat. Remove the wishbone from the breast. Cut at the shoulder joint (arrow) and along the breastbone (arrow). Pull the breast meat off in one piece. Repeat on the other side.

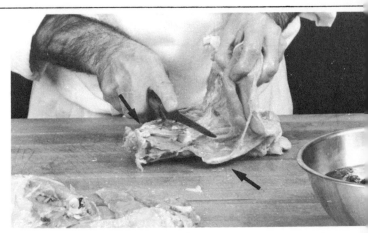

5. Remove the skin from the breast. Trim the wings. (Use the carcass, trimmings, etc., to make a stock for future use.) Cut each individual breast into 2 pieces. You now have 8 pieces of chicken with all fat and visible skin removed. Sprinkle the chicken pieces with salt and pepper.

6. Melt the butter in a skillet. When foaming, place the pieces of chicken in it. Gently sauté on medium heat for 4 minutes. The chicken should be browned lightly, but a crust shouldn't form on the flesh. After about 2 minutes on one side, turn and brown 2 minutes on the other side. The butter should be foaming nicely, but not burning. Add the white wine, cover and simmer another 2 minutes, then remove the lower 2 pieces of the breasts. These boneless pieces of white meat will get cooked first. After another 2 minutes, remove the other 2 pieces of white meat where the wing is attached. Leave the dark meat simmering gently for another 5 to 6 minutes, then remove and set aside with the breast meat. Add the shallots to the pan drippings for about 1 minute. Add the Sherry, bring to a boil and reduce on high heat for 2 to 3 minutes, or until the mixture is almost completely reduced.

7. Add the morels, stir and add the cream. Bring to a boil and reduce about 1 minute on high heat. The sauce should be glossy and should just coat a spoon. Add salt and pepper to taste and a small cube of *glace de viande* (see technique 6) if you have any. If not, reduce the sauce for another 1 to 2 minutes. Pour over the chicken and serve immediately. This is a quick, elegant dish, ideal as a main course for a dinner served with braised endives or potatoes and green vegetables.

66. Chicken Stuffed under the Skin

(Poulet Farci sous la Peau)

YIELD: 4 to 6 servings

STUFFING A CHICKEN between the skin and the flesh not only flavors the bird but keeps it moist as well.

Stuffing

1½ *tablespoons sweet butter*
6 *ounces mushroom (about 3 cups loose), sliced*
½ *teaspoon salt*
¼ *teaspoon freshly ground black pepper*
1 *tablespoon chopped parsley*
2 *cloves garlic peeled, crushed and chopped fine (1 teaspoon)*
1 3½-*pound roasting chicken*
1 *tablespoon soft sweet butter to cook the chicken*

Sauce

2 *tablespoons finely chopped onion*
2 to 3 *cloves garlic peeled, crushed and chopped (1 teaspoon)*
2 *cups fresh, coarsely chopped tomatoes (peeled and seeded)*
Salt and pepper to taste
½ *cup oil-cured pitted olives*
1 *tablespoon chopped parsley or other fresh herbs (chives, tarragon, etc.)*

1. Melt the 1½ tablespoons of butter in a saucepan, add the mushrooms, salt and pepper. Cook on medium heat for 4 to 5 minutes, until the liquid given off by the mushrooms has evaporated. Add the parsley and garlic and mix well. Let cool. Remove the wishbone from the chicken and slide your finger between the flesh and the skin to loosen the skin from the breast.

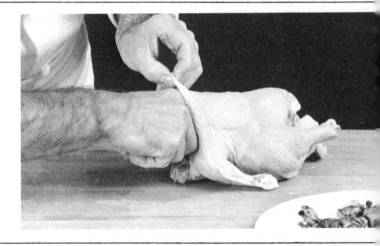

2. Keep pushing your fingers between the skin and the flesh to separate the leg meat from the skin. Slowly loosen the skin all around the chicken except along its back.

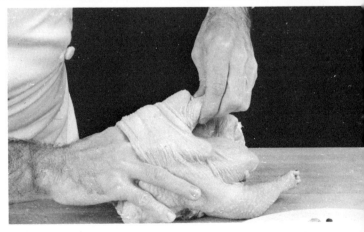

3. Lift the skin from the flesh and using a spoon or a spatula push the seasoned mushrooms inside.

4. Press the chicken back into shape and truss with or without a trussing needle. (You can find instructions for trussing on pages 218–224 in *La Technique*.)

5. Rub the skin of the chicken with 1 tablespoon softened butter, sprinkle lightly with salt and pepper and place the chicken on its side in a roasting pan or skillet. Roast in a preheated 400-degree oven for 45 minutes to 1 hour, turning from side to side the first 35 minutes and finally placing it on its back the last 10 to 15 minutes of cooking. Baste every 5 minutes during the last 10 to 15 minutes of cooking.

6. Lift the chicken from the roasting pan, trim the ends of the drumsticks and keep the chicken warm on a platter, uncovered in a 160-degree oven. Add the onions to the drippings in the saucepan and sauté for 1 to 2 minutes on medium heat. Add the garlic and mix for a few seconds, then the tomatoes. Bring to a boil and simmer gently stirring with a wooden spatula to melt the solidified juices. Season the sauce with salt and pepper. At serving time, pour the sauce on top and around the chicken, sprinkle with the olives and the herbs and serve im-

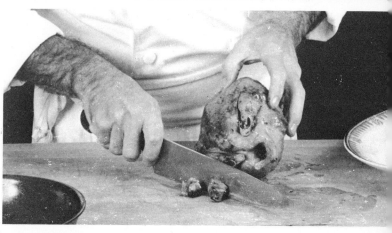

mediately. The chicken can be carved in the dining room or cut into portions in the kitchen and arranged on plates with the olives, sauce and herbs. The olives are not added to the dish prior to serving because they tend to blacken and make the sauce taste bitter.

67. Chicken Pie *(Fricassée de Poulet en Feuilletage)*

YIELD: 6 servings

THE CHICKEN PIE IS a stew made of boned chicken combined with a vegetable garnish and a cream sauce, topped with puff paste, and baked.

Braising the chicken

1 3½-pound chicken, quartered
⅜ cup thinly sliced onions
1 bay leaf
1 pinch thyme
1 cup dry white wine

Garnishes

2 carrots, peeled and cut into 2-inch chunks, split into ¼-inch-thick sticks, blanched 3 to 4 minutes in boiling water and drained
½ cup frozen baby peas, blanched 30 seconds in boiling water and drained
1 or 2 stalks celery, peeled, cut into 2-inch chunks and then into ¼-inch sticks, blanched 1 minute in boiling water and drained
1 cup fresh snow peas, cleaned, blanched 1 minute in boiling water and drained (Note: The vegetables can, of course, be varied at will.)

Sauce

1 teaspoon sweet butter
1 teaspoon flour
1 cup heavy cream
Salt and pepper to taste

Crust

1 pound puff paste (technique 91)
2 beaten egg yolks, for the wash

1. Sprinkle the chicken with salt and pepper. Brown in a saucepan, skin side down, without fat on medium heat for 8 to 10 minutes. There is enough fat in the skin to brown the pieces, without adding extra fat. Add the onions, bay leaf, thyme and wine to the chicken. Cover and simmer for 25 minutes. Remove from the heat and, when cold enough to handle, remove skin and take the meat off the bones. Cut the meat into 1- to 2-inch chunks.

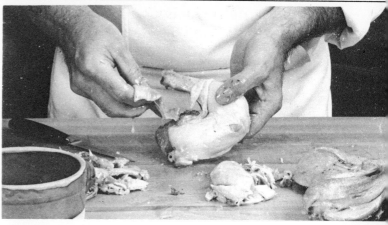

2. Reduce the juices left in the pan to 1 cup. Knead the butter and flour together (a *beurre manié*) and, using a whisk, whip the mixture into the juices vigorously. Bring the sauce to a boil stirring and simmer 5 minutes. Add the cream, bring to a boil again, taste for seasonings, and add salt and pepper if needed. Divide the meat and all the vegetable garnish among the crocks and pour the sauce over. The crocks should not be more than two-thirds full.

3. Roll the puff paste dough into ⅛-inch-thick rounds, and brush them with the egg yolk.

4. Place the dough on top of the crocks, egg-washed side down. Be sure to stretch the dough on top of the terrine so it does not sink in the center. Press to assure that the dough adheres firmly to the sides of the dish.

5. Brush the top and sides of the dough with egg yolk. Refrigerate for 1 hour, or place in the freezer for 15 to 20 minutes to firm up the dough.

6. Place the crocks on a cookie sheet in a preheated 375-degree oven and bake for 30 minutes. Serve immediately one crock per person or a large one for several people. For a large terrine, make a hole in the crust and serve the stew from the crock, with a piece of puff paste and some vegetables in each portion. The chicken pie is a complete main course with crust, vegetables, meat and sauce.

68. Boned Stuffed Squab *(Pigeons Désossés et Farcis)*

YIELD: 4 servings

THE SQUAB is a young domesticated pigeon about 4 weeks old, which has not yet flown and has been specially fed to be plump and tender. An older pigeon is tougher and should be braised but a dove (which is a wild species of pigeon) is quite tender. The squab is a good transition between regular domesticated poultry and real game, such as pheasant, woodcock, etc. It is all dark meat and though it doesn't have a gamey taste, it is probably as close as you can get to game if you have never had it. Squab liver, unlike other poultry livers, doesn't have a gallbladder (the little green sac filled up with bile which is removed from the liver). Squabs weigh from approximately 10 to 18 ounces. The squabs here weighed 1 pound each, cleaned. It is easier to eat the squabs if they are boned out, particularly if you are going to stuff them. The same instructions for boning squab also apply to Cornish hens and other small birds such as quail or woodcock. Serve one squab per person with the broccoli and cauliflower mold (technique 45) and potato cake (technique 51).

Stock

Carcasses, necks, gizzards, wings
½ cup sliced onion
½ cup coarsely sliced carrot
2 cloves garlic, skin on
¼ teaspoon thyme
1 cup dry white wine
4 quarts water (approximately)

Sauce

½ teaspoon salt
¼ teaspoon freshly ground white pepper
½ teaspoon arrowroot, diluted with 1 table-
  spoon water

Stuffing

(You may change the fruits in the stuffing, using figs, dates, raisins, etc.):

3 slices French bread, well toasted and blended
  into fine crumbs (about 1 cup)
¾ cup finely chopped mild boiled ham
1½ cups loose, finely chopped mushrooms (about
  4 ounces)
½ cup (about 4) sliced dry pitted prunes
½ cup (about 4) sliced dry pitted apricots
¼ cup melted sweet butter
½ teaspoon salt, depending on the saltiness of the
  ham
¼ teaspoon freshly ground white pepper

---

1. Trim the wings of the squab and eviscerate if needed. Lift the skin at the neck and cut around the wishbone. Remove the bone by pulling.

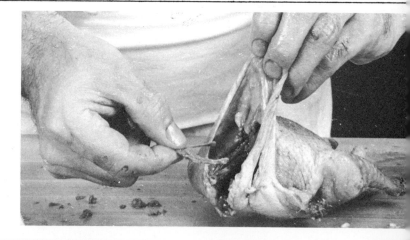

---

2. Put the squab on its side and push the piece of wing that remains back and forth to help locate the joint of the shoulder. Cut, twisting the blade back and forth, so it slides into the joint. Cut through. Repeat on the other side. Most of the boning from now on can be done with your fingers.

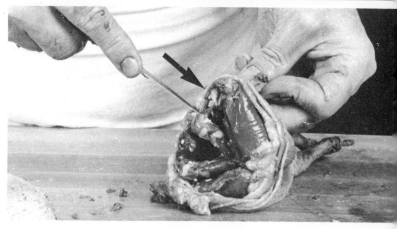

---

3. With the bird still on its side, push your thumb through the cut joint to release the meat from the carcass. Repeat on the other side.

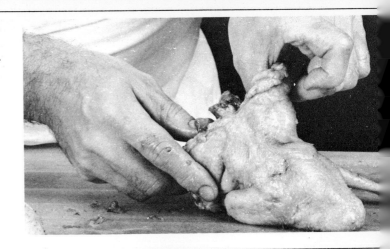

4. With the squab on its back push your finger between the flesh of the breast and the carcass to loosen the meat on both sides of the central breast bone (sternum). The skin will still be attached to the long cartilage part of the central bone.

5. Place the squab on its breast. Now separate the skin from the back bone. Be careful when pushing with the tip of your finger, not to go through the skin. (If you make a hole, it is not crucial, but try not to.) Keep pushing gently but firmly with your finger until you are close to the tail of the squab. All the skin should be loose.

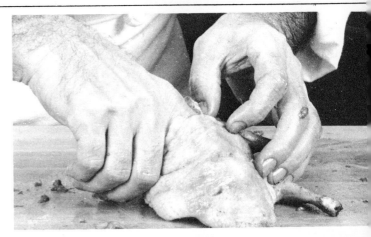

6. Put the squab on its back and separate the meat from the long cartilage of the breast. Use your thumbs as levers to tear the skin from the central bone (arrow). Notice that some of the cartilage will still be attached to the skin.

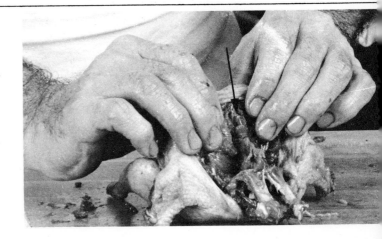

7. Now, with the skin completely loose from the central carcass, turn meat and skin gently inside out.

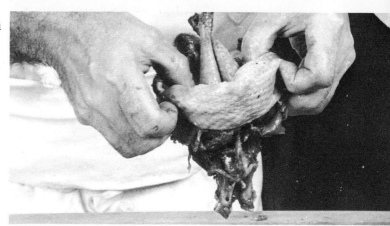

8. The only part of the squab still attached to the carcass is at the joint that joins the thigh bone to the body. Twist the bone at the joint (arrow) to tear it out of its socket on both sides.

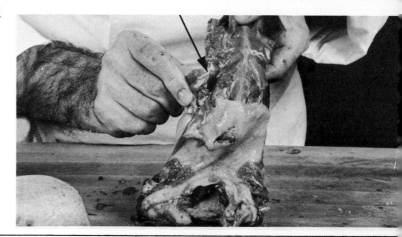

9. Keep pushing the skin from the bone and cut it off at the tail which should be left with the carcass. The carcass is now completely free from the rest of the squab.

10. Remove the thigh bones from the leg on each side. With your knife scrape the bone free of all meat and cut at the joint where it meets the bone of the drum.

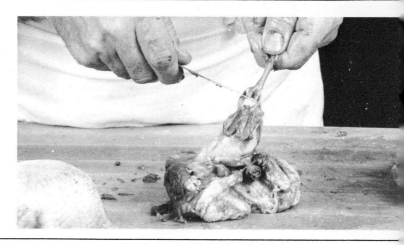

11. Turn the squab right side out again. The only bones left are little pieces of the drum and the first joint of the wing.

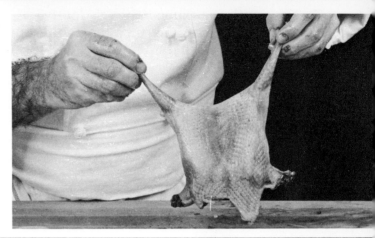

12. Place the neck, gizzards, heart, carcass, trimmings, etc., in a large saucepan without any fat. Brown on high heat for 1 to 2 minutes, then on medium to low heat for 25 minutes, stirring once in a while with a wooden spatula. (There is enough fat in the skin to brown the bones.) The saucepan should be large enough to hold the bones in one layer. When the bones are nicely browned all around, and a nice crust of solidified juices has formed at the bottom of the pan (do not cook too fast or the juices will burn and the sauce will be bitter), add the onions, carrots, garlic and cook, still browning, for another 10 minutes. Hold the cover on top of the saucepan and discard the fat. Add the white wine, thyme and approximately 2 quarts of water. Bring to a boil, lower the heat and simmer slowly for 1 hour. Remove the scum with a skimmer. After another hour, add another 2 quarts of water and cook another hour. Strain the liquid through a fine strainer. You should have approximately 4 cups left. Remove as much fat as possible then reduce the liquid to 1¼ cups. This reduced stock will be the base of the sauce.

13. While the stock cooks, prepare the stuffing. Toss all the ingredients of the stuffing gently and using a pastry bag, your finger, or a spoon, stuff the four squabs.

14. Cover the opening at the neck and tail by wrapping the loose skin under. Gently press the squab back into its original shape.

15. To truss, place a piece of string under the squab at the tail opening and cross above the drums.

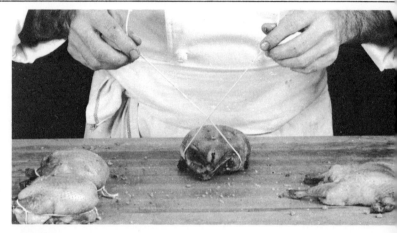

16. Bring the string back under the tip of the drumsticks in a figure 8. Pull gently on both ends of the string to close the opening at the tail and bring around the sides of the bird to tie in front.

17. Make a knot under the breast. Trussing holds the squab in shape while cooking. Sprinkle the squabs with the salt and pepper and place in a roasting pan breast side up. To brown properly, the squabs should not touch one another, and the sides of the roasting pan should not be too high. Because squabs are fatty enough, you don't have to rub them with butter before roasting. Roast in a preheated 400-degree oven for 30 minutes. After 15 minutes, baste with the fat which has melted from the birds, then baste every 5 minutes.

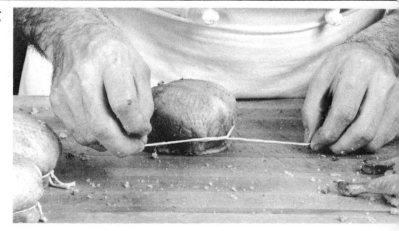

18. Untie and trim the ends of the drumsticks and the ends of the wing bones. Place the squabs on a platter and keep warm uncovered in a 160-degree oven while you finish the sauce. If the pan drippings are separated into solidified juices and clear fat, pour the fat out and retrieve the solidified juices by dissolving with stock. If not, cook the juices on top of the stove (see technique 62) until the fat separates completely from the solidified juices. Then pour the fat out and add the 1¼ cups of stock. Boil the mixture for a few seconds while stirring with a spatula to dissolve the juices. Strain into a small saucepan and add the arrowroot, stirring. Season with salt and pepper. You should have a generous cup of sauce. Serve on a large platter or on very hot individual plates. Coat each squab with about 2 to 3 tablespoons of sauce.

69. Rabbit with Prunes *(Lapin aux Pruneaux)*

YIELD: 6 to 8 servings

RABBIT IS PLUMP, tender, high in protein, low in fat—and much too infrequently eaten in this country. The wild rabbit and hare have a much stronger taste as well as darker meat than the domesticated rabbit. The former is excellent for pâtés, but for stews most people prefer the latter with its white, lean and tender meat. A rabbit is tender at about 2½ to 3 months old. A good size is approximately 5 pounds, which is how much the one pictured below weighed, eviscerated but with the head and skin on and liver and kidneys inside. There are countless recipes for rabbit—roasted, boiled, with red or white wine sauces or with jams and cream. Ours is prepared with prunes and onions and a slightly acidic sauce. Though we show you how to skin a rabbit, your butcher will do it for you if you prefer.

Stew

1 *rabbit, about 5 pounds, eviscerated but with
    skin and head on*
½ *teaspoon freshly ground black pepper*
½ *stick (2 ounces) sweet butter*
2 *tablespoons flour*
1½ *cups dry white wine*
2½ *cups chicken stock*
3 *garlic cloves, peeled and crushed*
Liver and kidneys of the rabbit
½ *cup dry white wine*

30 *small, white pearl onions the size of a large
    olive, peeled (about ¾ pound)*

Sauce

¼ *cup good red or white wine vinegar*
3 *tablespoons sugar*
⅓ *cup water*
2 *cups large prunes, pitted*

---

1. Make an incision with a knife through the skin in the middle of the rabbit's back.

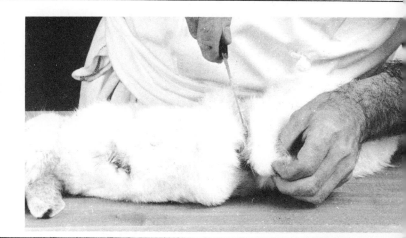

2. Place both hands in the incision and pull on each side to separate the skin from the flesh. You need strength but the skin should come off easily.

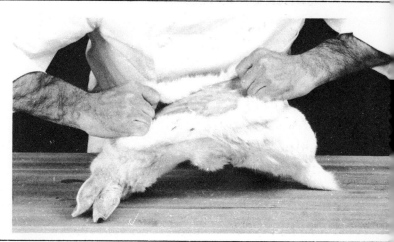

3. As you pull the skin off and expose the meat, you will notice that it is almost completely free of fat.

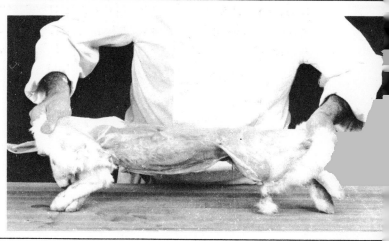

4. Pull off the skin toward the tail to expose the back legs. Cut at the tail, then break the foot bone with the back of a large knife, and cut through.

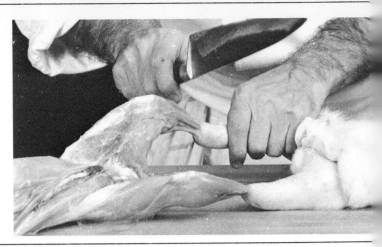

5. Proceed in the same manner with the front legs. Pull the skin toward the head and cut at the neck. (In France the head is often used in stock or stew. Although the fur can be kept and processed for use as clothing, it is rarely done.)

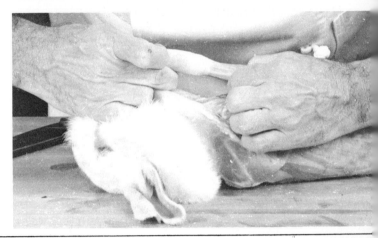

6. When the rabbit is clean, place on its back and cut through the pelvic bone.

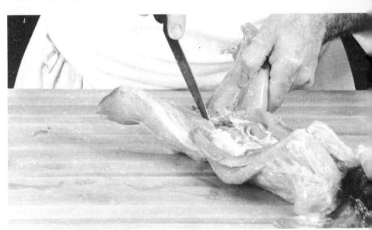

7. Stretch the pelvic bone open to expose a piece of the intestines which runs in between the bone.

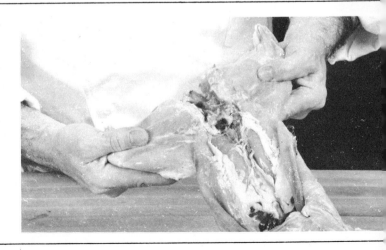

8. Pull and cut out the intestine and discard.

9. Separate the two back legs, then the flanks which run along the saddle or the back part of the rabbit.

10. Sever the two front legs from the shoulder by sliding your knife along the shoulder blade. Cut the back loin into 3 pieces cut across the ribs, then the rack into 3 pieces. Then cut each of the back legs in half.

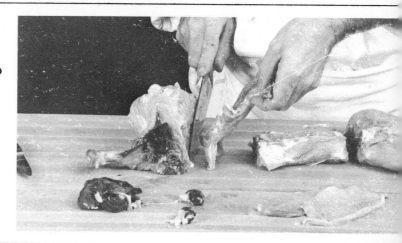

11. You now have the rabbit cut up into 12 to 14 pieces. The liver and the kidneys are kept aside. You should have approximately 3½ pounds of meat. Sprinkle the meat with salt and pepper. Melt the butter in a very large saucepan and brown the pieces all around on medium heat for 10 minutes. Sprinkle with the flour, stir well and cook for another 1 or 2 minutes. Deglaze with 1½ cups of white wine and the chicken stock. Cover and cook on low heat for 20 minutes. Place garlic, liver, kidneys and ½ cup white wine in a food processor and

purée. Add this purée to the rabbit and stir well. Cover and simmer another 15 minutes then add the onions. Keep cooking on medium heat for 15 more minutes. Meanwhile, prepare the vinegar mixture that finishes the sauce.

12. In a saucepan, combine the vinegar and sugar and cook 4 to 5 minutes, until it caramelizes. Add the water to liquefy the caramel (be careful as it may splash). When the caramel is melted, add to the rabbit with the prunes. Cover and simmer slowly for another 10 minutes. Taste for seasonings and add salt and peper if needed. Serve with fresh mashed potatoes, a purée of celery root, the *pommes savonnettes* (technique 50) or other fried potatoes.

70. Savoy Sausage in Brioche
(Saucisson en Brioche)

YIELD: 4 to 6 servings

SAUSAGE CAN BE POACHED and served with a potato salad or roasted with tiny potatoes around. It can be poached then cooked in a puff paste as well as in a *pâte brisée*. Cooking it in brioche dough is a classic way of preparing sausage. The aluminum foil keeps the dough from separating from the sausage while cooking.

Sausage

1 *bought or homemade sausage (about 1¼ pound)*
1 *teaspoon vinegar*
1 *teaspoon salt*

To finish

1 *egg, plus 1 egg yolk*
1 *teaspoon butter*
1 *tablespoon bread crumbs*

Brioche (enough to make 2 sausages)

1 *package dry yeast*
¼ *cup lukewarm milk*
½ *teaspoon sugar*
1½ *sticks (6 ounces) sweet butter*
3 *cups flour*
4 *large eggs*
1 *egg yolk*
1 *egg plus 1 egg yolk for the wash*

Combine the yeast and the lukewarm milk in a small bowl and let the mixture work and bubble for 5 minutes. Place all the remaining brioche ingredients in the large bowl of an electric mixer. Start mixing slowly then add the yeast mixture and beat on medium speed (number 4) for 5 to 6 minutes. After 2 minutes, scrape the bottom of the bowl with a large rubber spatula to combine all the ingredients and start beating again. At the end of the beating time the dough should be very elastic and should release from the beater easily when pulled. Remove the dough and place in a bowl in the refrigerator if not needed right away. You can keep the dough in the refrigerator overnight and use it the day after. Even though the refrigerator is cold, the dough will still work and develop slowly. The day after, push the dough down, and use as needed.

1. If you want to use the dough right away, let it rise in a lukewarm place, covered, for 2 hours. Knock it down by kneading it a few seconds. Cut the dough in half, dust with flour, and spread or flatten each piece with your hand to a thickness of ⅜ to ½ inch. The dough will make 2 sausages. If you are only making one sausage use the extra dough to make small brioches or freeze it for future use.

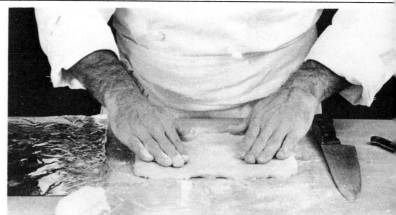

2. The best sausages are *cervelas, cotechino* or Savoy sausage (which are made of raw chopped and seasoned pork meat). They are sometimes studded with pistachio or even with truffles or other seasonings. You can buy it or make your own (see pages 288–291 in *La Technique*). Prick the sausage with a fork, cover with cold water and add the vinegar and salt. Bring to about 180 degrees barely simmering. It should not boil. Let the sausage poach for about 10 minutes and remove from heat. When cool enough to handle, take the skin off.

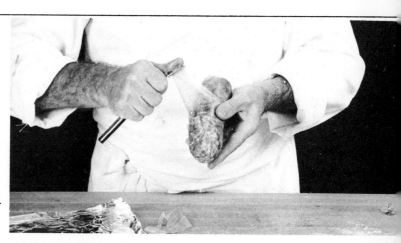

3. Beat the egg and egg yolk together to make a wash. Brush the sausage with egg wash and also the piece of dough. Sprinkle flour on the dough. The light sprinkling of flour will mix with the egg wash and form a "glue," which will hold the sausage to the dough while cooking.

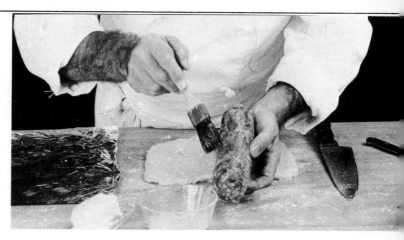

4. Lay the sausage on the dough and wrap the dough toward the top. Encase and seal the sausage tightly.

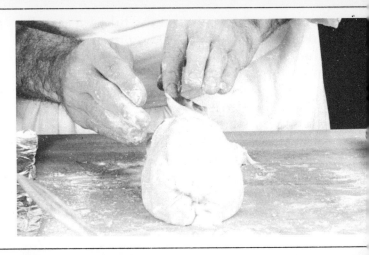

5. Spread butter on two-thirds of the surface of a square piece of aluminum foil. Sprinkle the buttered part with 1 tablespoon of fresh bread crumbs.

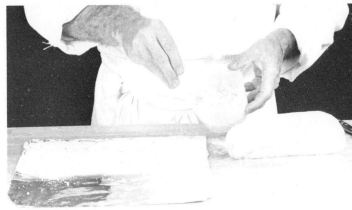

6. Place the sausage on the buttered part and wrap the foil around. Do not wrap too tightly so the dough has a little bit of space to expand.

7. Tighten both ends securely and place in a roasting pan, seam side down. Let the dough rise in the aluminum foil and "push" for about ½ hour in a warm (about 80 degrees) part of the kitchen. Roll the package seam side up and place in a preheated 375-degree oven for 40 minutes. Every 10 to 15 minutes, roll the sausage a quarter of a turn so the sausage does not sink into the dough on one side more than the other.

8. After about 40 minutes, take the sausage out of the oven, remove from the aluminum and brush again with egg wash. Raise the oven temperature to 400 degrees and bake for 5 to 8 minutes to brown better. Let set for 10 to 15 minutes before carving. If made ahead, the sausage can be reheated in a preheated 300-degree oven for 15 minutes. Serve in slices, as is, or with a little bit of melted butter on top. Excellent as a first course, or as a main course for lunch or brunch.

71. Pork Spread *(Rillettes de Porc)*

YIELD: 12 first course servings

THE WORD *charcuterie* implies different manners of cooking meat, but most particularly different pork preparations: pâtés, sausages, galantines, ham, etc. By extension the word *charcuterie* is also the store where these dishes are sold. In addition most *charcuteries* sell take-out food from pike *quenelles* to different salads of fish, shellfish, stuffed tomatoes, smoked fish, salami, *rillettes*, etc. The following techniques cover *rillettes*, pig's feet, headcheese, black pudding, chitterling sausages, tripes, parleyed ham—the typical preparations available from *charcuteries*.

The *rillettes* is seasoned pork cooked a long time, cooled and shredded into tiny pieces, bound together by fat and seasoned highly with salt and pepper. It is eaten cold with Dijon mustard and crunchy French bread as a first course or as a snack. The *rillettes* can also be made out of goose, rabbit or duck, but most of the time pork will be added to enrich the *rillettes* with fat and make it the right consistency. The *rillettes* are usually packed in small crocks and served as such with bread. *Rillettes* can be seasoned with wine or stock, thyme, bay leaf, etc., but the simple recipe given below and made with water retains the true taste of that country dish. The crocks should be covered tightly with plastic wrap and kept refrigerated up to 10 days. To keep longer the crocks have to be sealed with melted fat. When frozen the texture changes and the taste tends to grow rancid.

2¾ *pounds fresh pork from the chuck, butt or*
  neck (the meat should have about one-third
  lean meat to two-thirds fat)
1 *tablespoon salt*
½ *teaspoon freshly ground black pepper*
1 *clove garlic, peeled*
Water

1. Cut the meat into 2- to 3-inch cubes and place in a large heavy saucepan with the salt, pepper, garlic and enough cold water to reach 1 inch above the surface of the meat. Bring to a boil and cover. Simmer very, very slowly for 4 hours, covered. Uncover and cook another hour to evaporate the extra liquid. Skim the scum which comes to the top of the liquid every 20 minutes during the first 2 hours of cooking. The meat should poach gently in the liquid.

2. You may have to add water during the cooking process because if the water reduces completely and the fat melts, the meat will fry in the fat instead of poaching in the water. After 5 hours of cooking, nearly all water should have evaporated and the liquid in the pot should be fairly clear. Let the mixture cool overnight. The pieces of meat should be embedded in a nice, clear, white fat. If there's any liquid under the fat, pour it out.

3. Shred the pieces of meat between your fingers to separate the fibers of the meat. The *rillettes* are really meat fibers bound with fat. The easiest way to shred the meat into fiber is by hand.

4. Place in a bowl and mix with a wooden spatula until the mixture is smooth.

5. To make the mixture whiter and fluffier, place in the bowl of an electric mixer with the flat beater and beat for 30 seconds on speed #4 to 6. Do not overwhisk or the fat will become too white and too creamy. Add salt and pepper as you are beating. Remember that the *rillettes* should be well seasoned.

6. Divide the mixture into crocks. Smooth the top, cover tightly with plastic wrap and let set a few hours, preferably one day in the refrigerator before serving.

7. Just before serving, decorate with a fork. Serve very cold with crunchy French bread and cold white wine.

72. Stuffed Pig's Feet *(Pieds de Porc Farcis)*

YIELD: 6 servings

ORDINARY PIG'S FEET can be a delicacy whether you stuff them or not. They are excellent just simply boiled and served with a mustardy vinaigrette. They can be used to make aspic because they are very gelatinous in texture. They enhance the flavor and texture of tripe and cold jellied dishes, such as *Daube de Boeuf.* For our recipe the feet or "trotters" are first soaked in brine for six days. This improves the taste as well as the color. However, it is not absolutely necessary. If you omit the brine be sure to increase the salt in cooking and expect them to be grayish in color rather than pink. Use the front feet because although they are shorter, they are meatier. Prepare a brine as explained in technique 73.

Cooking

6 *pig's feet (about 12 ounces each)*
¼ *cup white wine vinegar*

Stuffing

1 *tablespoon butter*
½ *cup finely chopped onions*
2 *cloves garlic, peeled and finely chopped*
2 *cups (loose) mushrooms, finely chopped*
Dash of thyme leaves

½ *teaspoon salt*
¼ *teaspoon pepper*

To finish the feet

2 *cups fresh bread crumbs*
¾ *stick (3 ounces) sweet butter, melted*
2 *tablespoons strong Dijon-style mustard*

1. Soak the feet in the brine for 6 days, in a cool place, with a plate on top to keep them immersed in the brine. After 6 days wash in cold water and soak for 30 minutes in clear cold water. Place in a saucepan in one layer with the vinegar and cover with cold water. Cover and bring to a temperature of approximately 170 degrees. Poach at that temperature for 3½ to 4 hours. The water should not boil or the meat will come off the bones. If the feet have not been soaked in brine previous to cooking, add 2 teaspoons of salt to the cooking liquid.

2. Let the feet cool in the stock. When luke-warm, remove from the cooking liquid and pick all the bones off. Be careful to remove all the small bones in the hoof. Try to keep the meat together in a piece as best you can.

3. Sauté the onions in butter on medium heat for about 1 minute. Add the garlic, mushrooms and thyme. Cook until most of the liquid released from the mushrooms has evaporated (3 to 4 minutes). Allow the stuffing to cool. Then stuff the feet when they are still at room temperature. If they are allowed to cool off completely, they will harden and will be less easy to work with. Form little packages.

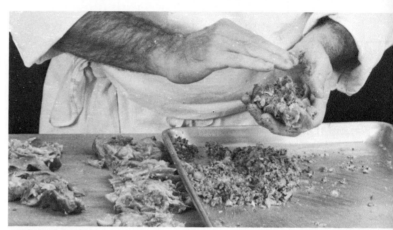

4. Place the stuffed feet, stuffing down, on a tray, one next to another, and place another tray on top with a weight. Refrigerate overnight. The "packages" will harden considerably when cold.

5. Trim each foot into a nice rectangular shape.

6. Brush the feet with the French mustard, covering the top and sides. The stuffed side should be underneath and the skin side on top.

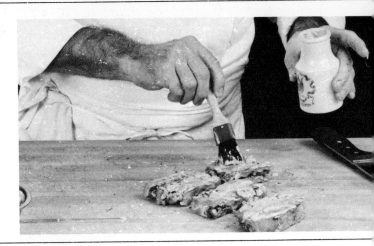

7. Mix the bread crumbs with the melted butter and pat firmly onto each package to coat. Up to this point the feet can be done ahead and kept covered in the refrigerator for a few days. To finish them, heat on a tray in a preheated 400-degree oven for about 12 minutes or until hot inside. Finish the browning under the broiler for a few minutes. Serve immediately with more French mustard and French bread for a lunch dish. It can also be served with boiled or mashed potatoes or various types of fried potatoes.

73. Rolled Headcheese *(Hure de Porc)*

YIELD: 16 to 18 servings

Headcheese is jellied meat and rind of the pig's head. There are different ways of making headcheese. The meat is sometimes cut into 1- to 2-inch pieces, cooked with stock and seasonings and the whole mixture placed into molds and allowed to cool and harden in the refrigerator. Then, the "loaf" is cut into slices and served with a vinaigrette. In this recipe, however, the meat and rind are rolled into a large headcheese sausage. It is a bit more work this way but the headcheese is meatier with less aspic. Curing the meat in a brine before cooking (although it is not imperative) makes it tastier and gives it a nicer color. If it is not cured in brine, the meat will be more grayish than pink. The brine can be used for ham or other pieces of pork, spare ribs (*petit salé*), shoulder, feet, loin, etc.

1 *whole pork head with bone, weighing approximately 12 pounds (Be sure the head is perfectly cleaned of hair.)*

1 *teaspoon thyme leaves*
4 *bay leaves crushed*
½ *teaspoon allspice*
½ *teaspoon coriander*
½ *teaspoon cloves*

Brine

6 *quarts water*
4 *cups kosher-type salt (1 ¼ pounds)*
1½ *cups brown sugar (about 10 ounces)*
1 *tablespoon saltpeter (potassium nitrate), optional*

First cooking

1 *small leek, cleaned and chopped fine, white only (½ cup)*
4 to 6 *shallots, peeled, chopped fine (¼ cup)*
¼ *cup chopped parsley*
½ *cup dry white wine*

Second cooking

1 *teaspoon freshly ground black pepper*
½ *teaspoon salt*
2 *cups dry white wine*
3 *cups well-seasoned chicken or beef stock, or a mixture of both*

1. To prepare the brine, crush the spices with a rolling pin or the bottom of a heavy saucepan. Place the water, salt, sugar and saltpeter in a large non-aluminum kettle and bring to a boil. Add the thyme, bay leaves, allspice, coriander and cloves, cover and remove from the heat. Let cool covered before using.

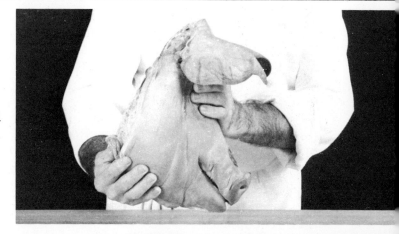

2. Split the skull into halves using a saw or a large cleaver. Remove the brains which can be poached, and fried in black butter or used with scrambled eggs. Do not cut through the skin under the chin.

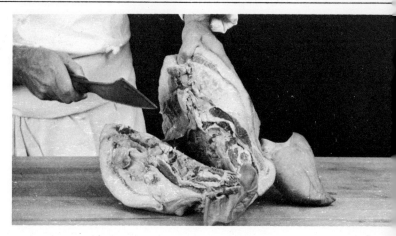

3. Bone the head all around the central bone. Do not worry if some meat is left on the bone because the meat can be removed easily after cooking. You should have approximately 6½ pounds of meat, rind and fat plus the remaining bones.

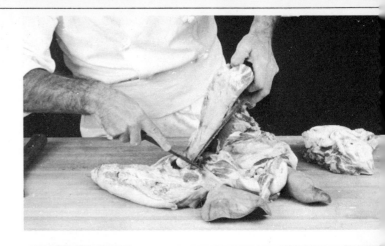

4. Place the meat and bones in the brine solution with a weight on top to keep the meat immersed. Keep in brine for 6 days in a cold place or refrigerate if possible. Wash bones and meat well under cold running water. Cover the meat and bones with cold water (salt is not necessary because the meat has been cured in brine) in a huge kettle and bring to a boil. Keep the meat submerged in the cooking liquid by placing a plate or lid and a weight on top. Simmer slowly for 1½ hours.

5. Let cool for ½ hour and remove the meat and bones to a tray. The headcheese should not cook too long because it will crumble and lose elasticity; it tastes better if it is a bit chewy. When the meat is cold enough to handle, start to pick the meat off the bones and discard the bones. Remove as much fat as you can from between the layers of meat and skin. There will be large chunks of fat which must be removed and either discarded or kept to make *rillettes* (technique 71) or used in stews or to sauté potatoes or other vegetables.

6. Spread out the largest pieces of skin on a towel—outside skin down.

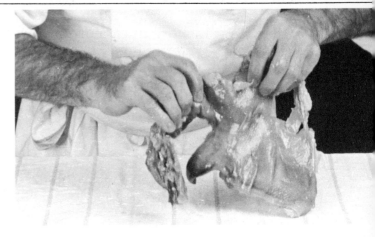

7. Place the ½ cup of wine, shallots, parsley and leek in a small saucepan. Simmer 4 to 5 minutes until the vegetables are wilted and most of the wine has evaporated. Cover the skin with the mixture and sprinkle black pepper and salt to taste on top of the meat.

8. Place the remaining pieces of meat on top of the shallot mixture and roll in the towel to form a large sausage with as much skin as possible on the outside. If you do not have a large fish poacher or *pâté* mold to accommodate the headcheese, make two smaller sausages instead of one large one. Smaller headcheese are easier to handle and serve.

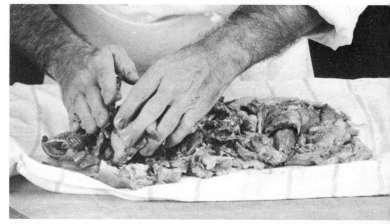

9. Tie the ends and center of the head-cheese with sturdy cotton kitchen twine.

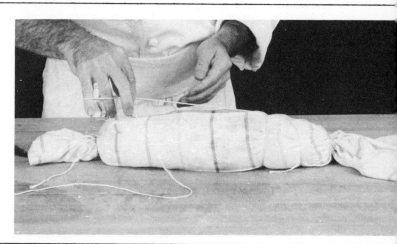

10. Place the sausage in a fish poacher or a large *pâté* mold and cover with white wine, the stock, salt and pepper.

11. To make sure the meat is immersed, weight it down with something heavy. Bring to a boil on top of the stove and simmer very gently for approximately 15 minutes. Allow to cool with the weight in place.

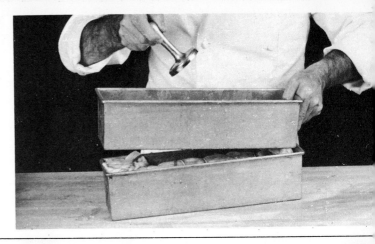

12. Cool overnight, then unmold and unwrap the towel. Keep the stock for later use. (It can be frozen or used to make aspic.) Cut the headcheese into thin slices and serve with sour pickles, French mustard, a dry white wine or light red wine and crunchy bread. Excellent as a snack or as a first course, for a country-type dinner.

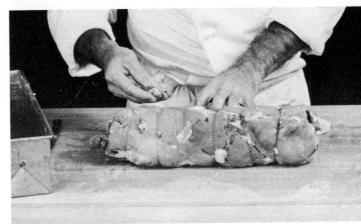

74. Black Pudding *(Boudins)*

YIELD: *20 boudins*

THE BLACK PUDDING or *boudin* is a very common country dish in France. Each region has its own variation, each one pretending to be the one and only original recipe. Some use apples, some leeks, some spinach, some chestnuts, etc. Regardless of the seasoning used, the *boudin* is bound with blood and enriched with pork fat.

The recipe given below is classic and simple. Pork blood gives the best result but it is hard to find in this country. Calf's blood or beef blood is a good substitute. The blood can be ordered from your butcher and will very likely come frozen, although, of course, it is better fresh. It is usually packed in half-gallon containers which will make approximately 40 *boudins*. The casing used for the *boudins* can be hog casing, approximately 1 to 1½ inches in diameter, or a small beef middle casing, as used in our recipe, which is also approximately 1½ to 2 inches in diameter. Casings usually come packed in salt. When served, the natural casing is usually discarded although some people like to eat it. (For more information about casings see pages 287–288 in *La Technique.*) Serve one *boudin* as a first course and two as a main course.

8 to 10 *feet hog or beef middle casings*
1 *quart pork or beef blood*
1½ *pounds* panne, *the pork fat around the kidney*
1¼ *pounds onions, peeled and chopped (about 2½ cups)*
4 *leeks, peeled, white and light green parts only, sliced very thin (1½ cups)*
1½ *cups heavy cream*
1¼ *teaspoons salt*
½ *teaspoon freshly ground white pepper*
¼ *teaspoon thyme*

1. The *panne* or pork suet is white, very waxy and surrounds the kidneys and lines the tenderloin. It is the best fat for *boudins*, *pâtés* and salamis. Grind the fat in a meat grinder or food processor. (If chopped in the food processor, it should first be cut into 1-inch chunks.) Place one-third of the fat in a large saucepan and melt for about 10 minutes on medium to high heat. Add the onions and leeks and cook for another 5 minutes on medium heat.

2. Add the remaining fat and cook for another 10 minutes. Let cool for at least 15 minutes and stir in the blood, cream and seasonings. Run the dry casings under water. Place the opening of the casing over the end of the faucet and let tepid water run through. Let the casings soak in lukewarm water for about 10 minutes, then squeeze to get rid of the water and place on a large cookie sheet.

3. Tie one end with kitchen string and fit the other end over as large a funnel as will fit. Ladle the mixture into the casing.

4. When filled, tie the other end of the casing with kitchen string. Leave a few inches of casing empty before the knot. The bit of extra space is for expansion during cooking and to accommodate the amount of casing taken in when you divide the *boudins* into individual portions.

5. Divide the filled casing into 5-inch lengths. You can simply twist the casing (reversing the twist for each different sausage) in order to separate the portions.

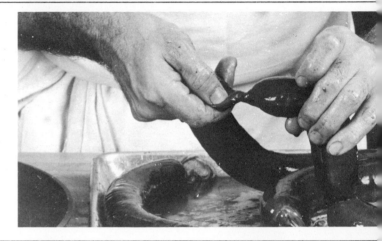

6. Or you can tie off the portions with pieces of kitchen string.

7. Place the *boudins* in a large saucepan into a coil. Use a wide saucepan that can hold the *boudins* in one layer. Add hot tap water to at least 1 inch above the meat. Place over high heat and bring the water to approximately 170 to 180 degrees. Do not boil or the *boudins* will burst.

8. Poach at the same temperature for 20 minutes. Prick the *boudins* with a needle to check the cooking. It is cooked when the liquid coming out of the casing is clear and only a few drops come out and stop.

9. When cooked, lift the *boudins* from the poaching liquid and let cool on a cookie sheet. When cold, separate into serving portions.

10. The *boudins* can be covered and stored in the refrigerator. It is at this stage that they can be bought in a *charcuterie* in France. At serving time, place in a skillet on medium heat. No fat is necessary. Cook for about 2 minutes on each side. Reduce to low heat, cover and let cook slowly for 10 minutes. Serve with freshly made mashed potatoes and/or sautéed apples on the side. This lovely country-style main course can be served for lunch as well as for dinner.

75. Chitterling Sausages *(Andouillettes)*

YIELD: 12 *andouillettes*

T HE *andouillettes*—chitterling sausages—are a delicacy of French *charcuterie.* They are usually served grilled or baked accompanied by mashed or sautéed potatoes. The *Andouille de Vire* is an extra large *andouillette,* a specialty of Normandy, served cold in slices and recognizable by its thick black skin. *Andouille* or *andouillettes* are made from the fatty, small intestine (chitterlings) and stomach of pig or calf, or a mixture of both. In our recipe, we use only pig chitterlings because veal chitterlings are not available in this country

6 to 8 feet hog or beef middle casings, same size
   as for **Boudins** (technique 74)
10 pounds pork chitterlings
1 clove garlic, peeled, crushed and finely chopped
8 to 10 shallots, peeled and chopped fine (¾ cup)
1½ tablespoons unsalted butter
1 cup dry white wine
3 tablespoons good Dijon-style mustard
1 tablespoon salt
2 teaspoons freshly ground black pepper

To poach

3 cups good chicken, beef or veal stock or a
   mixture of these
2 cups dry white wine
Dash of salt and pepper

1. If the chitterlings are frozen, thaw slowly in the refrigerator for about 48 hours. Chitterlings look like fatty casings. They are usually well cleaned and no further cleaning is necessary. Place the chitterlings in a large kettle, cover with cold water and bring to a boil. Lower the heat and simmer slowly for 2 hours. Drain and set aside. The chitterlings shrink considerably.

2. Cut the chitterlings into 1-inch chunks. Melt the butter in a large saucepan, add the shallots and sauté for 1 minute on medium heat. Add the garlic, mix well and remove from the heat. Combine with the chitterlings, then add the white wine, mustard, salt and black pepper and mix well together. The mixture is now well seasoned and ready to be stuffed in casings.

3. Close the casings (see step 2, technique 74), then, using a large funnel and the back of a wooden spoon, push the chitterling pieces through.

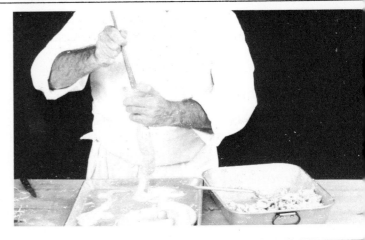

4. Massage the mixture down into the casing. Do not pack it too tight because the meat will expand during cooking and it will burst if it is too tight.

5. Separate the casing into 5-inch-long sausages, either by twisting, as explained in the previous technique, step 5, or by using a piece of kitchen string.

6. Prick the sausages with a fork. This will prevent them from bursting while poaching.

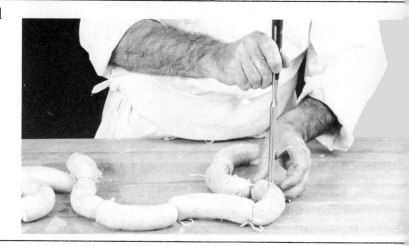

7. Use a large roasting pan or a saucepan which can accommodate the chitterlings in one layer. Add the stock and wine. It should cover the sausages by ½ inch.

8. Place an upside-down plate on top to keep the *andouillettes* immersed while cooking. Place on medium heat and bring slowly to 170 to 180 degrees. Do not boil or the sausages will burst. Add a dash of salt, depending on the seasoning of the stock, and a dash of pepper. Remember that the cooking liquid should be well seasoned. Poach for 15 minutes. Remove from the heat and let the sausages cool in the liquid. When cold, remove from the liquid and refrigerate. This is the stage at which chitterling sausages are bought in a French *charcuterie*. The sausages will keep in the refrigerator for a week or can be frozen. The liquid can be frozen, used for other sausages, or made into an aspic.

To finish four sausages

At serving time, melt 1 tablespoon of butter in a skillet and brown the sausages over very low heat (or they will burst). Brown for 2 minutes on each side. Add ¼ cup white wine and simmer covered, very slowly, for 10 minutes. Serve as such with the juices.

76. Tripe with Wine and Calvados
(Tripes à la Mode de Caen)

YIELD: Serves 8 to 10 servings

TRIPE usually refers to the stomach of ox or beef, although in France certain parts of the intestine are considered to be tripe as well. The tripe (also known as the honeycomb or *estomac* or *panse* in France) is thicker and fattier on one side and this side is what is used for the *gras-double,* a specialty of Lyonnaise cooking. The *pieds paquets* is a specialty of Marseille, made from lamb tripe mixed with the *feuillet* (part of the huge intestine), formed into little packages and cooked slowly for a long time. There are many different recipes for tripe and the one given here is the classic version cooked in Normandy and finished with Calvados. Beef feet are usually added to give a more gelatinous consistency to the dish. The tripe should be cooked slowly for a long time—the longer the better.

Tripe

10 *pounds beef tripe (honeycomb)*
2 *beef or calf feet, 1½ to 2 pounds each*
3 *carrots, peeled (about ½ pound)*
2 *large onions, peeled and cut into halves*
2 *teaspoons salt (depending on stock seasoning)*
1 *large leek or 2 to 3 smaller ones, cleaned*
2 *to 3 stalks celery*
3 *bay leaves*
1 *teaspoon thyme*
1 *teaspoon ground black pepper*

2 *quarts light, good chicken or beef stock or a
    mixture of both*
1 *quart dry white wine*

To finish the dish

Calvados
1¼ *cups flour*
½ *cup lukewarm water*
1 *egg, beaten, for glaze*

---

1. The tripe will come cleaned and already blanched. If you are unable to obtain it fresh, defrost it slowly under refrigeration.

---

2. Split the beef feet into halves. Cut the meat all around the central bone and in the middle of the hoof. It is not necessary to cut through the bone.

---

3. Arrange the feet and all the seasonings in a large kettle. Place the tripe on top and add the stock and wine. Cover and bring to a boil. Lower the heat and simmer very slowly for at least 4 hours. Set aside to cool.

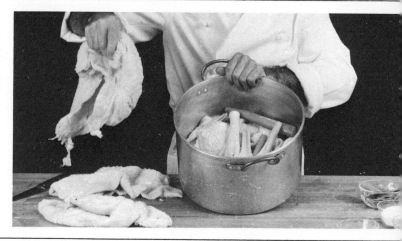

4. When cool enough to handle, lift the tripe, feet and vegetables from the liquid. Reduce the liquid on high heat to 2 quarts. Meanwhile, bone out the feet and cut the meat into 1-inch pieces. Discard the bones. Cut the tripe into 2-inch pieces and chop all the vegetables coarsely. Combine with the reduced stock. You should have just enough liquid to cover the tripe.

5. Bring to a boil. Taste for seasoning. You may have to add salt and pepper depending on the strength of the stock. It should be well seasoned. When we prepared this dish for photography we found it needed another ½ teaspoon of pepper and 1 teaspoon of salt.

6. At this point, the tripe could be divided into containers and frozen. When ready to use, defrost under refrigeration for 48 hours, and simmer gently another 2 hours. Serve with a sprinkling of Calvados (apple-jack brandy), approximately ½ teaspoon per person. The tripe is customarily served in bowls with boiled potatoes.

7. For a fancier way of serving tripe, place in earthenware crocks, seal the lid with dough so no steam escapes and bake in the oven. Make a dough by mixing the flour with water and kneading for 1 minute. Roll pieces of dough into 1-inch-thick strips, wet with water and place around the lid. Press to flatten the dough to make sure it adheres well. Brush with the egg wash, and place on a cookie sheet in a preheated 325-degree oven for 2 hours. Serve as is from the oven. At the table, break the dough and lift the cover in front of your guests. Tripe

is customarily served as a main course with boiled potatoes. You will notice that after the first cooking—after the 4 hours, at the point when the tripe can either be frozen or placed in terrines in the oven—there is still a lot of liquid and the seasoning is not strong. Keep in mind that it has another 2 hours of cooking and the liquid will reduce and the taste will become more concentrated.

77. Cured, Raw Country Ham

(Prosciutto/Bayonne-style) *(Préparation du Jambon Cru)*

IT ALWAYS COMES as a surprise to people that prosciutto, as well as salamis, French *rosette*, or even the Swiss *bunderfleish* of the Grisons (cured dried beef), is just plain, uncooked, raw meat served cut into thin slices. The greatest hams in the world, such as Bayonne from the southwest of France, Westphalia and Czechoslovakia as well as Parma from Italy, are all uncooked hams, served raw in very thin slices with bread and butter or sweet fruits such as melon or figs. Great American hams, such as Smithfield, Virginia or the Nashville country ham, can be served the same way.

To make a prosciutto-type at home you have to cure a piece of pork, preferably the hind leg of the pig. A shoulder, a piece of the front leg, as well as a piece of chuck (used for Italian *coppa*), give excellent results. In many parts of Europe farmers cure and dry their own hams as well as smaller pieces of meat and use them either raw (cut in thin slices) or cooked with sauerkraut or beans for a country casserole dish.

There are two basic ways of curing ham: either you immerse it in a liquid brine (mostly salt, sugar and water), or you cure it in dry salt. The salt drains the liquid out of the meat, depriving the bacteria of the moisture it needs to survive, and therefore preserving the meat from spoilage. We prefer not to smoke our ham, just cure it then dry it. After the salting, the meat is sometimes smoked, then it's dried. Professional producers dry at exact temperatures with controlled humidity. Too much heat and humidity can spoil the ham. A home-cured ham—hung in a cellar, a garage or an attic—should be processed in winter so it has a chance to cure and start drying before the warmer, more humid months.

1 15-pound fresh ham with "quasi" (pelvic bone)
   removed
1 3-pound box kosher-type salt
½ cup granulated sugar
Cognac
Whole black peppercorns

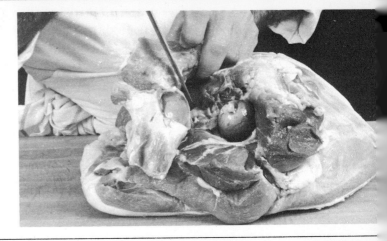

1. Buy the freshest and highest quality hind leg, or fresh ham, that you can find. Ours weighed 15 pounds with the pelvic bone removed. Using a sharp, sturdy knife, remove the pelvic bone attached to the joint of the femur (or thighbone).

2. Make a hole around the tip of the femur and massage the ham to help release some liquid and blood (if any) through the opening. Pour some Cognac into the hole around the bone and massage the meat around it. (Although we have never frozen the pork and have never had any problem, at this point, some people recommend freezing the meat for a few days to eliminate any possibility of trichinosis.)

3. Mix the salt and the sugar together (kosher-type salt is purer and sweeter than table salt) and rub inside the ham around the thighbone, forcing it into any openings, then place the ham in a large plastic bag. Pour plenty of salt under, around and on top of the ham, using the whole 3-pound box. Leave the bag slightly open so the meat can breathe and place in a cool place, skin side down. The ham should be completely saturated with salt and the holes around the bones should be packed full of salt because these areas are prone to souring. Check every few days to make sure that the meat is still entirely covered with salt. Some liquid will be leeched out and absorbed by the salt. Leave the ham curing in a cool place for at least a day per pound. Try to avoid handling the meat too much with your fingers.

4. After 16 days, clean the salt off the ham with paper towels. Be sure that the ham is clean and well dried. Rub 2 large cloves of peeled garlic all over the ham. Then sprinkle one tablespoon of good Cognac on the meat. Place ½ cup of black peppercorns in a coffee mill for a few seconds to crush coarsely (*mignonnettes*). Cover the ham with crushed peppercorns, especially where there is no skin where it will adhere best.

5. Place the ham in a large canvas bag or wrap it in a large kitchen apron.

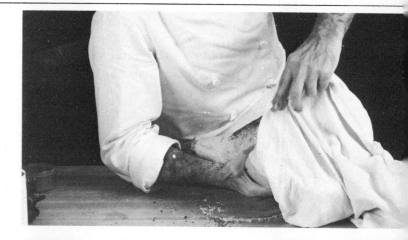

6. The cloth allows the air in so the ham will dry, but keeps flies or other insects out.

7. Tie with heavy kitchen string and make a loop at the end. Hang the ham in a cool, drafty place. There must be ventilation or the ham will spoil. If it is hung in a garage in the winter it may freeze slightly on the outside. This will not harm the ham in any way. (The salt lowers the temperature at which the ham will freeze and it will have to get very cold before the ham freezes through.) On the other hand, if the weather is warm and especially humid, the ham may get covered with mold. If this happens, unwrap, clean the ham, and re-wrap in a

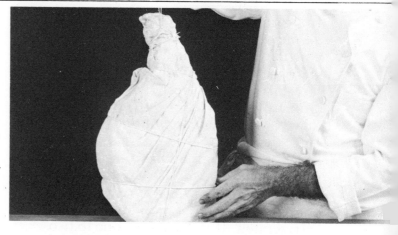

clean canvas. Place in front of a fan to dry.
(In a hot, humid climate, simulate a cold
and drafty environment by placing the ham
in a refrigerator with a fan for a couple of
weeks so it gets a good start drying.) Let the
ham hang for a minimum or 5 to 6 months.
It will then be ready, although still slightly
soft inside. The longer it dries, the harder it
becomes and the more weight it loses. After
approximately 6 months of drying the ham
will have lost close to half its original
weight.

8. When ready to eat, use a steel brush wetted with water and paper towels to brush
and dry the ham. The thick rind will clean
easily but the underneath will be covered
with mold. Start trimming on the thickest
side (the top round and meatiest part of the
ham). The rind as well as the beautiful
white fat underneath can be used to cook
lentils, beans, soups, stews, etc. It is a won-
derful seasoning.

9. There is a special piece of equipment
used to hold the ham in place during carving—a stainless steel metal strip on top of a
piece of marble. Unless you have it, the best
way to keep the ham in place is to put it in a
long pâté mold or squeeze it in a drawer.

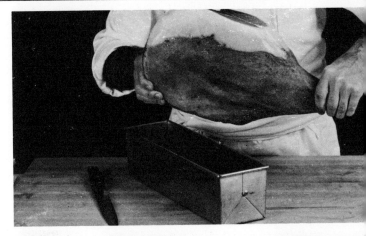

10. Using a long, thin knife, cut out the
thinnest possible slices. Do not apply too
much pressure on the knife. An electric
knife makes the carving easier. Serve the
slices plain with cornichons, mustard and
crunchy bread. Or fry with eggs in what is
called a *pipérade* in the south of France.
Once the ham has been started, it is advis-
able to go through it fairly quickly, though
it will last a few weeks. Cover the cut end
with a piece of plastic, secure it with a rubber band and keep it hung in a cool place or
refrigerated. If not used for one to two

weeks, the first slice will discolor but will still be perfectly edible. This home-cured ham makes a beautiful centerpiece and is enough for a buffet of 40 to 60 people.

78. Ham in Crust *(Jambon en Croûte)*

YIELD: 18 to 20 servings

A WHOLE HAM in crust makes a beautiful presentation for a buffet or an Easter or Christmas dinner. It is very difficult to slice a ham into thin slices without the crust crumbling which is why we cook the ham first, slice it, then wrap the dough around it and bake. The crust is used to encase the completely carved ham.

What in the market is called a "fully cooked ham" greatly improves when recooked. Place in a large kettle, covered with cold water, and bring slowly to a simmer. Keep the water barely "shivering" for 1 hour at about 185 to 190 degrees. Do not boil or the meat may split open. Let the ham cool in the stock for at least 3 hours at room temperature, or preferably overnight. Using the tip of a small sharp knife, remove the hip or pelvic bone from the ham (see step 1, technique 77). Try not to cut too deep into the meat. Remove the skin and most of the fat from the top, which can be kept for other uses, leaving at the most a ¼-inch layer of fat on top of the ham. Trim all around, especially underneath, where the surface may be a little tough.

Cooking the ham

1 10- to 12-pound fully cooked, lightly smoked ham, with pelvic and shank bone in, recooked for 1 hour and trimmed according to above instructions
3 tablespoons good apricot jam
1 tablespoon dry mustard
3 tablespoons brown sugar
1 egg beaten, for the wash

Dough

1 pound unsifted flour (about 3 ½ cups)
1½ sticks (6 ounces) sweet butter, softened and cut into pieces
2 tablespoons vegetable, peanut, grape-seed or almond oil
½ teaspoon salt
1 teaspoon sugar
3 egg yolks mixed with ⅓ cup cold water
1 egg, plus 1 egg yolk for the wash

Sauce

4 *cups concentrated* demi-glace *(see technique 6)*
¾ *cups dry Madeira wine or dry Sherry if Madeira is not available*
⅓ *stick (1⅓ ounces) sweet butter, cut in small pieces*
Salt and pepper to taste

To make the sauce, reduce the wine and stock on medium to high heat for about 20 minutes. You should have about 3 cups of liquid left and the mixture should be just thick enough to coat a spoon and be glazy. Add the butter piece by piece, stirring with a whisk to make a smooth and shiny sauce. Add salt and pepper to taste and keep warm until serving time.

1. Blend together the jam, mustard and sugar and spread on top of the ham. Place the ham on a cookie sheet in a preheated 425-degree oven for 30 minutes. Let the ham reach room temperature and carve in thin slices on a slant, arranging the slices neatly on the table as the carving progresses. (At this point the ham could be served just as is.) Keep carving until the central bone is exposed. Do not carve out whole slices from the center of the ham because the slices would be too large. Slice on one side of the bone then on the other side. To re-form the ham, arrange the slices back on the ham in their proper order. Do not worry if they are not exactly in order or not perfectly neat, since they will be covered with the dough.

2. To make the dough, place all the ingredients in a mixer, and using the flat beater, mix on medium speed until smooth and well combined—about 1 minute. It can also be made by hand using the technique of *fraiser* (technique 98). Roll the dough to ¼-inch thickness into a large wheel and brush with egg wash.

3. Place the carved ham on a cookie sheet lined with parchment paper and cover it with the dough, wet side touching the ham.

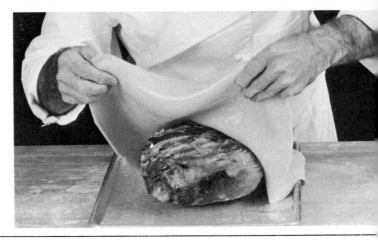

4. Press the dough all around the ham so it adheres and trim the excess dough. The ham at the shank should be well encased in the dough. We don't encase the whole ham but only cover the top and sides. It makes it easier to handle and moisture released during cooking can escape without the dough becoming soggy underneath.

5. Brush the dough all over with egg wash and decorate with strips of dough. Arrange two strips on top to outline the lid. When the ham is cooked a lid will be created by cutting between these two strips.

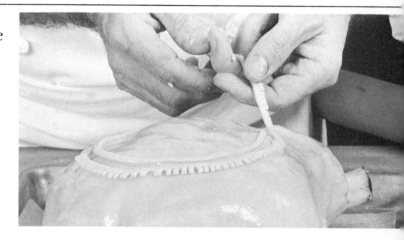

6. Decorate the lid with flowers made of dough. Make a long, thin strip and let it fold on itself to imitate the petals and stem of a flower.

7. Cut stems, leaves and other patterns and place to your fancy on top of the lid.

8. Decorate the outside of the lid by making a relief of cherries. Shape rounds with a pastry tube and arrange with stems.

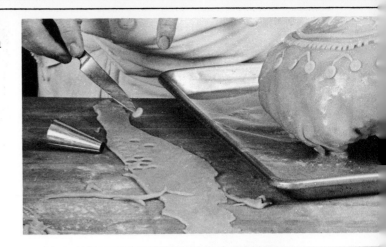

9. Cut leaves and place them in relief all around the cherries. Press the top and bottom of each leaf to keep them in position. The egg wash helps the decorations adhere.

10. Place another piece of dough with "teeth" around the shank.

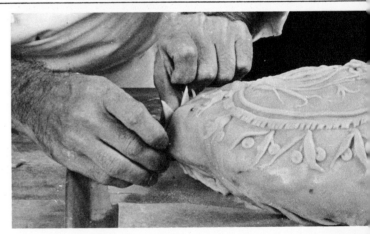

11. Brush the top of the decoration with more egg wash and place the ham in a cool place to let it set for an hour.

12. Place the ham in a preheated 425-degree oven for 10 minutes. Reduce the heat to 400 degrees and cook another 30 minutes. The ham should be beautifully glazed and shiny. Let the ham rest for 30 minutes in a lukewarm place before serving. Cut the lid following the outline of the dough.

13. Lift up the lid to expose the meat. Place the lid back loosely on the ham. Place the ham on a serving platter and secure a frill to the end of the bone. Serve one or two slices of ham per person with some of the Madeira sauce spooned on top. The ham goes well with a purée of spinach as well as with the little papetons of eggplant or the cauliflower and broccoli mold (techniques 45 and 46).

79. Cold Parsleyed Ham *(Jambon Persillé)*

YIELD: 10 to 12 servings

THE *jambon persillé,* a great way to use leftover ham, is pieces of ham imbedded in parsleyed aspic. The pink of the ham and the green of the parsley make a very attractive presentation as well as a delicious dish. It is usually served as a first course with a dry white wine or a light red wine, crunchy bread and *cornichons.*

Approximately 1¾ pounds ham (4 cups), cut into 2- to 3-inch chunks
¾ cup chopped parsley
½ cup chopped parsley
2 pig's feet (use the front leg which is fleshier, about 1½ to 2 pounds together)
2 cups good beef or chicken stock
2 cups water
1 teaspoon salt
½ teaspoon freshly ground pepper
2 cups dry white wine

½ cup chopped shallots (about 6 to 8), chopped fine
½ cup finely chopped leeks

1. Separate the meat from the bone on the leftover ham and cut into chunks. Keep the bone to season lentils or bean soups.

2. Split the pig's feet in half by cutting through the middle of the hoof and around the bone.

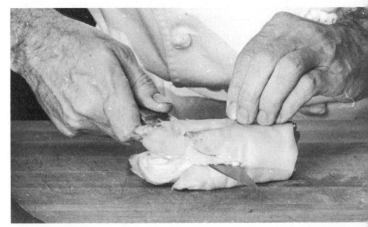

3. Use a cleaver to split the bones in half. Place the feet, stock, water, salt and pepper in a large saucepan and simmer for 1 hour, covered. Add the wine, shallots, leeks, ½ cup of parsley, cover, and simmer for another hour. Remove the feet from the liquid. There should be about 2 to 2½ cups of liquid left.

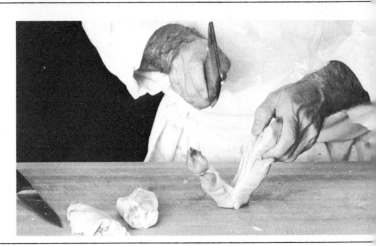

4. Pick the meat off the bones and chop coarsely. Be sure to remove all the tiny bones from the hoof.

5. Strain 1 cup from the reserved liquid and set aside. Add the chopped feet and the ham to the remaining stock, cover, bring to a boil and simmer 5 minutes. Let cool, stirring occasionally until it starts to set.

6. Meanwhile, add the ¾ cup of parsley to the cup of strained stock and bring to a boil. Cool in a metal bowl over ice. As the liquid starts to set, twist the bowl and use a brush to spread the liquid so that a thin layer of parsleyed aspic coats the bowl all around. Roll the bowl on ice as you are spreading the aspic so the sides get cold and the aspic sticks.

7. Place the ham mixture (it should not be completely set) in the lined bowl, packing the pieces together tightly and making sure that the chopped feet and the loose mixture surround the pieces of ham.

8. Cover with a piece of wax paper, place a small plate on top and flatten with a weight. Cool overnight in the refrigerator.

9. Run the bowl lightly under hot water for a few seconds, run a knife around the bowl and, using a kitchen fork, pry the ham out.

10. Cut into wedges and serve cold as a first course.

80. Stuffed Pork Chops with Sour Sauce *(Côtelettes de Porc Farcies Charcutière)*

YIELD: 6 servings

ALTHOUGH in our recipe we use the pork chops from the rack, loin chops can be used as well. The chops do not have to be stuffed and can be broiled or sautéed in different ways; for example, Normandy-style with apples, cream and Calvados.

Stuffing

6 *pork chops, center cut (6 to 7 ounces each)*
1 *tablespoon (½ ounce) sweet butter*
1 *leek, cleaned and diced very thin (white and light green parts only) (¾ cup)*
1 *stalk celery, peeled and finely diced (2 table-spoons)*
1 *pound cooked leaf spinach (see technique 40), coarsely chopped*
½ *cup finely diced boiled ham*
½ *teaspoon salt*
¼ *teaspoon freshly ground black pepper*

Sauce Charcutière

2 *medium sized tomatoes, peeled, seeds squeezed out and coarsely chopped (1 cup)*
½ *cup finely chopped onions*
3 *cloves garlic, crushed and chopped fine (1 teaspoon)*
½ *cup sour French gerkins (cornichons), thinly sliced*
¾ *cup* demi-glace *(see technique 6)*
½ *cup dry white wine*
2 *tablespoons chopped fresh herbs (parsley, tarragon, chives, etc.)*

1. When you buy a whole rack or a piece of rack you will find that it usually comes with the backbone. This makes it difficult to cut into chops or to carve in the dining room if it is roasted whole. To remove the backbone, place the rack flat and cut all along the bone to separate from the meat.

2. Standing the rack up and using the front part of a cleaver, cut through the end of the rib to sever the whole backbone.

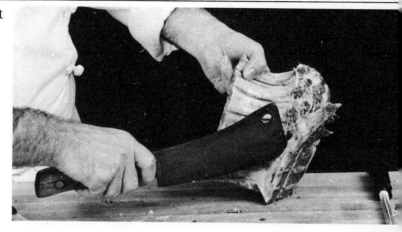

3. The backbone is now separated from the rack. The rack at that point could be roasted whole, seasoned with carrots and onions, and served with natural juices. Prepared this way, it is easy to carve in the dining room.

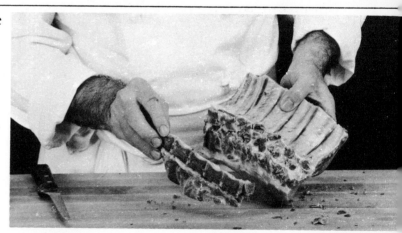

4. Cut in between each rib to make individual chops. The chops should weigh approximately 6 to 7 ounces each.

5. Trim each chop along the rib of sinews and fat. Trim if the pork is a few days old, as this is where the meat usually spoils first. In addition, trimming makes the chop a bit more elegant. However, if the pork is very fresh it is not absolutely necessary to trim it.

6. To make the chop still more attractive, clean the end off the rib. (Use the trimmings in stocks or soups.) Cut the meat all around the bone (it will be mostly fat), and scrape it off to expose the end of the rib.

7. Place the chop flat and holding it down with one hand, slice it through the middle with the point of a knife. Do not slice the ends. It should form a pocket. Cut deep enough to touch the rib with the knife.

8. Open the chop and flatten each half with a meat pounder to make it a bit larger so it can hold more stuffing and form a better pocket.

9. Melt the butter in a small skillet, add the leek and sauté for 1 minute on medium to low heat, then add the celery and sauté for a few seconds. Mix the spinach in with a fork and sauté for another minute. Combine with the ham and season with salt and pepper. Mix well. Let the stuffing cool, then divide among the chops.

10. Push the stuffing in the cavity and close the meat on top. If the chops are not over-stuffed and if the meat has been pounded nicely, it doesn't need to be tied or secured with a skewer.

11. Sprinkle the chops with salt and pepper. Melt 1 tablespoon of butter in a wide skillet with a cover. Add the chops and cook, uncovered, on medium heat, for 5 minutes on one side. When browned, turn, cover and cook on low heat for another 10 minutes on the other side. The pork chops should cook slowly or they will become dry and stringy.

12. Place the chops on a platter and keep warm, uncovered, in a 160-degree oven. Add the onions to the drippings and sauté for 1 to 2 minutes on medium heat, then add the wine. Boil for a few seconds, stirring to melt all the solidified juices. Add the tomatoes and garlic and cook for 1 minute. Add the *demi-glace,* bring to a boil and reduce for 2 to 3 minutes until it coats the spoon and has the consistency of a sauce. Add salt and pepper if necessary. Stir in the cornichons, pour the sauce over the chops, sprinkle with herbs and serve.

81. Loin of Veal *(Carré de Veau)*

IN TECHNIQUE 80 we trimmed and sliced a rack of pork. Here we are trimming a loin—in this case a loin of veal. The loin is divided by a "T" bone with the tenderloin (filet) on one side and the loin on the other. The loin as well as the tenderloin is the choicest, tenderest and most expensive piece of the veal. The loin is sometimes roasted whole, stuffed or unstuffed. It is also boned out, trimmed of all fat and sinew and divided in small *mignonnettes* (small scallopini) or *grenadins* (larger steaks). The filet is usually roasted whole or used in *pâtés*. The bones and trimmings should be kept for stock and the sinewy piece of the flank used in stews, *pâtés* or stuffing.

1. Lift up the flank to expose the filet. Trim off most of the fat on top of the filet.

2. Place the rack on the table, loin side down, and cut along the bone to loosen the filet. Note how the bone forms a "T" and the filet can easily be scooped out from one side.

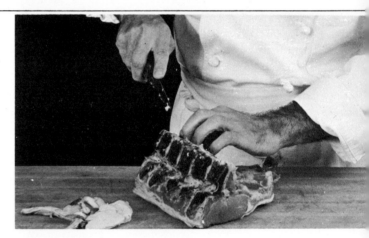

3. Remove the loin by cutting along the center bone and backbone.

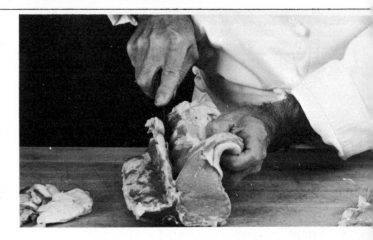

4. Cut underneath to separate the loin from the backbone in one piece.

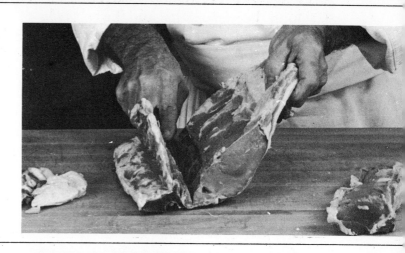

5. Cut the flank at the tail end of the loin. Trim the top of the loin of sinew and fat.

6. Clean the filet of all sinew and fat. Use the sinew in stocks and the flank in stews.

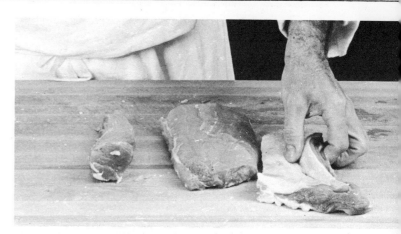

7. Cut small *médaillons* of veal (*mignonnettes*), about 1½ ounces each. *Mignonnettes* take only a few seconds to cook (see technique 6). They should be served three per person. Cut the loin into larger 4-to-5-ounce steaks (*grenadins*), to be served one per person with sauce and garnishes.

8. Pound the *mignonnettes* and the *grenadins* gently to make them of equal thickness and shape.

9. The whole loin carved: 5 *mignonnettes*, 3 *grenadins*, and the filet left whole. Be careful not to overcook the veal. *Mignonnettes* should be sautéed in butter that's not too hot for no more than 30 to 40 seconds on each side. The *grenadin* steaks will take 3 to 4 minutes, and the whole filet about 12 to 15 minutes.

82. Boning a Saddle of Lamb
(Désossage Selle d'Agneau)

THE SADDLE is comprised of the two loins, the two tenderloins, the flanks and the kidneys. An expensive cut of meat, it can be roasted whole and carved (see page 323 in *La Technique*), as well as boned out and cut into small *médaillons* (technique 81) or stuffed (technique 83). The loin (which is a half saddle) can be cut into loin chops or boned out and stuffed. The lamb fat is strong and cannot be used in any dish. The bones can be used for stocks or soups.

1. This photograph shows one saddle and one loin (half saddle). Place the saddle on its back to expose the filets. Remove the filet on each side, cutting along the central bone.

2. Keep your knife flat and cut along the T-bone on each side to expose the loins.

3. Turn the saddle and cut on each side along the backbone, to release both loins.

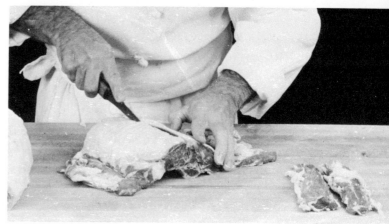

4. Trim the loins and tenderloins of all fat and sinew. Bone the half saddle in the same manner.

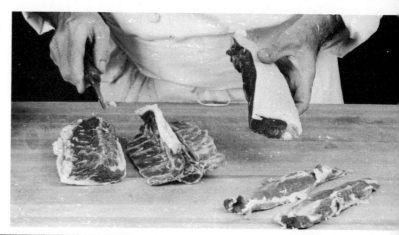

5. The saddle of lamb with the two loins and two filets, and the half saddle with its loin and tenderloin, all boned out. The bones can be used for stocks and the meat can be cut into scallopini and sautéed, or roasted whole, as well as stuffed.

83. Saddle of Lamb in Crust
(Selle d'Agneau en Croûte)

YIELD: 8 servings

A 5½-pound saddle of lamb yields about 2 to 2½ pounds of meat, completely trimmed and boned. In this technique, the boned-out meat is re-formed into a saddle with spinach replacing the bone. It is encased in puff paste and baked. The pink of the meat contrasts beautifully with the green of the spinach and the golden color of the crust. The spinach-stuffed saddle *en croûte* makes an elegant dish for a dinner party.

Roasting

1 *boned saddle (technique 82)*
2 *tablespoons (1 ounce) sweet butter*
½ *teaspoon salt*
¼ *teaspoon freshly ground black pepper*

Stuffing

2 *pounds spinach, cleaned and cooked (technique 40)*
½ *teaspoon salt*
¼ *teaspoon freshly ground black pepper*
2 *tablespoons shallots, chopped fine (about 3 to 4 shallots)*
1 *clove garlic, crushed and finely chopped*

To finish the dish

1 *pound puff paste for the crust (technique 91)*
1 *egg yolk mixed with 1 tablespoon milk or cream for the wash*

Melt the butter in a large skillet and when hot, salt and pepper the meat and brown on high heat for about 1 minute on each side to sear. Set the meat aside to cool. Heat the drippings until they turn dark brown and add the spinach with salt and pepper. Stir

with a fork to separate the leaves and add the shallots and garlic. Sauté on medium heat for about 1 minute, stirring occasionally. Remove the spinach to a plate and cool. Roll out the puff paste into a large rectangle about ⅛ inch thick.

1. Set the two loins in the center of the dough. The meat, as well as the stuffing, should be cool.

2. Arrange the spinach between and on top of the loins, and place the two tenderloins on top with more spinach in between. The meat and spinach are arranged to reconstruct the saddle. Brush the sides of the dough with egg wash and fold one side over the meat carefully. Bring the other side on top so it overlaps slightly.

3. Trim the dough to leave only a bottom flap on each end of the saddle. Fold the flap back on the meat to enclose the saddle tightly.

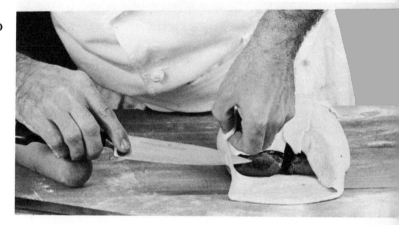

4. Place the saddle, seam side down, on a parchment-lined cookie sheet. Brush again with egg wash and decorate with strips of dough in a crisscross pattern. Brush the decorations with egg wash and let set in the refrigerator for 1 hour before cooking, if possible, or in the freezer for 15 to 20 minutes.

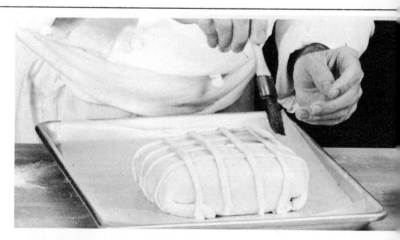

5. Place in a preheated 425-degree oven for 30 to 35 minutes for a medium-rare saddle. Remove from the oven and let the saddle rest in a warm place for at least 15 minutes before carving. The carving is a little tricky. Use a long, thin, sharp knife and cut ½-inch slices to reveal the two pieces of loin and the two pieces of tenderloin. To help carve, place a large flat spatula against the slices to keep them from breaking apart. Serve with the sauce (see step 6, technique 84).

Loin of lamb in crust (Demi-selle d'Agneau en Croûte)

YIELD: 4 servings

1. This variation on the lamb *en croûte* uses just one loin—not the whole saddle— and a "ham dough" instead of puff paste. The ham dough (the recipe appears in technique 78) is easier to make than puff paste and is less fragile. It is not as flaky as puff paste and won't brown quite as deeply. Bone-out one loin as explained in technique 82. Prepare half of the stuffing and sear the meat in butter. Prepare about 1 pound of ham dough. Roll into a rectangle and arrange the loin, spinach and tenderloin on top.

2. Bring one side of the dough on top of the meat and brush the top and sides with egg wash. Overlap the other side on top and trim both ends of the dough.

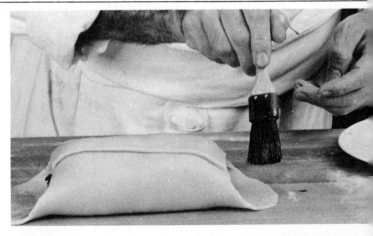

3. Brush the ends with the wash, fold and press gently on top. Turn the loin upside down and place it on a parchment-lined cookie sheet.

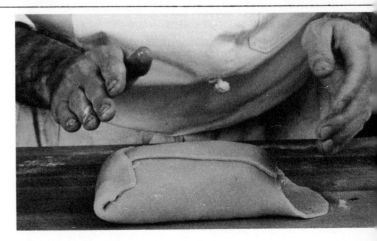

4. Decorate the top with a rose made of dough: Wrap a thin strip of dough around a lump of dough.

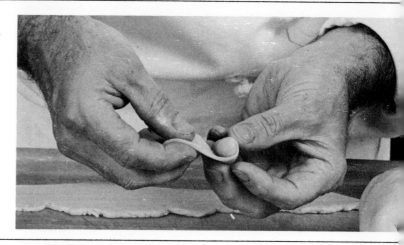

5. Make thin "petals" and wrap one after the other around the flower. Turn the edge of the petals outward to make them more lifelike (see technique 139).

6. Place the flower in the middle of the loin with one leaf on each side. Brush the dough with the egg wash and mark crisscross lines with the back of a knife. Cook in a preheated 425-degree oven for about 25 minutes. Let the meat rest at least 10 to 15 minutes before carving. The single loin is easier to carve than the whole saddle. For a sauce to serve with the saddle or loin, cut the bones and sinew in 1-inch pieces. Place in a large saucepan and brown over medium heat for 25 minutes, without adding fat. Add 1 quart brown stock (see technique 6) and 1 quart of water. Cook slowly for 2 hours, removing the scum as it rises to the top. Strain and reduce to about 1¾ cups *demi-glace* of lamb. Test for seasonings and add salt and pepper if needed. Serve with the carved saddle or loin.

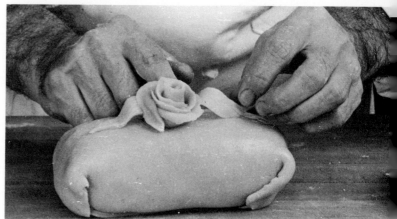

Breads, Pastry and Desserts

84. Country Bread (Pain de Ménage)

YIELD: 2 to 3 round loaves and 4 to 5 baguettes, about 1 pound each

VERY SIMPLE RECIPES are often the most deceptive because they are the hardest to make well. What is wine? Simply fermented grape juices. What is salami? Seasoned ground meat dried in a casing. What is French bread? Water, flour and yeast. Yet these ultra-simple recipes demand years of practice to achieve perfection. Once a recipe becomes complicated, the list of ingredients expands and the recipe becomes easier to adjust, change and control. But try to improve a hard-boiled egg! In addition to years of knowledge, professional bakers have the right flour, special equipment, temperature control, humidity control, and especially the brick-lined oven which gives enormous amounts of heat as well as forced steam which gives the texture and the crust of the French bread. We have a friend, a professional *boulanger*, who makes bread at home once in a while with results that are never as good as the bread he makes at his shop.

There are a few things to keep in mind when making bread. Use a hard wheat flour, high in gluten, which is the protein part of the flour and gives you the elasticity needed for the bread to develop (unbleached all-purpose flour is satisfactory). Keep in mind that the thick, crisp crust is usually caused both by forced steam and dough made only with water. Bread made with milk and with fat will have a soft crust. If a bread collapses, it is likely that it was not kneaded enough or that there was too much water in the dough. The smaller the amount of yeast used, the longer the rising time, and the larger the air bubbles in the bread. Some bakers add ascorbic acid (vitamin C) to the dough to make the air bubbles hold better and the bread stronger. Sugar, as well as a warm temperature helps the enzymes (the yeast) to develop better and faster. If the water or temperature is cold, the bread rises very slowly. Under a certain temperature, the enzymes won't develop any more. Salt is often added at the end of a recipe because it tends to prevent the development of the yeast. Fresh yeast usually comes in .6-ounce packages, and dry yeast comes in 7-gram (¼-ounce) packages. They can be used interchangeably. A *levain* or a dough starter can also be added to the dough to start the fermentation; this gives the dough a slightly nutty, sour taste. It is usually supplemented with yeast. The starter can be made by taking a piece of finished dough and keeping it in a jar with water. Refrigerated, it will keep there for a week to ten days. Through all the bread-making techniques that follow, we will use all-purpose, unbleached flour. To measure out the flour, scoop a cup directly from the flour bag. This produces a fairly tightly packed cup and 3 generous cups will amount to 1 pound of flour. The moisture in the flour varies from season to season. Humidity will be absorbed by the flour in the summer and water should be decreased in the recipe. Vice versa in winter. The following recipe makes a basic dough used to make large country breads as well as thin *baguettes* or small breads.

9 *cups all-purpose, unbleached flour (about 3 pounds)*
3 *envelopes yeast or 3 fresh yeast cakes (.6 ounce each)*
3½ *cups water at about 80 degrees*
1 *tablespoon salt*

1. Mix the yeast and water together, and place two-thirds of the flour, about 6 cups, in the bowl of an electric mixer.

2. After 2 or 3 minutes, stir the water and yeast mixture again. Wait another 5 minutes until the water starts to bubble on top. Add the yeast mixture to the flour and using the dough hook, beat on medium speed (#4) for 5 minutes. Add the salt and keep mixing for a few seconds.

3. Notice that the dough at this point is still quite soft. All the flour cannot be added to the mixture at first because the machine is not strong enough and would stop. However, working two-thirds of the flour with the water for 5 minutes allows us to still let the machine do the hardest part of the work. Add 2 more cups of the flour and keep beating on low speed (#2) for 1 minute.

4. Place the dough on the table and knead by hand with the rest of the flour. More or less flour will be needed, depending on weather, humidity, etc. Reserve at least ½ cup flour for the end. Work the dough by folding it with the palms of your hands.

5. Keep folding and pushing down to get some air in the dough and develop the gluten which gives the dough elasticity.

6. Keep pressing the dough and folding it for at least 7 to 8 minutes. Sprinkle it with flour if it is sticky and absorbent. The dough should be satiny and resilient.

7. To know if the dough has been sufficiently kneaded, place your hand flat on top and leave it on the dough for 5 seconds. Then, remove your hand; the dough should only stick slightly to your palm and spring back like rubber. It should be soft and shiny, already forming some small bubbles on top.

8. Sprinkle the dough with flour and place it in a large bowl to allow for expansion. Place the bowl in a plastic bag to prevent a skin from forming on the top and to retain moisture. Allow to raise for 2 hours in an 80- to 85-degree area. The dough will more than double in volume.

9. To make a starter, take a piece of dough and place it in a jar. Fill the jar with cold water and place in the refrigerator. When making dough, add the whole mixture to the flour at the beginning. Reduce your yeast by one-third and reduce the water so the dough won't be too soft.

10. After 2 hours, check the dough by plunging two fingers into it. If the depression made by your fingers remains, the dough has risen enough.

11. Knead the dough for a few seconds to knock down the air bubbles. You can now let the dough raise a second time or knead it for 1 to 2 minutes and divide it in whatever shapes you wish (see technique 85).

85. Baking Country Bread and Baguettes *(Pain de Campagne et Baguettes)*

1. To simulate as closely as possible a baker's oven lined with fire bricks, arrange clay tiles or fire bricks on a large cookie sheet which fits your oven. You may have to cut the tiles to fit the cookie sheet. Place the tile-covered tray in a preheated 425- to 450-degree oven. Place a can of water in the oven to generate steam.

2. Use the country bread dough (technique 84). Let the dough rise once or twice. If the dough has risen twice the bread will be a bit lighter, with larger air bubbles inside. Knead the dough on the table for 1 to 2 minutes to make it tighter and push out all the air bubbles.

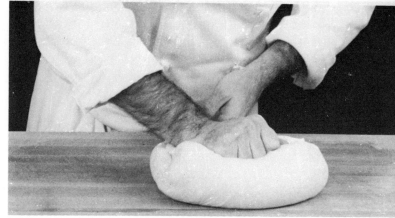

3. Using a dough scraper or a knife, cut the dough into the size you desire. If you want *baguettes*, cut long strips so you just have to pull them a bit, without having to do much more shaping after they've been cut. Each *baguette* should weigh approximately ¾ to 1 pound.

4. To mold the *baguette* use a flat piece of wood and a kitchen towel with wood sticks in between. This technique is similar to what is done in a professional kitchen, where long canvas is folded continuously and all the *baguettes* arranged in the pleats of the canvas.

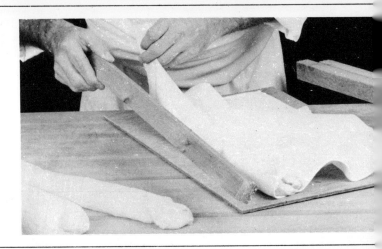

5. Once the *baguettes* are molded in the kitchen towel, let them raise in an 80-degree humid place (if possible) for about 1 hour. The dough can also be placed into special gutter-like bread molds.

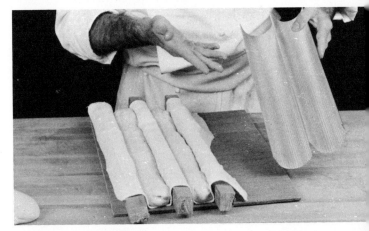

6. Let the *baguettes* raise until they have approximately doubled in volume (about an hour in a warm area). Wash the dough with a beaten egg or sprinkle with flour. Then mark with a knife and bake.

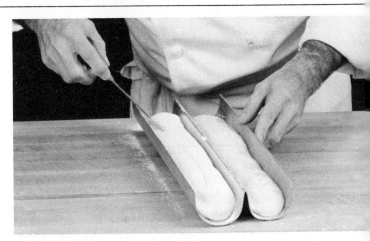

7. For the baguettes which have been molded with the towel, sprinkle a board with semolina, farina or any coarse-grain flour, then invert the baguette right on top of the coated surface. The bottom of the dough, which is the softer part, is now on top. Sprinkle the top with flour or wash with the egg wash.

8. Then make long diagonal slashes along the top of the loaf with a razor blade. Note how the end of one slash and the beginning of the next correspond. They are on the same plane. Make approximately 5 slashes in each loaf.

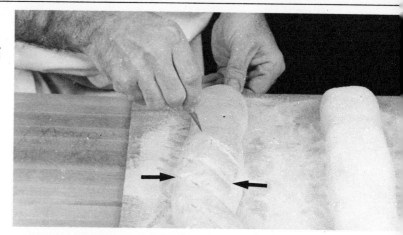

9. It requires practice to cut with a razor blade and the dough cakes and sticks. You may find it easier to use a long thin knife. Hold it on an angle and slide it gently on top of the dough until it cuts through.

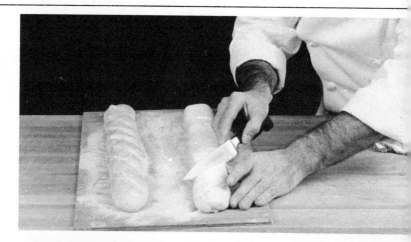

10. Slide the bread in one stroke onto the preheated tiles. It should be done directly in the oven but as it is difficult to photograph, we did it on the table. Sprinkle about ¼ cup water in the oven and close the door immediately. It creates steam along with the can of water already in the oven. Bake 30 minutes for the *baguettes* until nicely brown and hard. The bread should sound hollow when tapped.

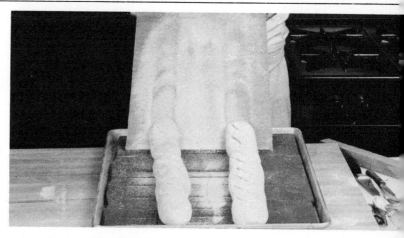

11. The metal-molded *baguettes* should be removed from the mold and cooled on a rack. Knock the *baguettes* with the handle of a knife. A hollow sound is an indication that they are well cooked. This *baguette* had only one long slit on top.

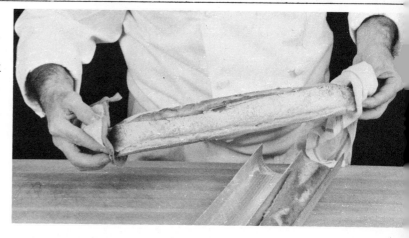

12. This bread was brushed with egg wash, slit across with the razor and cooked on the quarry tiles.

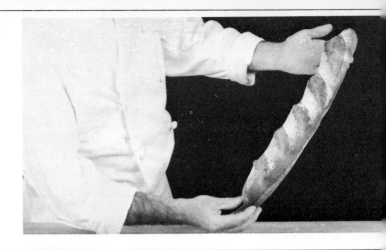

13. The *baguette* on the left was washed with the egg wash and cut diagonally with the knife. The one on the right was sprinkled with flour and cut in a crisscross pattern. Both were cooked on the tiles.

14. This large country bread was made with ·1¾ pounds of dough and had risen 1½ hours. It was sprinkled with flour, cut in a crisscross pattern with a knife, cooked in a preheated 425-degree oven for 50 to 60 minutes and cooled on a rack.

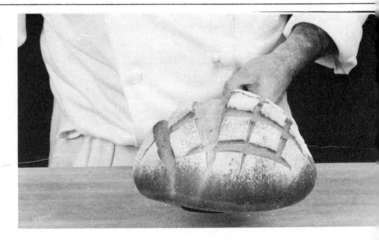

86. Milk Bread *(Petits Pains au Lait)*

YIELD: About 2 dozen 2½-ounce rolls

DOUGH MADE WITH MILK and butter will have a more tender crust and a slightly more delicate inside than the regular country bread. This type of dough is used to make individual "rolls" usually served for breakfast. The dough is started in the machine and finished by hand although it can be made entirely by hand.

2⅓ cups milk at about 90 degrees
2 packages dry yeast or 2 packages fresh yeast
6 cups all-purpose, unbleached flour
2 teaspoons salt
1 teaspoon sugar
½ stick (2 ounces) sweet butter, softened

1. Mix the milk, yeast and sugar together and let the mixture "work" for 20 minutes at room temperature. Meanwhile, place 4 cups of flour in the bowl of the mixer. Add the butter and salt. After about 10 minutes, stir the milk and yeast mixture. Let it rest another 10 minutes, then combine with the flour. Beat on medium speed (#4) for about 7 to 8 minutes.

2. Add another cup of flour to the bowl and mix to incorporate the flour. The dough should come out of the bowl soft but rubbery.

3. Place the dough on a board and work in more flour by hand, depending on the humidity and temperature. You may need all the flour or even a few tablespoons more or a few tablespoons less.

4. Knead for about 5 minutes, until the dough doesn't stick to your fingers. It will be slightly softer and stickier than the country bread dough in technique 85.

5. Place the dough in a buttered bowl, turning the dough around so it is buttered on top. Cover with a towel and let raise in an 80-degree place for 1 hour.

6. To approximate the type of heat in a baker's oven, line a cookie sheet with quarry tiles and place them in the lower shelf of the oven preheated to 425 degrees. Set a tray of water between the lower shelf and the oven floor to generate humidity and steam. Cut the dough in about 2½-ounce pieces and roll in a ball with the palm of your hand, pushing out the air bubbles. Shape the rolls into rounds, ovals or any shape you fancy.

7. For the *épi* ("head of wheat"), shape about 1 pound of the dough into a long loaf about 2 inches in diameter. Butter a tray lightly, place the dough on top and cut with a pair of scissors. Divide the dough into wedges to simulate a blade of wheat. Alternate from one side of the dough to the other, without cutting completely through. Pull out each "wheat" so it forms a pointed head. Let the breads and *épi* raise for 45 minutes to 1 hour at room temperature. Brush with egg wash and place in a preheated 425-degree oven for 25 minutes for

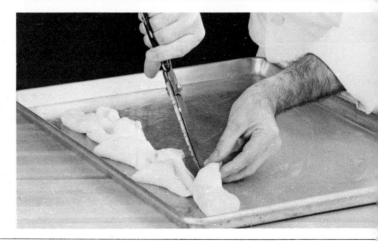

the small breads and 30 minutes for the *épi*. Every so often check that there's water in the oven, throwing in some water to produce steam during the first 10 to 15 minutes of cooking.

87. Pullman Bread *(Pain de Mie)*

YIELD: 1 16-inch loaf (4 inches wide by 4 inches high)

THE PULLMAN BREAD is often hollowed out and filled up with little sandwiches to serve at a buffet. Whereas sandwiches are usually trimmed on four sides, and the trimmings used for bread crumbs, in this technique, the whole loaf is trimmed of its crust and the crust becomes a receptacle. After the party it can be transformed into bread crumbs. The dough for the pullman bread is softer than for the *petits pains au lait*.

6 cups all-purpose unbleached flour (2 pounds)
2 cups milk
1 cup hot water
1½ envelopes dry yeast
1 tablespoon sugar
1 tablespoon salt
1½ sticks (6 ounces) sweet butter, softened

1. Mix the water and milk (the temperature should be about 95 to 100 degrees). Mix in the sugar and yeast and stir until dissolved. Place 5 cups of the flour in the bowl of an electric mixer and add the yeast mixture. Using the dough hook, place on medium speed for 5 to 6 minutes. Then add the rest of the flour, the salt and the butter. Mix again on low speed (#2) for 2 minutes. The dough will be sticky when you pull it off the hook, but it will come off clean and spring back as though it were rubber.

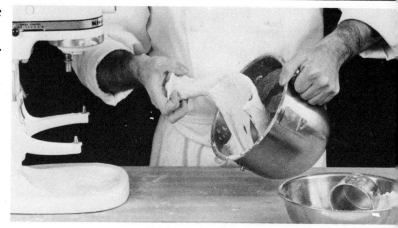

2. Butter a large bowl and place the dough in it. Turn the dough in the bowl to coat the top with a film of butter. Place the bowl in a large plastic bag and set it in an 80-degree oven or a warm area for 2 hours. The dough, when pushed in with your fingers, should hold the indentation, which is an indication that it has risen enough. Knock the dough down by kneading it a few seconds in the bowl.

3. Place in a buttered 16- by 4- by 4-inch mold or two smaller molds. Be sure to butter the mold well. The dough should come about one-third of the way up the mold. Let it raise again for 1 to 1½ hours, depending on the humidity, until the dough comes about three-quarters of the way up the mold. Brush with the egg wash (one whole egg, beaten).

4. A pullman bread mold has a special lid that slides in; or you can improvise a cover for the mold. Butter a cookie sheet, place on top of the bread and place a rock on top to hold it down. Place in a preheated 425-degree oven for 20 minutes, then remove the cookie sheet or the cover. By then the dough is set and will not rise further. Bake for another 40 minutes until the bread sounds hollow when tapped. If the top browns too much, top with a piece of aluminum foil to prevent further browning. Unmold the bread and cool on a rack.

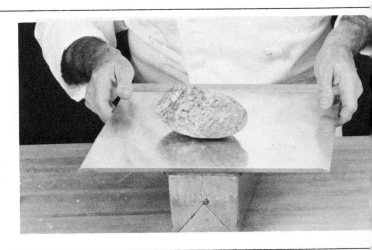

5. Pictured here is the round country bread, crisscross cut on top (technique 84), and the long, cooked pullman bread. If the pullman bread is baked without a cover, it will be rounded on top.

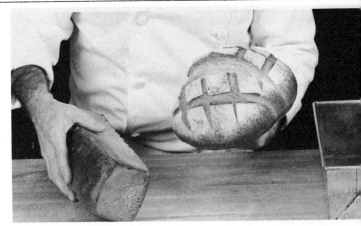

6. After cooling, cut off the top of the bread to form a lid. Using a small pointed knife, cut all around the bread, about ¼ inch from the edge, to loosen the inside. It is now holding only from the bottom.

7. Place the bread on its side. Insert the knife into the bread about ¼ inch from the bottom crust and pivot the blade back and forth to loosen a section of the bottom.

8. The object is to loosen the bottom of the bread without cutting the bottom crust off. Make a few incisions along the base of the loaf, jiggling the knife back and forth at each point of entry to eventually loosen the whole inside.

9. Remove the inside, which should come out easily. Notice that the bottom crust is attached to the sides, except for a few holes along the edge where the knife was inserted.

10. Slice the bread into ¼- to ⅜-inch slices. You should have approximately 40 slices, enough for 20 sandwiches. Make different varieties: sliced chicken with fresh herbs and mayonnaise; prosciutto with butter; anchovies fillets and butter; boiled ham and mustard; salami with a mixture of butter and mustard; watercress and mustard mayonnaise; etc. Avoid fillings that could bleed on the other sandwiches. Pack the sandwiches together, cover with the lid and place on the buffet table. The bread container can be dried and used as a basket.

88. Provence-style Pizza *(Pissaladière)*

THE *pissaladière* is a French pizza that's usually made from a bread dough rolled very thin and covered with onions, garlic, anchovies, olives and olive oil. Other ingredients such as tomatoes, green peppers, tuna and cheese are used to vary the filling.

Dough for one large *pissaladière*

1 *pound all-purpose flour (3 generous cups)*
1¼ *cups water, at about 80 to 90 degrees*
2 *¼-ounce packages dry yeast or 2 .6-ounce*
*   packages fresh yeast*
2 *tablespoons olive oil*
1 *teaspoon salt*

Filling

3 *tablespoons good olive oil*
8 *cups sliced onions, loosely packed*
4 *to 5 cloves garlic, peeled, crushed and chopped*
*   (1 tablespoon)*
½ *teaspoon salt*
3 *2-ounce cans anchovies in oil*
Generous dozen Spanish or Greek oil-cured black
*   olives*

1. Mix the water and yeast and let rest at room temperature for 10 minutes. Meanwhile, place 2 cups of the flour in the bowl of an electric mixer. Add the salt and 2 tablespoons olive oil and beat on medium speed (#4) with a dough hook for about 3 minutes. Then add the remaining flour. Mix to incorporate the flour, then turn the dough out on a board and knead by hand for about 2 minutes until the dough is smooth and satiny. Oil a bowl, place the dough in it and turn over to coat with the oil all around. Cover with a towel and let

raise for 1 hour at room temperature, at about 75 to 80 degrees. The dough should double in volume. Check by making indentations with your fingers. If the holes remain, the dough has raised enough.

2. Make the filling. Heat the oil in a saucepan and add the onions. Cook on medium to high heat for about 10 minutes, until the onions are cooked and lightly brown. Add the garlic and salt. (It is a small amount of salt because the anchovies are salty.) Add the pepper. Spread the dough out by hand on the table or directly on the cookie sheet.

3. Oil a 16- by 12-inch cookie sheet or 2 round pans. Spread out the dough with your hands to enlarge and line the pans. The dough should be about ¼ inch thick all around.

4. Arrange the cooked onions on the dough and the anchovies in a crisscross pattern on top. Remove the pits from the olives, cut them in half, and position one in each anchovy diamond. Sprinkle the "pizza" with 1 tablespoon of olive oil and bake for 30 minutes in a preheated 425-degree oven.

5. Allow it to cool in the pan for at least 10 to 15 minutes. Brush again with olive oil before serving. It should be served at room temperature.

89. Crescent Rolls *(Croissants)*

YIELD: Approximately 16 small croissants

ROISSANTS are the essence of the French breakfast. They are never eaten at other meals. The large twisted croissants bought in *cafés* in the morning are often made with a mixture of shortening and butter. The small straight croissants are usually made with only butter. Croissant dough requires skill to make. It has some of the qualities of puff paste as well as of brioche. It acquires flakiness through the rolling and folding technique of puff paste, but it is also a yeast dough, which needs proofing before cooking. We made our croissants with all-purpose flour (which is a high-gluten, hard-wheat, elastic flour), because we found that using pastry flour (a soft wheat flour with less gluten) did not make much difference. Small croissants are about 1¼ to 1½ ounces each; large croissants are about 3 ounces each. See technique 91 for puff paste before starting the croissant dough.

1 *pound all-purpose, unbleached flour (a good 3*
   cups tightly packed)
2 *tablespoons extra flour to mix with the butter*
3 *sticks (12 ounces) sweet butter, softened*
1 *generous cup milk, at approximately 90 to*
   100 degrees
1 *¼-ounce package dry yeast or a .6-ounce pack-*
   age fresh yeast
1 *tablespoon sugar*
1½ *teaspoons salt*

1. Place the yeast, sugar and milk in a bowl. Mix well and let it work for about 5 to 10 minutes at room temperature. Meanwhile, place 2½ sticks (10 ounces) of the butter in the bowl of an electric mixer with the 2 tablespoons of flour and mix well with the flat beater for about 5 to 10 seconds, until you have a creamy, homogenized mixture.

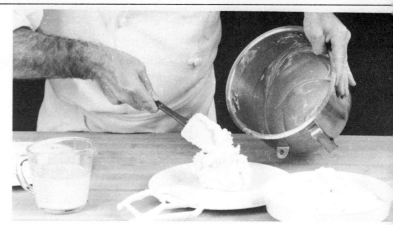

2. Place the flour with the remaining 2 ounces of butter, salt and yeast-milk mixture in the bowl of an electric mixer and mix on low speed (# 2), using the flat beater for about 10 seconds, until it forms a ball. Shape the dough into a rectangle.

3. Place on a floured board and roll the dough into a rectangle 20 inches long by 12 inches wide. Use extra flour to help in the rolling. With the palm of your hand or a spatula, spread the butter mixture from step 1 over two-thirds of the dough.

4. Leave about 1 inch along the edges of the dough unbuttered.

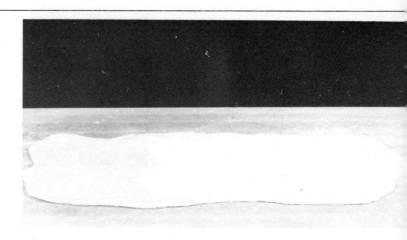

5. Lift the unbuttered third and fold on the buttered part.

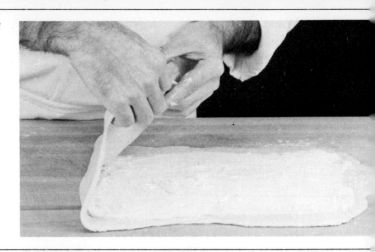

6. Fold the remaining third over and press all around the edges.

7. Place the dough in a plastic bag and refrigerate for 2 hours or longer. The object is to get the dough and the butter well set and to the same temperature so it rolls out uniformly. On a floured board roll the dough into a 24- by 12-inch rectangle and give it a double turn (see technique 91). Roll the dough once again into a 24- by 12-inch rectangle and give it another double turn. Refrigerate the dough for 1 to 2 hours so it relaxes and becomes workable again (without refrigeration the dough becomes too elastic to roll). Then roll the dough into a 24- by 12-inch rectangle once again and give it a third double turn. Refrigerate for another 2 hours, at which point the dough can be cut into croissants or left refrigerated overnight.

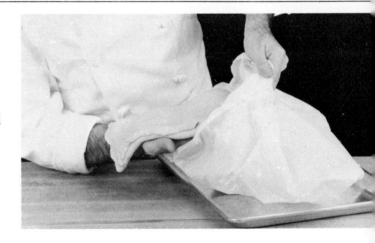

8. If you refrigerate the dough overnight, it will still proof somehow despite the low temperature in the refrigerator. Flatten it with the palm of your hand. We reserved approximately one-quarter of the dough to make *petits pains au chocolat* in technique 90. Roll the remainder of the dough in a rectangle approximately 12 inches wide by 25 inches long. It should be quite thin.

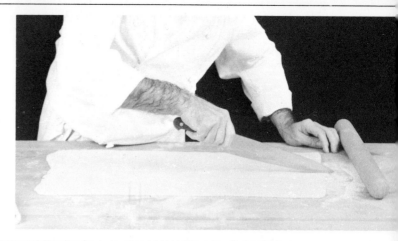

9. Cut the rectangle in half lengthwise to make 2 strips, approximately 6 inches wide by 25 inches long. Cut into triangles about 5 inches at the base. Each triangle will weigh about 1¼ to 1½ ounces. If the dough gets rubbery at any time, just let it rest again in the refrigerator. Remember that cold temperature and time are allies.

10. Take each triangle and roll it to enlarge it both in width and length.

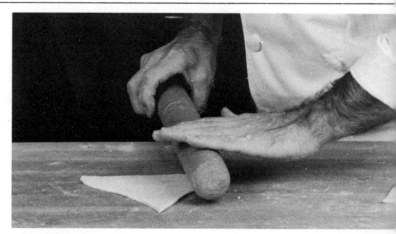

11. With the rolling pin, crush the point of the croissant so it sticks to the table. Starting at the base of the triangle, use both hands to roll the dough, spreading it as you roll to extend the croissant.

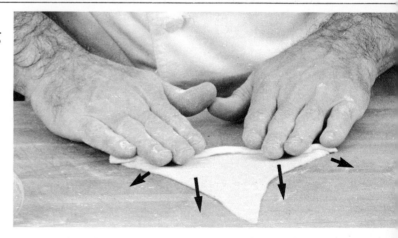

12. Wet the apex of the triangle with water. Keep rolling the dough on itself until you reach the apex which will stick.

13. Line a cookie sheet with parchment paper and arrange the croissants, bent into a crescent shape or straight, on top. Be sure that the point of the croissant is on top, curving inward toward the tray. Let proof in a moist 80- to 90-degree oven with a pilot light, or in a warm, humid place. In very dry weather, the dough tends to dry out and form a crust on top which prevents proofing. Make sure that the croissants proof in a humid area. If proofed in an oven, place a pot of warm water close by to create humidity. The croissants should proof a good hour.

14. Brush with a glaze (made of 1 egg plus 1 egg yolk beaten together) about 15 minutes before you put them in the oven, then brush once again just before you put them in. Bake in a preheated 425-degree oven for 15 to 18 minutes, until well browned and crisp. Let cool on the tray for at least 20 minutes before serving.

90. Small Chocolate Rolls *(Petits Pains au Chocolat)*

YIELD: 6

THE SMALL *petits pains au chocolat* are common in all the *boulangeries* (bakeries) in France and are often made with regular bread dough shaped into small breads stuffed with a piece of chocolate. In *patisseries* (pastry shops), however, the *pains au chocolat* are often made with croissant dough rather than bread dough and this is the version explained below.

1. You will need approximately one-third of the croissant dough made in technique 89 and 3 ounces of either sweet or bitter-sweet chocolate (approximately ½ ounce per roll). Cut the chocolate bar into strips. Don't worry if it breaks into pieces because it will melt during the cooking. Roll the dough into a long strip, 8 inches wide by 12 inches long, and cut into 2 strips lengthwise. Cut each strip into three 4-inch squares.

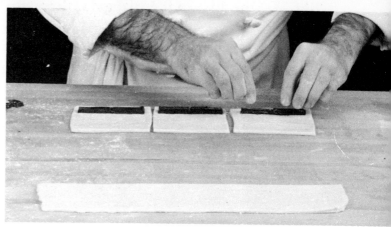

2. Brush the dough with water and place approximately ½ ounce chocolate on each square of dough and roll the dough into cylinders.

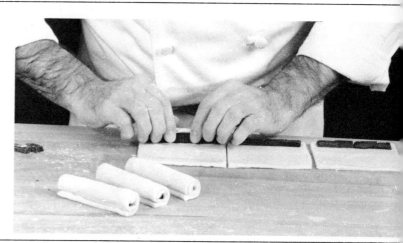

3. Place on a tray and proof in a moist 80- to 90-degree oven with a pilot light or in a warm place for about 1 hour (see step 13, technique 89). Glaze with egg wash (as in technique 89) and bake in preheated 425-degree oven for 15 to 18 minutes. Remove from the oven and cool for ½ hour before eating.

91. Egg Yolk Puff Paste *(Feuilletage à Pâté)*

THERE ARE SEVERAL DIFFERENT TYPES of puff paste. We featured two in *La Technique*, a fast one and a classic 6-turn dough made with cream. In this recipe we have added egg yolk which makes the dough stronger and particularly well suited to pâtés and other situations where it has to withstand pressure from the steam building inside. (For a lighter version, omit the egg yolk and increase the butter to 14 ounces.) Work very fast with ice-cold ingredients and equipment so the mixture will not have time to get too elastic before the dough is finished. Place the flour in a bowl in the freezer for a few hours so it gets extremely cold. Cut the butter into tiny ¼-inch dice. (Cut the sticks of butter in half lengthwise, then cut each half into halves, lengthwise, and then dice the strips.) Spread the butter pieces on a plate and place in the refrigerator. Owning a piece of marble also makes it easier. If it is winter, place the marble outside to cool or cool it in a refrigerator or freezer or by placing a tray full of ice cubes on top. If the ingredients and marble are cold, the dough doesn't stick and almost no flour is needed in the rolling. The dough can be made in not much more than 10 minutes.

1 *pound flour (3 cups tightly packed)*
3 *sticks (12 ounces) sweet butter*
2 *egg yolks mixed with enough cold water to give*
      1 *cup (8 ounces) of liquid*
1 *teaspoon salt*

1. Combine the egg yolks with the water and place in the refrigerator for a few hours, or in the freezer until very cold. Refrigerate the butter and flour, too.

2. Stir all the ingredients in a bowl fast, so it barely holds together.

3. Place the dough on the cold marble. Gather and press it together until it holds a shape.

4. Flatten the dough with the palms of your hands by pushing and pressing it down so it extends to about 1 inch in thickness.

5. As you spread the dough, you will see pieces of butter distributed throughout. Use the dough scraper to lift the dough if it sticks. Keep rolling, using as little flour as possible, into a rectangle about 15 inches long and 10 inches wide. Fold the dough like a letter into thirds. This is a single turn.

6. Working as fast as you can, roll the dough into a rectangle about 18 inches long by 10 inches wide and ½ inch thick. Fold so the edges join in the center.

7. Press to flatten and then fold in half. This is called a double turn (four layers). Moving as fast as you can, roll the dough out again into a rectangle about 18 inches by 10 inches. Fold again into a double turn. Turn the dough and roll again, this time into a longer and wider rectangle about ¼ inch thick. Fold again into a double turn. A lot of physical strength is needed in the rolling. Use a rolling pin at least as big as the one in the picture. A large ball bearing or *tutove* pin will make the rolling easier and faster.

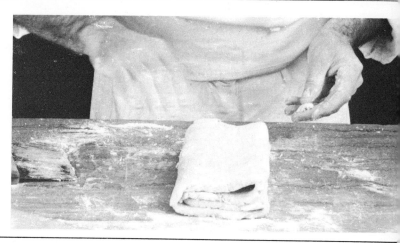

8. At this point the dough will be too elastic to use. After refrigeration, the dough can also be cut and frozen.

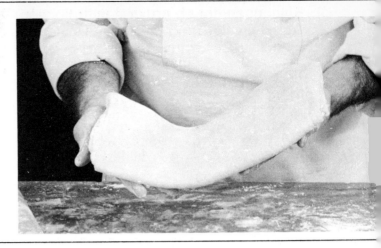

To recap the process: The mixture was first crudely spread by hand and folded into thirds. Then, rolled and folded into a double turn. Then rolled and folded double again, then finally rolled and folded double once more. The 3 double rolls or turns are equivalent to 5 single turns. If the mixture gets too sticky and the ingredients tend to blend together, give it one less turn. If the dough becomes too elastic to be worked, do not fight it. Refrigerate for 30 minutes. Remember that cold, as well as time, is your best ally.

92. Brie in Brioche Dough *(Brie en Brioche)*

YIELD: 12 to 14 servings

THE BRIE in brioche makes a nice presentation to be served at the end of a dinner. Serve the cheese in slices with its own brioche. In the photographs that follow, the decorations were made with regular pie dough. It stands out because it doesn't brown as much as the brioche dough during baking. Of course the decorations can be made with strips of brioche dough. You need a ripe, 2-pound brie and the brioche dough described in technique 70.

1. Spread out a piece of the brioche dough with your hands or roll it with a pin to about ½ to ¾ inch larger than the brie all around and about ¼ inch thick. Place on a cookie sheet lined with parchment paper. Place the brie on top. Fold the edges of the dough back onto the brie.

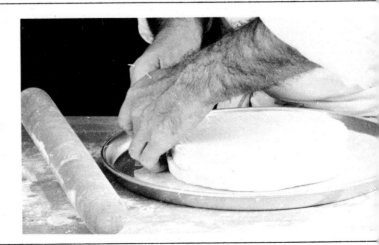

2. Roll out another piece of dough ¼ inch thick and 1 to 2 inches larger than the brie all around. Brush with egg wash (1 egg plus 1 egg yolk, beaten).

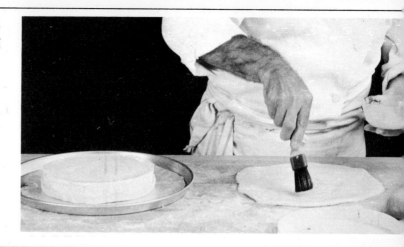

3. Cover the brie, egg-washed side down, and press the dough on the sides so it sticks to the bottom layer. Trim it all around.

4. Brush the dough with egg wash and decorate with little strips of pie dough, puff paste or brioche dough. Decorate to your fancy with strips to imitate flowers with borders, etc. (For ideas, look at the decoration of the ham, technique 78.) Brush the decorations with the egg wash and let the brie proof for about 20 minutes at room temperature.

5. Bake in a preheated 350-degree oven for 25 to 30 minutes until golden brown. Let the brie rest at room temperature for a couple of hours, otherwise the cheese will be too runny inside. If done several hours ahead, and the brioche is cold, place in a preheated 400-degree oven for 5 to 6 minutes, just to warm up the brioche without heating the cheese. Cut into slices and serve.

93. Yeast Cake Babas and Savarin

(Savarin et Babas)

YIELD: 1 savarin and 12 babas

THE BABAS AND THE SAVARIN are made with the same dough, but raisins are usually added to the baba dough. Both cakes are usually made ahead and kept in a tin box unrefrigerated or packed in plastic bags and refrigerated or frozen. Before serving, the cakes are soaked in a rum syrup and glazed with preserves. In addition they can be coated with a sugar frosting as we did here. Babas are generally served plain while the savarin is usually filled with whipped cream (below) or with fruit salad.

Dough

1¼ pounds all-purpose, unbleached flour
1 cup milk, at about 90 to 100 degrees
1 ¼-ounce envelope dry yeast or one 6-
    ounce package fresh yeast
2 teaspoons sugar
1½ sticks (6 ounces) sweet butter, softened
6 large eggs
1½ teaspoons salt
1 2-ounce package raisins

Syrup for savarin and babas

3 cups sugar
4 cups lukewarm water
1 tablespoon pure vanilla extract
3 tablespoons dark rum
½ cup strained apricot preserves

Frosting

1 cup powdered sugar
2 tablespoons light Karo syrup
About ½ teaspoon lemon juice
4 drops red food coloring
1½ tablespoons water

Filling

2 cups heavy cream
2 tablespoons sugar
A few candied violets

1. Mix the milk, yeast and sugar together and allow to work for about 5 minutes in a warm place, about 80 degrees. Place the flour, salt and 3 eggs in the bowl of an electric mixer and add the milk mixture. Beat with the flat beater on low speed (# 2) until smooth. Add 2 more eggs and work 1 minute on medium speed (# 4). Finally add the last egg and work another 2 to 3 minutes on medium speed. Then add the butter piece by piece, still beating for 1 minute on the same speed. Cover the bowl loosely with a towel and let proof in a warm place, about

80 degrees, for 25 minutes. The dough should have almost doubled in volume. Knock down. Place some of the dough in a buttered savarin mold. Add the raisins to the remaining dough and divide between the buttered baba molds. The dough should come no higher than one-third of the way up the molds. Cover loosely with a towel and let proof for 35 to 45 minutes in a warm place until it reaches almost the top of the mold. Do not overproof or the cakes will expand too much and will be dry and crumbly after cooking. Brush the babas and savarin with an egg wash (1 egg, plus 1 egg yolk, beaten), and bake in a preheated 400-degree oven for about 35 minutes or until well browned and cooked inside. The savarin may take 5 to 8 minutes more than the babas, depending on its thickness.

2. When the savarin and babas are cooked remove from the oven and let set about 10 minutes, then remove from the molds and place on a wire rack to cool. At this point they can be refrigerated, frozen or packed in tins and stored for future use.

3. Stir the sugar with the water and vanilla to dissolve. Place the babas and/or savarin into a deep pan and pour the syrup on top. Let the cakes absorb the syrup for about 30 minutes. Turn them from time to time. Allow the cakes to absorb as much syrup as they can.

4. When well impregnated, drain the cakes on a rack for 15 to 20 minutes. Reserve the extra syrup for other uses. Brush the savarin and babas with the dark rum. By brushing the rum on the cakes instead of putting it in the syrup, you get a stronger rum taste.

5. Strain the apricot preserves and brush the tops and sides of the cakes with it. Decorate with slivered almonds with crystallized violets in the center to simulate flowers. Serve the babas as is.

6. Mix all the frosting ingredients with a whisk and spoon over the top of the savarin. Place on a serving platter. Combine the cream and sugar and whip until firm. Place two-thirds of the cream in the cavity of the savarin and the remaining cream in a pastry bag fitted with a fluted top. Decorate the top with the cream and top with the candied violets. Serve at once.

94. Proust's Small Coffee Cakes

(Madeleines de Commercy)

YIELD: About 18 madeleines

Here are the famous small cakes so dear to Proust in *A la Recherche du Temps Perdu*. They originated in the small town of Commercy. The madeleines can be made in a special tray or in small individual brioche molds.

1 stick (4 ounces) sweet butter, softened
½ cup sugar
½ teaspoon baking powder
½ teaspoon pure vanilla extract
½ teaspoon grated orange rind
2 eggs
1 cup all-purpose flour

1. Place the butter and sugar in the bowl of an electric mixer and work on medium (# 4) to fast speed (# 6) until light and fluffy, about 1 minute. Add the baking powder, vanilla, orange rind and 1 egg. Beat on

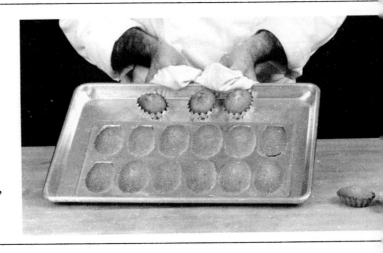

low speed (# 2) for about 1 minute, until smooth and light. Add the other egg and mix another minute at the same speed. Finally, stir in the flour with a whisk until the mixture is smooth. Do not overwhisk. Butter a madeleine tray well and place 1½ tablespoons of the soft cake dough in each mold. Hit the tray on the table to flatten the dough in the molds or push it down with the tips of your fingers. Bake in a preheated 400-degree oven for about 20 minutes.

2. Let the madeleines rest or set 10 minutes before unmolding. Unmold, cool on a wire rack and, when cold, place in a plastic bag or a tin box to prevent drying. Use as needed. They are the ideal coffee cake but are also served as garnish for ice cream, or with berries and whipped cream as a type of shortcake.

95. Puff Paste Almond Cake *(Pithiviers)*

THE PITHIVIERS is usually served as a coffee cake. Although it is a specialty of the town of Pithiviers in the south of France, it has become a classic made in most good pastry shops. Make puff paste following technique 91 or use a recipe of your own. You will need about 1½ pounds of puff paste.

Almond cream mixture

¾ cup finely ground almonds or almond powder
2 tablespoons sweet butter, melted
½ cup granulated sugar
2 tablespoons dark rum
3 egg yolks
2 tablespoons heavy cream

1. Roll the puff paste to ¼ inch thick. Unroll on a cookie sheet or a pizza plate lined with parchment paper. Using a flan ring as a mark, cut a circle about 10 inches in diameter. Combine the almond cream ingredients together and spread in the center of the puff paste, being careful to leave about 1 inch uncovered all around.

2. Brush the uncovered edge with an egg wash (1 egg, plus 1 egg yolk, beaten). Roll another circle of puff paste, cut it with the flan ring and place on top of the almond cream mixture.

3. Press the edges together so the two layers adhere. Invert a cake pan on top of the dough to help press it down and act as a guide to mark a scalloped edge.

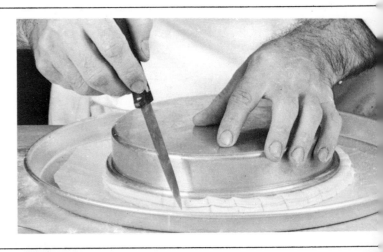

4. Brush the top of the cake with the egg wash, make a hole in the center with the point of a knife and, using the point, mark a spiral from the edges toward the center hole, cutting into the dough about ¹⁄₁₆ inch deep. Place the cake in the refrigerator for 2 hours or in the freezer for 1 hour, then bake in a preheated 400-degree oven for ½ hour. Cover loosely with foil, reduce the temperature to 375 degrees and bake for another 20 minutes.

5. Remove the aluminum foil and generously sprinkle the top with powdered sugar. Return the cake to the oven for 5 to 10 minutes until the sugar melts and forms a beautiful glaze on top. If the sugar doesn't melt fast enough, place under the broiler for 1 minute. If the sugar melts in one place first, cover the melted spot with aluminum foil to prevent further cooking and place the pithiviers under the broiler so the remaining sugar melts evenly on top.

96. Galettes of Lemon *(Galettes au Citron)*

YIELD: 2 galettes serving about 12

THE GALETTE is an open-faced tart, very thin and crunchy, usually made in a round shape and cut into large, pizza-type slices. Although it is usually a country dessert, it can become very elegant with the addition of a sauce. The lemon galette is made with a *pâte sucrée* (sweet dough) and the apple galette (technique 97), with a *pâte brisée* (pie dough). It is a good dessert for a large party. It's easy to make and serve, and keeps quite well for hours.

Pâte sucrée
3 cups all-purpose flour
2½ sticks (10 ounces) sweet butter, softened
½ cup granulated sugar
¼ teaspoon salt
1 egg, plus 1 egg yolk, beaten

Sauce
3 egg yolks
½ cup powdered sugar
3 tablespoons Grand Marnier
2 cups sour cream

Lemon filling
10 egg yolks
1 tablespoon, plus 1 teaspoon, cornstarch
¾ cup granulated sugar
Grated rind of 2 lemons (approximately 1 tablespoon)
Juice of 3 lemons (approximately ⅔ cup)
1 lemon, peeled and cut into very thin slices

1. To make the dough, combine the ingredients in a bowl and work until it holds together. Place on the table. Crush or smear the mixture with the palm of your hand a few times until the mixture is well blended (see technique 98). Divide into two pieces. Roll the first piece into a 14-inch round, about ¼ inch thick. Roll the dough on your rolling pin and unroll onto a cookie sheet.

It is a delicate dough to roll as it tends to break. Remembering that the *pâte sucrée* cannot be rolled as thin as a *pâte brisée* or a puff paste or it will burn. Trim the edge of the dough and fold it back onto itself all around.

2. Fold the dough over once again to make a border approximately ½ inch high. Press the border with your fingers to bring it to a point on top. The base will be wide and the top pointed like a triangle (see arrow). This keeps the border from collapsing during cooking.

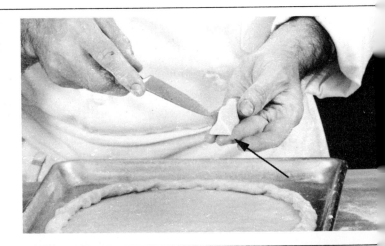

3. Use your fingers to pinch and press a decorative border all around.

4. Roll the rest of the dough and trim it into a rectangular or square shape. Make the border.

5. Place both "shells" in a preheated 400-degree oven for 12 to 15 minutes to pre-cook lightly. They will be baked again later with their fillings. (For a different dessert, cook the shells entirely, which will take about 25 minutes, and fill with a *crème patissière*, top with fresh berries such as strawberries, raspberries, or slices of bananas and glaze with a fruit jam that complements the fruit used.) If there are any holes in the crust, patch with a bit of extra dough or water mixed with flour.

6. The lemon galette batter is liquid and if there are any holes it will seep through during cooking. To prepare the lemon filling, mix the yolks and sugar together and whip with a whisk for 2 to 3 minutes, until it reaches the ribbon stage. Add the cornstarch and lemon rind, mix well, then add the lemon juice. Divide the mixture onto the two pre-cooked shells.

7. Arrange the slices of lemon on top and immediately place in a preheated 375-degree oven. The oven rack and the cookie sheet must be very flat or the batter will run on one side or spill over. Bake for 18 to 20 minutes.

8. As the dough cooks, the batter will pleat and pull around the slices of lemon and form a design by itself. Let cool and cut into wedges. For the sauce, mix the 3 egg yolks and sugar together and work with a whisk for 1 to 2 minutes. Stir in the Grand Marnier and sour cream. Serve 2 tablespoons next to each slice.

97. Galette of Apple *(Galette de Pommes)*

YIELD: About 10 servings

THE GALETTE OF APPLE, thin and crunchy, done free form, is real country-looking and perfect to take along on picnics or to serve on a buffet. Whether you use puff paste or *pâte brisée,* it is important that the dough be very thin and the layer of apples very thin. The galette should be well browned and very crisp. The apricot glaze is not always used in country cooking, but it makes the tart taste and look beautiful.

Pâte brisée

2 *cups flour*
1½ *stick (6 ounces) sweet butter, cut in ¼-inch*
    pieces and kept very cold
¼ *teaspoon salt*
½ *teaspoon sugar*
⅓ *cup water, very cold*

Apple filling

5 *to 6 large apples, pippin, golden delicious,*
    greening, etc.
⅓ *stick (1⅓ ounces) sweet butter, cut into small*
    pieces
⅓ *cup sugar*

Apricot glaze

½ *cup quality apricot preserves, strained, com-*
    bined with 1 tablespoon Kirschwasser,
    Calvados or Cognac

1. Combine all the dough ingredients together and work just long enough for it to hold together. You should still see pieces of butter spotted throughout the dough. Refrigerate for a good hour. Sprinkle the board with flour and roll out the dough as thin as possible. It should not be more than ⅛ inch thick. Roll the dough onto the rolling pin.

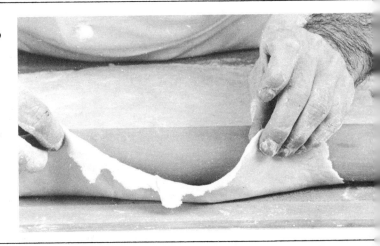

2. Unroll onto a 16- by 12-inch cookie sheet.

3. Peel the apples, cut them into halves and remove the central core. Cut each half into slices about ¼ inch thick. Arrange the slices in diagonal rows, overlapping to simulate the tiles of a roof. Leave approximately a 1½-inch border of dough arround the apples.

4. Fold the border back onto the apples. Patch holes, if any, or the juices will run and burn on the tray during cooking. Dot with pieces of butter and dust with the sugar. Dust some sugar on the border where it will crystallize while cooking and form a crunchy cookie-like edge. Bake in a preheated 400-degree oven for 75 minutes. It needs this long cooking time to be really crunchy. The dough is better if it's slightly too dark than too light.

5. Let the galette rest for a few minutes, then spoon the apricot glaze on top. Spread gently so as not to disturb the pattern.

6. After 15 or 20 minutes cut into large slices. Eat at room temperature or slightly warm, but never cold straight from the refrigerator.

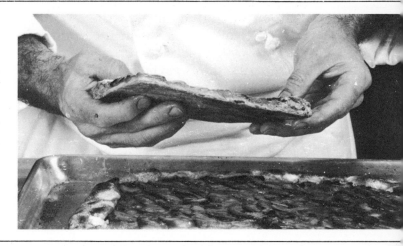

98. Linzer Torte *(Tarte à la Confiture)*

THE LINZER TORTE is a specialty of Austria. The dough, extremely rich and delicate, is easier to spread than roll. The torte is easy to make and is well suited to buffets or whenever desserts have to hold for a few hours.

YIELD: 8 servings

Linzer dough

1¾ *cups flour*
1 *cup ground almonds*
⅓ *cup granulated sugar*
2 *sticks (8 ounces) sweet butter, softened*
3 *egg yolks*
¼ *teaspoon powdered cinnamon*
½ *teaspoon pure vanilla extract*
¼ *teaspoon mace powder*

Jam filling

1 *12-ounce jar quality raspberry preserves*
1 *tablespoon raspberry brandy*
Powdered sugar

1. Combine the flour and ground almonds on a work table and make a well. In the center, place the butter cut in pieces, and the remaining ingredients. Start mixing with your fingertips.

2. Gather the ingredients together. With the palm of your hand, smear the dough away from you, a piece at a time, in the technique called *fraser*. Gather the dough and repeat once more.

3. The dough will be very soft. Use a dough scraper to place it on a piece of wax paper.

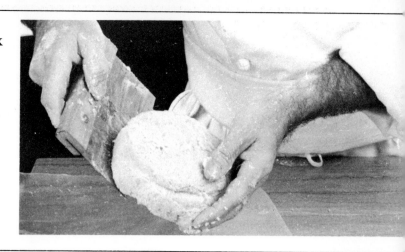

4. Set a 10- to 12-inch flan ring on a cookie sheet. Place about three-quarters of the dough in the bottom of the ring and spread it out, using a piece of parchment or wax paper to help spread. It should be about ¼ inch thick all over the bottom.

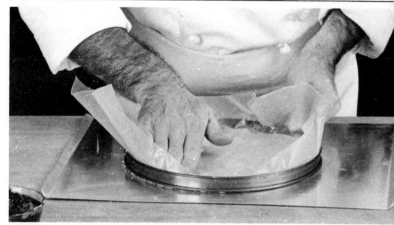

5. Roll some dough into strips and press inside to form the edges.

6. Use the wax paper again to thin the sides to about ¼ inch thick. Trim the excess dough.

7. Strain the raspberry preserves and combine with the raspberry brandy. Spread the mixture on the bottom of the dough.

8. Roll leftover dough into thin cylinders. Flatten the cylinders into strips and arrange on top of the jam lattice fashion—about four strips in each direction.

9. Fold the edges of the torte in toward the torte, on top of the jam and strips. Flatten gently with your fingertips.

10. Bake in a preheated 375-degree oven for 35 minutes until nicely browned and crisp. Let rest at least 10 minutes, then remove the ring. Sprinkle with powdered sugar and clean the crumbs of dough around the bottom edge.

11. Slide the linzer torte on a serving platter. Be careful as it is delicate and brittle. Serve in wedges at room temperature.

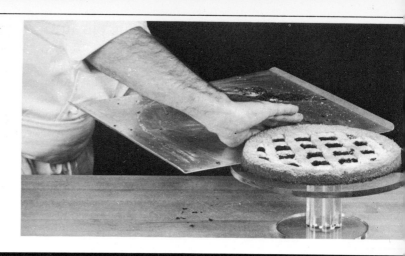

99. Strawberry Strip *(Bande aux Fraises)*

YIELD: 8 to 10 servings

THE DOUGH for the fruit strip can be cooked a day ahead but the custard (if any), as well as the fruits, should not be placed on the dough more than 30 minutes before serving or the dough will get soggy. *Pâte sucrée* (see technique 96) is less prone to becoming soggy than puff paste, however, the puff paste is lighter and more tender. The bottom of the cooked shell can be smeared with a *crème patissière* then covered with the fruits and finally glazed. Our version is done without the *crème patissière*. With the fruit and glaze ready and the dough cooked, the final assembly should not take more than 10 minutes.

1 *pound puff paste (see technique 91)*
2½ *baskets fresh strawberries or raspberries*
2 *tablespoons powdered sugar*
¾ *cup glaze made with raspberry preserve or warm currant jelly, strained, mixed with 1 tablespoon raspberry brandy, Kirschwasser or Cognac*

1. Roll the dough into a rectangle approximately 15 inches long by 10 inches wide and not more than ⅛ inch thick. Line a large cookie sheet with parchment paper.

2. Roll the dough on the rolling pin and unroll on the parchment paper. Trim the edges of the dough to make them straight. The dough should be about 9 inches wide after trimming. Brush the long edges with water then fold each in toward itself.

3. Remove a small strip from the outside edges so that instead of being folded the border is two layers.

4. Brush the borders and the dough between with an egg wash made of 1 egg plus 1 egg yolk, beaten together. Prick the center of the dough with a fork to prevent it from puffing too much and score the border with the point of a knife to form a design. Place in the freezer for 10 to 15 minutes or in the refrigerator for 1 hour so the dough sets before cooking. Then bake in a preheated 375-degree oven for 25 minutes. If the center puffs too much while cooking, push it down with a towel. The dough should be browned and well cooked.

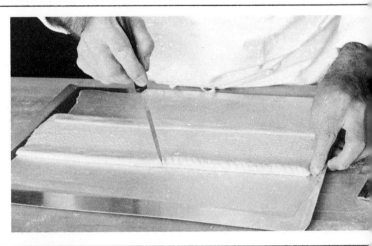

5. Clean the berries and set two-thirds of the nicest aside. Arrange the remaining fruit on the bottom of the baked, cooled strip, sprinkle with powdered sugar and press down to crush them slightly so they release a little of their juice.

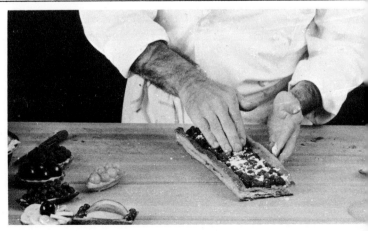

6. Arrange the nicer berries on top and, using a brush or a teaspoon, glaze with the glaze (cold strained raspberry preserves or warm red currant jelly). Serve as soon as possible.

100. Pears in Caramel on Puff Paste
(Feuilleté de Poires au Caramel)

YIELD: 6 servings

ROLLED PIECES of sugared puff paste, cut into ovals and baked, are called *carolines*. They are large puff-paste cookies and can be served with fruit, or whipped cream, or with poached pears and a caramel cream sauce as we do below.

1 *pound puff paste (half of the recipe technique 91)*
1 *cup sugar*
3 *medium-sized pears, ripe, peeled and cut in halves*
½ *cup sugar*
¼ *cup water*
1 *cup heavy cream*

1. Spread 1 cup of the sugar on the table. Using the sugar as if it were flour to prevent the dough from sticking, roll the dough to approximately ¼ inch thick. Sprinkle with sugar and fold into thirds like a letter.

2. Roll out the dough again into a rectangle about ⅜ inch thick. Using a large oval cookie cutter (about 5½ inches long by 3 inches wide), cut 6 *carolines*. Place them on a cookie sheet lined with parchment paper and set in the refrigerator for 1 hour or in the freezer for 30 minutes.

3. Bake in a preheated 400-degree oven for 25 minutes until nice and brown. Remove from the paper as soon as possible or the sugar which has melted around the dough will harden and make the paper stick. Let cool on a wire rack.

4. Peel the pears, cut them in half and core. Mix the ½ cup sugar and water together in a large saucepan and place on high heat. Cook until it turns into a caramel, about 6 to 8 minutes. Add the halved pears to the caramel, cover, and cook on low heat about 5 minutes or less, depending on the ripeness of the fruit. The pears will render some juice and will thin down the caramel. Do not let the pears fall apart. When they feel tender when poked with the point of a knife, add the cream, bring to a boil and simmer for about 3 minutes, uncovered. Remove from the heat and cool until lukewarm. Remove the pears from the caramel, slice each half and arrange on top of a *caroline*. Pour some of the sauce on top and around the puff paste and serve immediately.

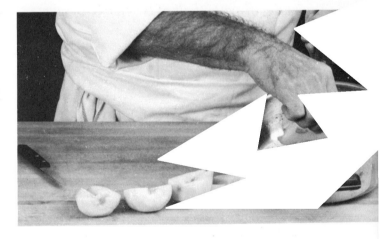

101. Small Fruit Tarts *(Tartelettes de Fruits)*

SMALL FRUIT TARTS are an ideal summer dessert. The shells are precooked, filled with a purée of fruit or *crème patissière,* topped with fruit and glazed. For raspberries, strawberries or blueberries, use a glaze of currant jelly or raspberry preserves. If a jelly is used, heat to liquefy, and brush on while still warm. Any preserve which is not jelled need only be sieved and flavored with alcohol. For fruits such as banana, pear, pineapple, oranges, etc., use an apricot or peach preserve, strained and seasoned with a bit of Kirschwasser or Cognac. Use the *crème patissière* in technique 135 but omit the gelatin.

1. Roll the *pâte sucrée* (see technique 96) out to ¼ inch thick. It should not be too thin. If too thin, *pâte sucrée* tends to burn. Line up your tartelette molds. (They line up better if they are all the same shape and size—unlike ours.) Roll the dough back onto the rolling pin and unroll on top of the molds.

2. Take a lump of dough, dip it in flour so it doesn't stick, and use it to push and stretch the dough into each mold.

3. Trim the dough by rolling the pin on top of the molds. The weight of the pin will cut through the dough. Finish by pressing with your fingers.

4. Place another mold on top of the dough and press it down, to keep the dough from puffing during baking. Alternatively line with wax paper and weight with rice or beans. Bake in a preheated 375-degree oven for 5 to 8 minutes. Remove the upper molds and return to the oven for 10 more minutes or until lightly brown. (*Note:* The molds can also be inverted and the dough cooked on the outside.)

5. Fill with about 2 tablespoons *crème patissière* per shell, then arrange the fruits on top. Glaze with the appropriate preserve and serve as soon as possible.

102. Fresh Fruit Cake *(Croûte de Fruits)*

YIELD: 8 servings

THIS EASY DESSERT is very simple to assemble. A base of *génoise* (sponge cake) or pound cake is covered with about a cup of *crème patissière*, topped with fruits and glazed with an appropriate glaze.

1 *slice sponge cake about ¾ inch thick and 8 inches in diameter*
¾ *cup* crème patissière *(technique 135)*
Ripe fruits
½ *cup apricot preserves, strained through a food mill and flavored with 2 teaspoons Kirsch, rum or Cognac*
½ *cup* génoise *crumbs (made from trimmings in a blender or food processor)*

1. Cut a piece of cardboard the size of your *génoise* and place the *génoise* on top. Cover the top and the sides of the sponge cake with the *crème patissière*.

2. Peel and cut the fruits into wedges. Arrange on top. In this case we used fresh peaches, grapes and cherries. Use any combination of fruits that are attractive in color.

3. Hold the cake in one hand and press the crumbs all around the cake with the other. Using a brush or a spoon, glaze the top with the apricot glaze. If you have the ingredients, this dessert takes just a few minutes to assemble. Do not assemble more than 1 hour before serving because the *génoise* will get soggy.

103. English Trifle *(Trifle Anglais)*

YIELD: 8 to 10 servings

T HE ENGLISH TRIFLE, like the preceding dessert, is simple to assemble. Unlike technique 102, it can be done a few hours ahead because in this case the cake should get soft. It is a colorful, festive and delicious dessert. It can be made with sponge or pound cake, with or without fruits, with custard or only whipped cream. Keep refrigerated until ready to serve.

2 génoises (8 to 10 ounces each) or 1 large
    pound cake

Custard

2 cups milk
¼ cup granulated sugar
½ teaspoon pure vanilla extract
4 egg yolks
2 tablespoons flour

Filling

½ cup quality raspberry jam
¼ cup good, dry Sherry
1½ cups heavy cream
2 tablespoons granulated sugar

Fruits

½ cup sugar
1½ cups water
Rind of ½ lemon
2 pears

1. Bring the milk to a boil. Place the sugar, egg yolks and vanilla in a bowl and work with a whisk until the mixture is pale yellow and thick, about a minute. Mix in the flour; then pour in the boiling milk. Mix well. Place the whole mixture back in the saucepan and bring to a boil, stirring with a whisk. Let it boil for a few seconds, then transfer to a clean bowl, cover with plastic wrap and allow to cool. Strain the jam through a fine strainer. Cut the *génoises* into 3 layers each and spread one layer with the raspberry jam. Cut into 6 triangles.

2. To poach the pears, boil the sugar, water and lemon rind for 2 minutes. Peel the pears and cut each one into 6 wedges. Drop in the boiling syrup and simmer for 2 to 3 minutes. Let it cool in syrup and drain. Line the bottom of a glass or crystal bowl with the triangles, jam side down.

3. Place a layer of plain *génoise* in the middle of the bowl and sprinkle with 1 tablespoon of Sherry. Pour the cooled custard on top. Break slices of *génoise* into pieces and embed in the custard to cover. Sprinkle with 2 tablespoons of Sherry.

4. Combine the cream with the granulated sugar and 1 tablespoon of the Sherry and beat until firm. Place a generous cup of the whipped cream into a pastry bag fitted with a tube, and spread the rest on top of the custard and *génoise* cake.

5. Spread the whipped cream with a spatula so that the top is smooth. Spread another layer of *génoise* cake with the jam, cut into triangles. Place on top of the whipped cream.

6. Arrange the wedges of pear between the triangles of coated *génoise* cake.

7. Decorate the edges and the center with the whipped cream.

8. The jam-coated *génoise* cake shows through the bowl as well as being visible on top. Refrigerate until serving time. Serve with a spoon.

104. Poached Peaches with Raspberry Sauce *(Pêches Pochées à la Purée de Framboises)*

YIELD: 8 servings

POACHED FRUITS are easy to make, light and elegant and particularly well suited as a finale to an elaborate meal. Make them in the summer when peaches are ripe and tasty. If you cannot find good peaches, you can substitute pears, apricots or even apples.

Poaching

8 *ripe peaches (about 2¾ pounds), at room temperature*
2 *cups water*
6 *cups water*
Juice and skin of 1 lemon

Sauce

1 *cup fresh raspberries*
1 *package (10 ounces) frozen raspberries*
½ *cup good raspberry preserves*
1 *tablespoon raspberry brandy, Cognac or Kirsch*

To finish the dish

1 *pound cake cut into 8 ½-inch slices, each slice cut into a disk with a cookie cutter (use the trimmings to make a pudding)*
1 *branch fresh mint, cut into sprigs, one for each peach*

1. To make the sauce, bring all the ingredients except the brandy to a boil and simmer for 2 to 3 minutes. Strain through a fine strainer or a food mill, cover with plastic wrap and let cool. When cool, stir in the brandy. Mix the sugar, water and lemon juice in a saucepan, bring to a boil and boil for 5 minutes. Add the peaches. Place a piece of paper towel on top of the peaches and push them down into the syrup so the paper towel gets wet with the syrup. If the peaches are in contact with air, they will discolor. Cover with a lid and simmer for 3 to

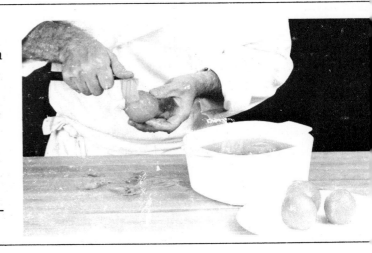

5 minutes. Let the peaches cool in the syrup. When the peaches are cold, remove from the syrup and peel the skin off. (Reserve the syrup to poach other fruit.) Spread approximately 2 tablespoons of raspberry sauce in each individual plate and place a disk of pound cake in the center. Place a peach on the cake and decorate with a sprig of fresh mint. For an alternate method, coat the peaches with the raspberry sauce, then arrange on the pound cake and decorate with the mint.

105. Poached Oranges with Candied Rind (*Oranges Pochées Pelures Confites*)

YIELD: 6 servings

CANDIED ORANGE RIND is useful to enhance desserts. Candied peels of lemon and grapefruit can be done in the same manner. They are excellent served with ice cream, poached fruit or ice-cold soufflés. The candied rind of oranges is good dipped in melted chocolate. Dip half of the rind in chocolate and leave the other half plain to have a contrast of colors and taste.

6 *large seedless oranges*
1 *cup sugar*
4 *cups water*
2 *tablespoons Grand Marnier*
¾ *cup extra sugar to coat the rinds*

1. Peel the oranges with a vegetable peeler, removing only the uppermost orange part of the skin (the zest) which is where you have the essential oils and most of the taste. Cover the peels with cold water, bring to a boil and boil for about 30 seconds. Drain, rinse under cold water, cover again with cold water, bring to a boil and boil for about 3 minutes. Drain and rinse under cold water. Set aside.

2. Using a sharp paring knife, remove the white skin of the orange, moving your blade in a jigsaw pattern. Make sure the orange is completely "nude."

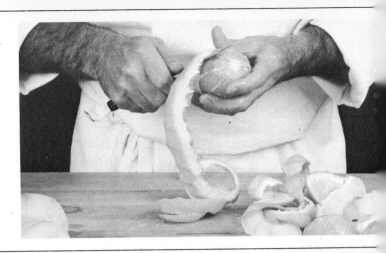

3. Return the peels to the pan, add sugar and water and bring to a boil. Simmer for 10 minutes. Place the oranges in the liquid, cover, bring to a boil and simmer for 10 minutes. Using a slotted spoon remove the oranges and set aside. Place the syrup and the rinds back on medium heat and allow to boil slowly for 40 minutes. There should be almost no liquid left.

4. Spread out the extra sugar on a piece of parchment paper and, using a slotted spoon, lift the peels from the syrup and place on the sugar. Toss and separate the rinds in the sugar until each piece is well coated. Because the rinds are still hot, they should separate easily. Allow the rinds to cool until crisp. When cold, arrange them on a platter or store in a jar. Pour whatever syrup is left over the oranges. When the oranges are cold, sprinkle with the Grand Marnier.

5. Refrigerated, the rinds will keep for months. To serve with the poached oranges, place each orange in an individual glass bowl or in a wineglass, divide the syrup among the oranges and, just before serving, sprinkle the top with candied orange rinds. If the rinds are positioned too early, they will get wet and the sugar coating will dissolve.

106. Glazed Strawberries *(Glaçage des Fraises)*

WHEN STRAWBERRIES are in season, fresh and abundant, they always make welcomed desserts, either plain with brown sugar and sour cream, or simply topped with a dusting of sugar. For a buffet or elegant dinner they are glazed and passed to the guests at the end of the meal. Here are three different ways of glazing strawberries. One is a currant jelly glaze, the other an egg white and sugar coating, and the third one—the most sophisticated and delicate—is a cooked sugar syrup.

Currant jelly glaze

1 *dozen medium-size strawberries, preferably with the stems*
1 *jar (12 ounces) quality currant jelly*

Frosted strawberries

1 *dozen medium-size strawberries, preferably with the stems*
1 *egg white, lightly beaten with a fork*
1½ *cups granulated sugar*

Sugar-syrup glaze

1 *dozen medium-size strawberries, preferably with the stems*
1 *cup sugar*
¼ *cup water*
½ *teaspoon cream of tartar diluted with 1 teaspoon water*

---

1. Currant-glazed strawberries. Place the currant jelly in a saucepan on the stove and bring to a boil. Mix with a spoon until smooth. If the mixture is not smooth it will have to be strained. Holding the strawberry by the stem, dip in the mixture, twist to coat and allow the excess jam to fall off. Place on a plate and refrigerate. The coating will harden as it cools. At serving time, transfer to a clean plate.

2. Frosted strawberries. Beat the egg white lightly with a fork until slightly foamy and loose. Brush the strawberries lightly with the egg white, then roll them in sugar until well coated.

3. Sprinkle sugar on a plate and place the strawberries on top. Let dry and set in the refrigerator for at least ½ hour before serving. The coating will get hard. Transfer to a serving dish and serve.

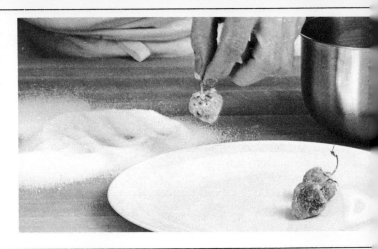

4. Sugar-syrup-glazed strawberries. Place the sugar and water in a heavy saucepan and stir just enough to wet the sugar. Bring to a boil but do not stir the mixture or the sugar may crystallize. Boil for 4 to 5 minutes, then add the cream of tartar. Boil for another minute at which point it should be at the hard-crack stage (300 to 310 degrees), which is the stage before it turns into caramel. Dip a teaspoon in the mixture, lift it and dip in cold water right away. If the mixture sets hard on the spoon, it is at the hard-crack stage. Incline the pan so the syrup gathers in one corner. Dip the strawberries one by one in the hot sugar syrup. Twist the berry and rub gently against the sides of the saucepan so the excess syrup drips off. The coating should be thin. Place on an oiled metal tray until hard. The hot syrup will begin to cook the berry and the berry will release juices, which, in about ½ hour, will start melting the sugar coating. The berries should be eaten just before the sugar coating starts to melt as at that moment the coating is the thinnest.

107. Candied Pineapple *(Ananas Confit)*

Candied pineapple is served with sherbet or cut into small pieces to decorate a soufflé. Canned pineapple packed in pure pineapple juice gives perfectly fine results.

8 *slices pineapple*
About ⅔ cup pure pineapple juice
1 *cup sugar*
1 *cup water*

1. Place the pineapple juice, sugar and water in a flat, large saucepan and bring to a boil.

2. Add the pineapple slices. They should lie flat on the bottom of the pan without overlapping too much. Boil on medium heat for 45 minutes to 1 hour until the juices have almost caramelized and the pineapple slices are almost transparent.

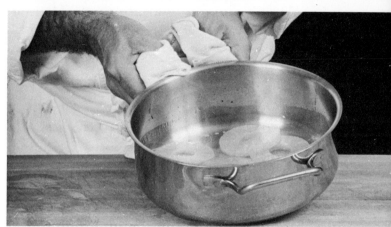

3. Place the pineapple slices in a dish with the syrup. Let macerate in the syrup for 4 to 5 hours, turning the slices every hour.

4. Place on a rack and allow to dry at room temperature for 48 hours. Then pack the slices in containers and keep in the refrigerator until needed.

108. Swan in Melon *(Cygne en Melon)*

A MELON like the honeydew, with its smooth and large graceful round shape, lends itself to carving. Here it gets transformed into a swan, then hollowed into an elegant serving receptacle for ice cream, sherbets, fruit salad, or whatever. Use the flesh to make a sherbet or cut into small pieces, sprinkle with sugar and serve for dessert.

1. Use a pen or the point of a knife to draw the outline of the swan on the melon. Draw the head so it looks like a question mark. With a sharp, small knife, cut along the outlined head and on both sides to form the wings. Cut the back of the swan in between the wings to accentuate their shape. When the whole outline is carved, remove the seeds with a spoon.

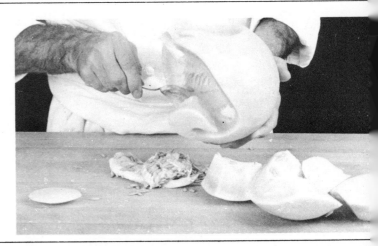

2. Cut inside about ¼ inch in from the rind to separate the flesh from the shell.

3. This is the swan seen from the back. Keep removing melon from the inside to make the shell thinner and more elegant looking. The shell shouldn't be much more than ⅜ inch thick.

4. Cut little dents in both wings to imitate the feathers. Cover with plastic wrap and keep refrigerated. At serving time, drain of any juices and fill.

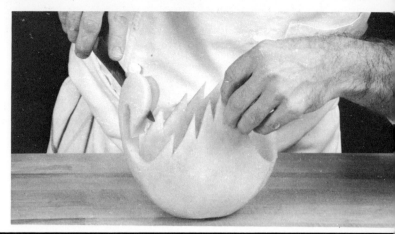

109. Fruit Salad *(Salade de Fruits)*

YIELD: 6 to 8 servings

Our FRUIT SALAD, enhanced with alcohol and sugar, is always served as a dessert. The mixture of preserves, lemon juice and sugar adds a certain acidity and preserves the color of the fruits. Taste improves if the fruit sits an hour in the syrup before serving. Keep an eye for colors. Remember that the bananas, pears, apples, pineapple, have about the same color after peeling. Use dark grapes, plums, cherries and also some dried fruit, such as figs, apricots or prunes, sliced thin and sprinkled in the salad. The fruit salad is beautiful presented in the swan melon described in the previous technique. Serve in glasses or on dessert plates, with small cubes of pound cake around or slices separately served.

Juice of 1 large lemon (⅓ cup)
3 tablespoons strained apricot preserves
2 tablespoons quality Kirschwasser or pear brandy
¼ cup sugar
4 small ripe plums, cut into wedges
2 ripe peaches, cut into wedges
1 ripe apple, peeled and cut into slices
1 ripe pear, peeled and cut into slices
1 ripe banana, peeled and sliced
Small bunch of white grapes, cleaned (about 1 cup)

Small bunch of dark grapes, cleaned (about 1 cup)

Vary the fruits according to availability

1. Mix the lemon juice, apricot preserves, Kirsch and sugar in a stainless steel or glass bowl until well combined.

2. Cut the fruits (bananas, peaches, etc.) directly into the bowl. If the peaches, plums and grapes are ripe, they don't need peeling. The apples and pears are usually peeled. Mix all the fruits in the marinade and let sit at least 1 hour before serving. Arrange in the swan.

110. Strawberry Sherbet *(Sorbet aux Fraises)*

YIELD: 6 servings

THERE ARE lots of different types of "iced desserts"—ices, *sorbet, spum, marquise, granité*. All are conventionally made from fruits or fruit juices or wines although different cooks may interpret them differently. In this and the next few techniques we'll keep to *sorbets* and *granités* (frozen sweetened purée of fruits) and ice cream made with egg yolks, milk and cream. Fruit sherbets or *sorbets* have a truer taste when made only with water, sugar and a fruit purée. With the addition of cream the fruit tends to lose its identity. Fruits like apples and bananas don't make good sherbet. Very juicy fruits like lemon or pineapple, or berries such as black currants, raspberries or strawberries, make the best sherbets. Commercial sherbets are made with ice-cream machines. We prefer to use the machine for regular ice cream only, because it tends to emulsify the mixture too much. Beating air into a mixture of milk, cream and eggs makes it light and smooth. However, in *sorbets* too much air changes the color and taste of the fruit. It makes it too light and too foamy and changes the texture, as well as diluting the fruit taste. The less distinctive the taste of the fruit, the less it should be emulsified. Melon *sorbet* for example is ruined if it's done in an ice cream machine. The color changes too much and the taste of the melon practically disappears.

1½ pounds fresh strawberries or raspberries, ripe, hulled
¾ cup sugar (or more or less depending on the sweetness and ripeness of the fruit)
Juice of ½ large lemon (¼ cup)
2 tablespoons corn syrup
Raspberry sauce (see technique 104)

1. Place all the ingredients in a food processor and process for about 1 minute. Strain if you object to seeds. Place the mixture in a stainless steel bowl in the freezer for 2 hours. Stir it once in a while.

2. When the mixture is partially frozen and grainy, place it back in the food processor for 1 minute to emulsify. It will liquefy and get softer, whiter and much smoother. Place back in a bowl, cover with plastic wrap and freeze to harden (for a few hours) before serving.

3. The mixture is usually spooned with an ice cream scoop and served with the raspberry sauce. To make individual *bombes:* Fill small containers with the sherbet and freeze. Plastic containers are easier to unmold than glass or metal (the plastic can be squeezed to let air between the frozen mixture and the container). When the mixture is hard, hollow the center with a spoon, place a piece of plastic wrap into the cavity and keep it in the freezer until needed.

4. Before serving time, fill the center of the mold with fresh berries, top with a plate and invert. Wait a couple of minutes for the sherbet to soften and unmold. Serve with the raspberry sauce around.

5. One way to facilitate unmolding is to line the container with plastic wrap then pack the sherbet on top of it.

6. Then you can unmold by pulling on the plastic wrap and serve with the sauce.

111. Melon Sherbet *(Sorbet au Melon)*

YIELD: 6 servings

FOR BEST RESULTS, choose melons that are very ripe and of the utmost quality. Read the introduction to technique 110 for some of the singular qualities of melon sherbet.

2 *ripe melons (about 3 pounds each), peeled and seeded*
⅓ *cup sugar (or more or less depending on sweetness and ripeness of fruit)*
⅓ *cup fresh lime juice*
2 *tablespoons honey*

1. Cut one melon in small chunks and place in the food processor just long enough to liquefy. Add the sugar, lime juice and honey. Place in a bowl and freeze for about 2 hours. Stir the mixture every half hour. When the mixture is frozen and grainy, place back in the food processor and whip for about 10 seconds to smooth and emulsify it a bit. Cover with plastic wrap and return to the freezer for a few hours to harden.

2. Serve with fresh melon. Cut a second melon in wedges, cut the skin off using a vegetable peeler. Slice into very thin slices.

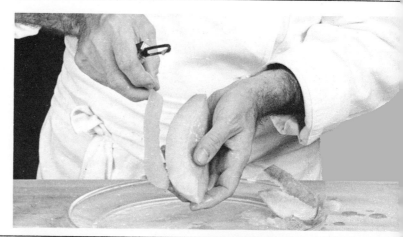

3. Arrange the slices in a round on individual plate. Make more slices and keep on the side.

4. At serving time, place a scoop of melon sherbet in the center of the plate and wrap melon slices around.

5. Cut the rind into thin triangles and arrange around the sherbet. Serve right away.

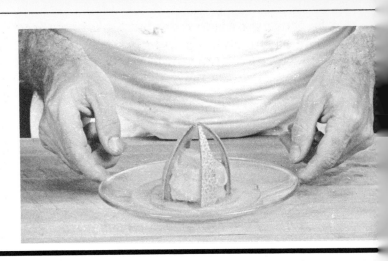

112. Pineapple Sherbet *(Sorbet d'Ananas)*

YIELD: 6 to 8 servings

T HE DELIGHTFUL AROMA of a ripe pineapple is unmistakable. You can recognize that the fruit is ripe if the center leaves can be pulled out easily. The following recipe calls for one pineapple. However, if you want to use an empty pineapple as a container, plan on using two pineapples to have enough sherbert to fill it to the top.

1 large ripe pineapple (about 3 ½ pounds)
⅓ cup sugar (or more or less depending on
*   sweetness and ripeness of the fruit)*
Juice of 1 large lime or lemon (about ¼ cup)

1. Using a long, sharp knife, cut straight down, about ¼ inch in from the skin. Cut all around several times until the inside flesh is loose.

2. Insert the point of your knife straight through the pineapple about ½ inch from the bottom.

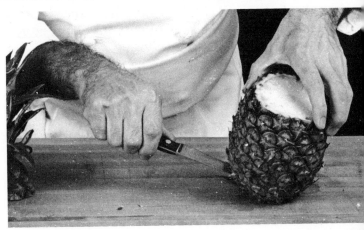

3. Move the blade from left to right without making the opening wider so the blade inside severs the pineapple flesh without cutting through the skin.

4. Use a kitchen fork and twist left to right to loosen the inside. Pull out in one piece.

5. Cut the flesh from around the core and discard the tough core.

6. Cut the flesh in chunks (you should have about 1¾ pounds of flesh) and, using a spoon, scrape out all the pulp left in the shell. Freeze the shell.

7. Do not freeze the top which will be used as a decoration.

8. Place the pineapple chunks in the food processor and blend for about 30 seconds. Mix in the sugar and lime juice and place the mixture in the freezer for 2 hours, mixing every hour so the mixtures freezes evenly into a grainy mush.

9. When frozen, place back in the food processor and emulsify for about 1 minute. The mixture will become slightly runny, whiter and smoother. Return to the bowl or place in containers or in the pineapple shell. Cover with plastic wrap and freeze for a few hours to harden before using.

113. Grapefruit Ice *(Granité de Pamplemousse)*

YIELD: 6 to 8 servings

THE *granité* is a rough unemulsified *sorbet*. The mixture is condensed, tight, grainy and not too sweet. *Granités* are usually served between courses in the middle of an elaborate meal to clear the palate and excite the appetite for the course to come.

4 *medium grapefruit (about 3¼ pounds al-*
    together, or ¾ pound each)
¾ cup sugar
2 tablespoons Vodka

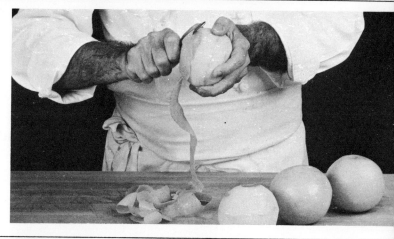

1. Using a vegetable peeler, remove the top
layer of the skin (the "zest") without getting
any of the white underneath. Cover the
skins with cold water, bring to a boil and
boil for 5 minutes. Drain and wash under
cold water. Set aside.

2. Cut the blanched skins coarsely and place
in a food processor until finely chopped. Set
aside.

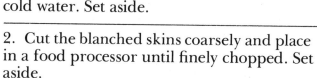

3. Cut the fruit in half and press the juice
into a bowl. (You should have about 2 to 2½
cups.) Strain the juice to eliminate the
seeds.

4. Use a spoon to scrape the pulp out of
the shells. Do not remove any membranes
or white skin. Add the sugar and Vodka and
stir well. Place the mixture in the freezer
for 4 to 5 hours, mixing every 45 minutes
until the mixture is completely frozen. The
addition of alcohol slows the freezing process. The mixture should be grainy and
coarse, but frozen. Pack in plastic containers
until ready to use. Serve in glasses with a
swirl of grapefruit skin on top or a sprig of
mint. *Granité* is always served in a glass.

114. Pralin Ice Cream *(Glace au Pralin)*

YIELD: 10 servings

ICE CREAM made with egg yolks and cream is usually called French ice cream and the mixture is close to a basic *crème anglaise* (custard cream). The addition of coffee to the basic ice-cream mixture makes it mocha ice cream, the addition of chocolate makes it chocolate ice cream, and so on. In this technique the custard is flavored with *pralin*. An ice-cream maker is needed for this ice cream. It emulsifies the mixture, making it light, smooth and voluminous.

Pralin

¾ cup sugar
3 tablespoons water
½ cup oven-browned hazelnuts with skins
½ cup oven-browned almonds with skins
1½ teaspoons almond or peanut oil

Ice cream mixture

8 egg yolks
1 cup granulated sugar
1 teaspoon vanilla extract
3 cups milk
1 cup heavy cream

To freeze

Crushed ice
Salt

1. The *pralin* is a *nougatine* (caramelized sugar and nuts) ground to a paste. The cold mixture is usually crushed and reduced to a paste by machine, in the process of which some of the essential oils from the almond are extracted. A food processor doesn't achieve the exact effect but produces a good enough fascimile. Place the nuts on a tray and roast in a preheated 350-degree oven until golden brown. Place the sugar in a heavy saucepan and mix in the water. Stir this just once then place on the stove. Cook until it turns into a nice golden caramel color, about 5 minutes. Add the nuts and shake to mix well. Oil a cookie sheet lightly and pour the mixture on top. Let cool until hard and brittle. Break in a mortar into large crumbs. Reserve a quarter of the crumbs to use as a garnish.

2. Place the remainder of the *nougatine* in the food processor and powder for 1 minute. It should begin to look crumbly and soft. Add the oil and blend for another 2 to 3 minutes, stopping the machine every 20 or 30 seconds until it looks pasty and slightly wet. Set aside. At this point the *pralin* can be placed in a jar in the refrigerator and kept for months, using it to flavor ice cream, custards or butter creams.

3. Place the milk in a heavy saucepan and bring to a boil. Meanwhile, combine the egg yolks, sugar and vanilla in a bowl and work with a whisk for 2 to 3 minutes, until the mixture is light, smooth, pale colored and has reached the ribbon stage. Add to the milk and place back on medium heat. Cook, stirring constantly with a wooden spoon, for about 2 minutes until the mixture thickens slightly. Be careful not to overcook the sauce (the temperature should be about 170 degrees) or it will scramble. Place the cream in a clean bowl and, as soon as the custard is ready, strain through a fine sieve directly into the cream and mix well. The cream, being cold, brings down the temperature of the mixture and eliminates any further danger of the eggs scrambling. Whisk in the *pralin* paste. Let cool to room temperature.

4. Pour the cream into the central container of the ice-cream machine and secure the beater and motor following the manufacturer's instructions.

5. Because of its sugar and fat, the cream mixture has to be brought lower than 32 degrees in order to freeze. A mixture of salt and water (this brine—like sea water—can withstand temperatures lower than freezing before it hardens) is used to lower the temperature until it's cold enough to freeze the viscous mixture. Place a layer of crushed ice all around the container of cream and cover with about ½ cup of salt. Place another layer of ice on top and sprinkle another ½ cup of salt. Turn the machine on and run for 15 to 25 minutes, adding more ice and salt as the mixture melts. Do not plug the hole on the side of the bucket. If there's too much brine in the ice-cream maker, it will leak out through the hole rather than seep in to the container of ice cream. Most electric machines stop automatically when the ice cream is ready.

6. Lift out the central container taking care that the salted ice doesn't drip into the ice cream.

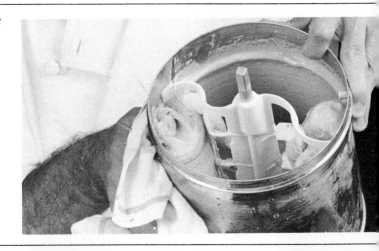

7. Pack the ice cream into containers, cover tightly and freeze until ready to use. Serve in lacy ice-cream shells (technique 116) with crumbled *nougatine* on top.

115. Cat's Tongue Shells
(Cassolettes en Langues de Chat)

YIELD: About 12 shells

CAT'S TONGUES are thin narrow cookies (about 3 inches long by 1 inch wide), which are customarily served with ice cream, fruit salads or custards. In this technique we use the same cat's tongue dough and shape it into shells to fill with ice cream, *sorbet*, fruits and the like. The shells can be formed in small tulip-shaped brioche molds or on the outside of a cup or small ramekin or bowl.

½ stick (2 ounces) sweet butter, softened
½ cup sugar
2 egg whites
¼ teaspoon vanilla extract
½ cup flour

1. Cream the butter and sugar together with a whisk for 1 minute. Add the egg whites and vanilla, mix a few seconds and finally fold in the flour with a rubber spatula. Take a piece of thin cardboard and cut out a disk about 6 inches in diameter.

2. Line a cookie sheet with parchment paper. Unless you have large professional cookie trays, you can only make two shells at a time. Lay the cardboard flat on top of the parchment paper. Place a heaping tablespoon of dough in the center and spread it thinly using a metal spatula. Keep the spatula flat, almost parallel to the table. The dough should be evenly spread (about ¹⁄₁₆ inch thick). If the dough is not spread uniformly the thinner part will burn during cooking.

3. Remove the cardboard and use it to make another disk next to the first one. You will have two thin pancakes on the parchment paper. Set in a preheated 350-degree oven and bake for 6 to 7 minutes.

4. Remove from the oven and slide a spatula underneath to lift the shell off the paper. Shape while still hot because if it is allowed to cool the cookie will become brittle and will break during shaping.

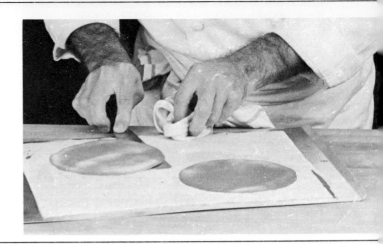

5. Push it into a mold, making it conform to the shape of the mold.

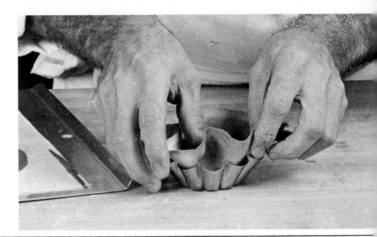

6. An alternate method is to place it on the outside of a plain cup and press it so it takes the shape of the cup. Notice that the dough will pleat in one or two places. The inside can be brushed with melted chocolate, then filled with whipped cream or a custard, or it can be used in one of the ways described in the introduction to this technique.

116. Lacy Ice Cream Shells *(Caissettes Dentelles)*

YIELD: 12 shells

THE DOUGH for the lacy ice cream shells doesn't need to be spread out like the cat's tongue dough in the previous technique. It spreads by itself during baking and forms little holes exactly like a lace. It is a brittle, delicate cookie and should be cooked on parchment paper to prevent sticking. If the cookie still sticks, butter and flour the parchment paper. The dough can be prepared a day ahead and refrigerated until ready to use.

1 cup finely ground blanched whole almonds
¾ cup granulated sugar
¾ stick (3 ounces) soft sweet butter
4 teaspoons flour
2 tablespoons milk

1. For this cookie to work perfectly, the quantities have to be exact and the directions followed exactly. Combine all the ingredients in a smooth paste. If the dough has been refrigerated, soften with a spoon or wooden spatula before dividing it into cookies. Cut parchment paper into 6-inch squares. You should be able to fit 4 squares on a large cookie sheet. Place 1 large tablespoon of the dough in the center of each square. Wet your finger with cold water and flatten the dough into rounds about 3 inches wide.

2. Bake in a preheated 350-degree oven for 12 to 13 minutes. The cookies should brown nicely and should have spread to about 6 inches in diameter.

3. Let the cookies set for about 1 minute. If you try to mold them right away they will fall apart. Lift each cookie on its own piece of paper and place upside down on a small pyrex or glass bowl. The bowls should be about 3 inches in diameter. Remove the paper before you start molding the cookie or the paper will get caught in the pleats and will be hard to remove. Press the cookie down so it takes the shape of the cup. Work fast because the cookies become brittle as they cool. Remove from the mold when hardened.

4. The cookie can also be molded around a metal cornet or horn. Place the horn on top of the cookie and roll the cookie around it.

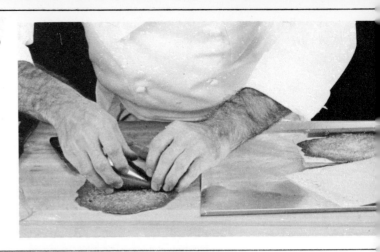

5. The cookie can also be rolled around the handle of a wooden spatula or a wooden stick into a large cigar shape.

6. The "horn of plenty" and the cigar can be served plain or filled with sweetened whipped cream or berries as a dessert.

7. For a variation, brush the inside of the cookie with melted chocolate. Then, fill with ice cream, whipped cream or fruit. The cookies will keep well in a tinned box in a dry place.

8. Shape the dough to your fancy. If the mold is small the cookie spreads out and looks more like a flower.

117. Glazed Puff Paste *(Allumettes Glacées)*

YIELD: 12

THE *allumettes glacées* are often served with ice cream or plain as a coffee cake.

About 1 pound puff paste (technique 91, or your own)

Glaze

1 *cup powdered sugar*
1 *egg white*
3 *tablespoons cornstarch*

1. Roll the puff paste into a rectangle about 14 inches long by 6 inches wide and ¼ inch thick. Combine the sugar and egg white in a bowl and work for about 2 minutes until creamy. Add the cornstarch and work for another minute. Pour on top of the puff paste right away. If the glaze is kept it should be covered with a wet towel or a crust will rapidly form on top.

2. Use a spatula to spread the mixture as evenly as you can on top of the puff paste. Refrigerate for at least 2 to 3 hours so the icing stiffens and forms a crust.

3. Trim the outside of the puff paste and cut into strips about 1½ inches wide.

4. Bake in a preheated 375-degree oven for 30 minutes. The icing should be beige in color, shiny and brittle. Let cool before using.

118. Jam Toasts *(Croûtes de Confiture)*

YIELD: 2 dozen

JAM TOASTS are easy to make and very decorative. They are ideally served with fruit sherberts, although they are good served with whipped cream or a custard. The shape and color can be varied at will. Ours are made with apricot and raspberry jams. Use a dense buttery pound cake.

1 pound cake, day old and preferably homemade
About ¾ cup quality apricot jam
About ¾ cup quality raspberry jam

1. Strain the apricot jam through a fine strainer, food mill or sieve and repeat with the raspberry jam. Cut the pound cake into ½-inch-thick slices.

2. Spread the slices of pound cake with the jams. You may flavor the jam with a little bit of brandy (about 2 teaspoons per cup). (As the alcohol will dilute the jam, and may make it runny, boil it down gently for 5 to 10 minutes to thicken it, then strain and cool off before adding the brandy.)

3. Cut into triangles.

4. And also rectangles, lozenges, squares or rounds with a cookie cutter. Keep refrigerated. Arrange on a nice platter when ready to serve.

119. Raspberry Soufflé

(Soufflé aux Framboises)

YIELD: 6 to 8 servings

EVEN FOR THE PROFESSIONAL, making a soufflé always involves an element of suspense. A soufflé is usually made of a base into which egg whites are folded. As the soufflé bakes, the air beaten into the egg whites, in the form of little bubbles, swells and pushes the soufflé up. Hot expands and cold deflates. Therefore a soufflé folds if allowed to cool.

Soufflés are served as first courses, main courses or desserts—for brunch, as well as lunch, dinner or supper. Although regularly made in a special soufflé mold, they can be made in any oven-proof container. Soufflés are also served unmolded or lukewarm and rolled. The ice-cold soufflé is a made-up soufflé—an unbaked mousse mixture shaped in the form of a soufflé.

There are two basic types of soufflés. The most common is made with a cream sauce base *(béchamel)* flavored with spinach, cheese, etc., into which egg yolks and beaten egg whites are added. The second type uses a purée of the main ingredient as a base, to which egg yolks and the beaten egg whites are added. It can be a purée of cauliflower or mushrooms, or fish or, in our case, raspberries. The flourless soufflé cooks faster and is lighter in texture.

Most soufflés can be prepared ahead, placed in a mold and kept refrigerated for a couple of hours before cooking. Our lobster soufflé (technique 29), cannot be assembled ahead because the top layer would liquefy into the hot lobster sauce. Remember that the smaller the soufflé, the easier and better it works. Large soufflés are harder to make and an 8- to 10-cup soufflé is about the maximum. It is important that large soufflés be cooked in the center of the oven so there's equal heat all around. The highest, best-textured soufflés are the ones cooked in a *bain-marie,* like the caramel soufflé (technique 120). However, other soufflés made this way won't get brown around because, being cooked in a bath of water, the outside is not exposed to enough heat to brown it. In the caramel soufflé, the caramel melts during cooking and colors the outside.

Remember that the equipment used to beat the whites must be immaculately clean. The egg whites should be at room temperature and there should be no egg yolk in them. If not, the egg whites will not expand to the right volume during beating. Beat the whites in an unlined copper bowl cleaned with vinegar and salt for the most volume. (Or add a dash of salt or lemon juice or cream of tartar for the same effect.) Do not beat the whites in aluminum or they will discolor. Have the base ready before you beat the whites. When you start beating do not stop. If you stop, the whites become grainy. As soon as they are ready, combine with the base as fast as possible. At that point the mixture can be placed in the mold and kept for a while. The base should be lukewarm when the whites are added. If too cold the mixture won't combine well and will be grainy; if too hot, the whites cook before baking and the soufflé won't raise properly. If the base is too light, the soufflé will run; if too thick, the soufflé will split. Whisk about a third of the egg whites into the base mixture to lighten it, then fold the rest of the whites in with a spatula. If all the whites are beaten into the base instead of being folded in, the mixture will lose volume and become too dense. The size of the mold is important and the mixture should fill it to the rim. A half-full soufflé mold will not look right after baking even if the mixture has risen properly. The soufflé should go from the oven directly to the table, so seat your guests in advance.

Be sure when separating the eggs that all the white is removed from the shell. If a bit is left it will amount to a whole egg white every five or six eggs. If the eggs are small add one or two egg whites. It is better to have too much egg white than not enough.

Conventionally, for a fruit soufflé, the fruits are cooked with sugar to a syrup, then folded into the egg whites. However, the taste of the fruits is truer when the fruits are mixed uncooked with the egg whites and sugar. They will bleed slightly during cooking and get soft. Serve with a raspberry sauce.

For the recipe that follows you will need a 5- to 6-cup soufflé mold. Butter the mold, coat with sugar and set aside.

Sauce

1 *cup fresh raspberries*
1 *10-ounce package frozen raspberries, including juice*
⅔ *cup raspberry preserves*
1 *tablespoon raspberry brandy, Kirsch or Cognac*

Bring all ingredients except the brandy to a boil and boil for 2 to 3 minutes. Strain through a fine strainer or a food mill. Cover and cool. When cold, add the brandy.

Soufflé

2 *cups very ripe raspberries*
6 *egg whites*
¾ *cup sugar*
Pinch of salt

1. Place the egg whites and the pinch of salt in the bowl of an electric mixer and beat on medium to high speed (#6 to 8) until they form a peak. Add the sugar gradually while continuing to beat. Keep beating at high speed for about 30 seconds. With a fork, crush ½ cup of raspberries coarsely and fold along with the whole ones into the egg whites. Fill the mold with the soufflé mixture. Smooth the top with a metal spatula and make ridges with the spatula to decorate. Place the soufflé on a cookie sheet in a preheated 400-degree oven for 20 minutes.

Remove from the oven and sprinkle powdered sugar on top. Serve immediately with the raspberry sauce. If, after 10 to 15 minutes of cooking, the soufflé appears to be browning too fast, place a loose piece of aluminum over it and continue to bake.

120. Lemon and Caramel Soufflé

(Soufflé au Citron et Caramel)

YIELD: 8 servings

THE LEMON AND CARAMEL SOUFFLÉ is cooked in a double boiler and this gives it a particularly good texture. The soufflé can be served sprinkled with powdered sugar, hot out of the oven, or, as in the case below, allowed to cool, unmolded and served in wedges with a caramel sauce, a whipped cream or a custard. When it cools it deflates and becomes denser like a pudding. For this recipe you will need a 1½- to 2-quart soufflé mold.

Caramel	Soufflé mixture
1 *cup sugar*	1½ *cups milk*
¼ *cup water*	4 *egg yolks*
	⅓ *cup sugar*
	1 *teaspoon vanilla extract*
	2 *teaspoons lemon rind*
	2 *tablespoons cornstarch*
	7 *egg whites*

1. Combine the water and sugar in a saucepan and cook over medium to high heat until it turns a light caramel in color, about 6 minutes. Immediately pour most of the caramel into a soufflé mold.

2. Tip the mold back and forth so the caramel coats the bottom and sides of the mold. Use a brush (not nylon) to spread it around the sides and edges well. Work as quickly as possible because the caramel hardens fast.

3. Bring the milk to a boil. Combine the yolks and sugar and work together for 1 minute with a whisk until they form a ribbon. Mix in the vanilla, lemon rind and cornstarch. Add the milk to the mixture. Return the whole mixture to the pot and bring to a boil, stirring with a whisk. When it reaches a strong boil, pour into a large stainless steel bowl. Beat the egg whites until stiff. Add one-third of the whites to the cream mixture and stir. Fold in the remaining whites. Work fast. Pour into the mold and place in a skillet.

4. Place tepid water around the mold and bake in a preheated 350-degree oven for 1 hour. If the scoufflé is brown enough on top after 35 to 40 minutes, place a piece of aluminum foil on top to prevent further browning.

5. The soufflé can be sprinkled with powdered sugar and served hot with or without a sauce.

6. For our "pudding," allow the soufflé to deflate and cool at room temperature. Note that the soufflé won't go lower than the rim of the bowl. Cool the pudding for a few hours or overnight in the refrigerator. To unmold, run a knife around the edge to loosen the caramel stuck to the rim.

7. Invert on a platter. If you have time, refrigerate with the mold on top. The soufflé will unmold itself slowly. Cut the pudding into slices and serve with whipped cream, a caramel sauce or a light sabayon. (See color plate 22, page 65.)

121. Chocolate Soufflé with Rum Sauce *(Soufflé au Chocolat Sauce au Rhum)*

YIELD: 6 to 8 servings

THIS SOUFFLÉ is better without flour, because the chocolate has enough body to hold the egg whites. More than any other soufflé, the chocolate soufflé should not be overcooked but slightly wet in the center. Serve hot right out of the oven with the sauce or let it cool, unmold and serve in wedges like a cake with or without a sauce.

Rum sauce

1½ cups milk
2 teaspoons cornstarch
1 teaspoon pure vanilla extract
3 egg yolks (reserve the whites for the soufflé)
¼ cup sugar
2 tablespoons good dark rum

Place the milk, cornstarch and vanilla in a saucepan. Mix with the whisk and bring to a boil. Meanwhile, combine the egg yolks and sugar in a bowl and whisk for 1 to 2 min-utes until the mixture is light, fluffy and pale yellow. Pour the boiling milk all at once directly on top of the yolks whisking to combine well. The hot milk will cook the egg yolks. Cover with plastic wrap and let cool. When cold, add the rum.

Soufflé

*4 large eggs at room temperature, separated, plus
the 3 egg whites leftover from the sauce*
*4 ounces bittersweet chocolate (or 3 ounces sweet
and 1 bitter)*
½ cup milk
3 tablespoons sugar

1. Butter and sugar a 6-cup soufflé mold and refrigerate until ready to use. Place the chocolate in a saucepan with the milk and melt on top of the stove. Stir until it comes to a simmer. Remove from the heat and whisk the yolks in. Beat the 7 egg whites until they reach a soft peak and add the sugar. Keep beating for about 1 minute until very stiff.

2. Whisk about one-third of the mixture into the chocolate. Pour the chocolate mixture back onto the beaten egg whites.

3. Carefully fold the chocolate mixture into the egg whites, then pour into the soufflé mold. It should reach the rim of the mold. At this point, the soufflé can be kept for a good hour, refrigerated or at room temperature.

4. Place on a cookie sheet in a preheated 375-degree oven and cook for 18 to 20 minutes. The soufflé should be moist in the center. Sprinkle with powdered sugar and serve immediately with the rum sauce around.

5. You can leave the soufflé to deflate and cool overnight and then unmold it, cut into wedges and serve with sweetened whipped cream or with the rum sauce. It will have the consistency of a very light cake.

122. Chocolate and Vanilla Soufflé *(Soufflé Panaché)*

YIELD: 6 to 8 servings

IN THIS TECHNIQUE two soufflé mixtures are cooked together in the same mold. The contrast of color and different tastes make it unusual and attractive. Serve it with a *crème anglaise* or the rum sauce from technique 121, or just plain.

Chocolate base

2½ ounces bittersweet chocolate
⅓ cup milk
2 egg yolks

Vanilla base

¾ cup milk
2 egg yolks
¼ cup sugar
½ teaspoon vanilla extract
1½ tablespoons sugar

For both mixtures

7 egg whites
3 tablespoons sugar

1. Butter and sugar a 2-quart soufflé mold and cut a piece of wax paper as wide as the bowl to act as a divider. Set aside until ready to use. The base mixtures are made separately but the egg whites for both mixtures are beaten together. Melt the chocolate in a saucepan with the ⅓ cup milk and when hot and smooth, whisk in the egg yolks and pour the mixture into a large bowl. You will notice that when the yolks are combined with the milk it thickens the mixture. For the vanilla base, bring the ¾ cup milk to a boil. Meanwhile mix the egg yolks and sugar and beat about 1 minute with a whisk. Stir in the vanilla extract and the flour until smooth. Pour the boiling milk into the yolk mixture, stirring constantly. Place the whole mixture back on the stove and bring to a boil, stirring with a whisk. Pour the mixture into a large bowl.

2. Beat the egg whites until they hold a peak, then add the 3 tablespoons of sugar and keep beating for ½ minute until the mixture is stiff. Place about a cup of the egg white mixture into the chocolate mixture and stir with the whisk. Do the same thing with the vanilla mixture. Then divide the remaining whites into each of the soufflés and fold it in with different spatulas. Work fast. Holding the wax paper in the center of the mold, spoon in the soufflés alternating each soufflé from one side to the other, so the paper is held in place.

3. Keep filling both sides until the mold is full. Then gently pull the paper divider out.

4. Place the soufflé on a cookie sheet and bake in the center of a preheated 375-degree oven for about 25 minutes. Sprinkle powdered sugar on top and serve immediately. If the top browns too quickly, cover with a piece of aluminum foil.

5. Sometimes the soufflé cracks during cooking. To prevent splitting, a "collar" of parchment or wax paper can be placed around. The paper should be wide enough to touch the cookie sheet and rise to about 2 inches above the mold. Butter and sugar or flour the paper to keep the soufflé mixture from sticking to it. Secure with a piece of kitchen string. Remove before serving.

123. Floating Island *(Ile Flottante)*

YIELD: 8 to 10 servings

THE FLOATING ISLAND is a type of cold soufflé cooked for a short time in a *bain-marie* at a low temperature, unmolded and served with a sauce. The mixture is the same as for *oeufs à la neige* (pages 336–338 in *La Technique*). Butter and sugar heavily a 1-quart charlotte mold. Set aside until ready to use.

Soufflé mixture

5 *egg whites*
½ *cup sugar*
⅓ *cup slivered almonds, roasted, plus extra for decoration*
½ *teaspoon vanilla extract*

Coffee cream

1 *cup milk*
½ *cup coffee extract (these are the first drops from a drip coffee maker) or*
1 *tablespoon instant coffee and boiling water to make ½ cup*
4 *egg yolks*
⅓ *cup sugar*
1 *cup heavy cream*

1. Beat the egg whites with a whisk until stiff but not dry and grainy and add the sugar. Keep beating for another 15 to 20 seconds. Fold in the almonds and vanilla extract.

2. Pour the mixture into the mold. It should fill the mold. Smooth the top with a spatula, butter a piece of parchment paper and cover the top of the mold. Place in a saucepan with tepid water around. The water should reach one-half to three-quarters of the way up the mold. Place in a preheated 325-degree oven for 15 minutes. The mixture will only rise slightly higher than the rim of the mold. Allow to cool at room temperature. It will deflate to the height of the mold.

3. To make the sauce, bring the milk and coffee to a boil. Meanwhile, work the egg yolks and sugar with the whisk until they form a ribbon, about 1 minute. Add the egg yolk mixture to the milk and place back on the stove. Cook, stirring, until it reaches about 170 degrees (see step 3, technique 114). The mixture should be thick enough to coat the spoon. Place the cream in a bowl. As soon as the custard reaches the right temperature, strain it at once through a sieve into the cream and stir. This will cool the custard and prevent it from curdling.

4. Unmold the floating island. Blot up any liquid that leaks out so it won't thin the sauce down. Put some of the mocha cream around and serve the rest on the side. Decorate with little pieces of slivered almonds.

124. Chocolate Truffle Cake

(Gâteau au Chocolat Albert)

YIELD: 10 to 12 servings

T HIS CAKE is made from layers of chocolate *génoise*, a cream *ganache* and a dense, buttery layer of cookie dough in between. It can be shaped round, square or rectangular. Its taste is even better when it is 1 day old. It freezes well provided it is properly wrapped.

Chocolate *génoise*

3 *extra large eggs, or 4 smaller ones*
½ *cup sugar*
½ *cup flour*
1 *tablespoon unsweetened cocoa powder*
2 *tablespoons unsalted butter, melted*

Chocolate cookie dough

3 *cups all-purpose flour*
3 *sticks (12 ounces) sweet butter, softened*
2 *ounces bittersweet chocolate*
⅓ *cup hot water*

Ganache cream

12 *ounces bittersweet chocolate*
1½ *cups heavy cream*
1 *tablespoon dark rum*
½ *stick (2 ounces) sweet butter, softened*

Syrup

2 *tablespoons sugar*
2 *tablespoons hot water*
2 *tablespoons dark rum*

1. For the chocolate *génoise*, place the eggs and sugar in the bowl of an electric mixer and mix well. Place the bowl in a pan of warm water for about 1 minute, mixing until the mixture is barely tepid. Whip on high speed (#6 to 8) for 8 to 10 minutes. (The mixture whips better when the eggs are slightly warm.) Combine the flour and cocoa and sift over the beaten egg mixture, folding it in with a spatula as you sift. Then fold in the melted butter gently. Do not overfold.

2. Cook the *génoise* in cake pans or flan rings or a mold shaped the way you want the cake to be. Our rectangular flan mold is 12 inches by 4½ inches wide. Butter and flour the cookie sheet and the mold. Place the mold on top of the cookie sheet. Pour the batter inside and level with a spatula. Bake in a preheated 350-degree oven for about 18 minutes.

3. Let cool for ½ hour before unmolding. Run a knife around the edges of the mold and remove the flan ring. When cool, wrap the *génoise* in a plastic bag. It can be kept this way for a few days.

4. When ready to be used, cut the *génoise* in half. Each half should be about ½ inch thick.

5. The *génoise* should be smooth and soft in the center without being wet or crumbly. (A dry *génoise* is a product of overbeating; a wet, tight one indicates underbeating or under-cooking.)

6. For the cookie dough, combine the chocolate and hot water and stir until melted. Place the flour in the bowl of a mixer and add the butter in pieces. Mix for about 10 seconds, add the chocolate mixture and mix for another 15 seconds. The mixture should be like a paste. Spread the dough with a spatula on a large cookie sheet. It should be at least as long as the rectangular mold.

7. Place a piece of parchment paper on top of the dough and spread the dough out with your hands. It should be twice as wide as the rectangular mold and no more than ¼ inch thick. It should be equally thick all over. If thinner in one place, it will burn. Remove the parchment and cook in a pre-heated 425-degree oven for 20 minutes.

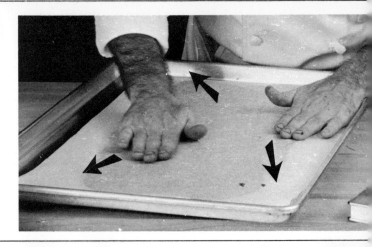

8. Let the biscuit cool for 5 to 6 minutes, then cut it into 2 strips, using the flan mold as a guide.

9. Use a large spatula and the bottoms from a removable-bottom cake pan to lift the strip which is fragile and may easily break. Place it on a platter, a piece of wood or a piece of cardboard cut to the exact size of the cake.

10. For the *ganache,* combine the cream and chocolate in a heavy saucepan. Bring to a boil, stirring. Remove from the heat and let cool until thick, but not too hard. Place in a bowl and add the softened butter and the rum. Beat with a whisk for 1 to 2 minutes, which will expand the volume and whiten the cream. The cream should not be overbeaten or it will absorb too much air and become grainy and hard to spread. If this happens, remelt slightly and stir gently until soft enough to use. Spread a thin layer of *ganache* on top of the biscuit.

11. Prepare the syrup by mixing the water, sugar and dark rum together. Place one layer of *génoise* cut side up on the *ganache* and moisten it all over with the rum syrup, using a brush. Cover with another layer of *ganache*, about ¼ inch thick, then with the other cookie strip, and again *ganache* and finally the last of the *génoise*, smooth side up. Moisten again with the rum syrup, then cover the top and the sides with the remaining *ganache* cream (about ⅛ inch thick all around).

12. Place the cookie trimmings in a food processor and crumble into fine crumbs. (The crumbs may also be mixed with powdered almonds.) Pat the crumbs all around the cake.

13. Then place the rest of the crumbs on top. Scrape the top of the cake gently with a spatula to remove the excess crumbs and make the top flat.

14. Cut pieces of wax paper and arrange on top of the cake. Sprinkle powdered sugar on top to make a design. In our case, we put two strips on each side and two at the end. Refrigerate until serving time. If the cake is to be kept several days, wrap well in plastic wrap to prevent it from picking up refrigerator odors.

125. Christmas Log with Chocolate Bark *(Bûche de Noël au Chocolat)*

YIELD: 8 to 10 servings

THE CHRISTMAS OR YULE LOG is usually made with a butter cream and a *génoise* batter. This version is made with a soufflé-like batter, rolled, filled with a coffee cream and covered with a light *ganache*. Read the introduction to technique 119 for more information about beating egg whites.

Cake

½ cup sugar
⅓ cup strong coffee
6 large eggs, separated
6 ounces bittersweet chocolate, melted

Filling

1 tablespoon freeze-dried coffee
3 tablespoons boiling water
½ envelope unflavored gelatin
2 cups heavy cream
2 tablespoons sugar

Ganache

3 ounces bittersweet chocolate, melted
½ cup heavy cream
1 teaspoon dark rum
1 tablespoon unsweetened cocoa powder to sprinkle on top

Chocolate bark (technique 126)

1. To make the cake batter, bring the sugar and coffee to a boil and boil gently for 1½ to 2 minutes. Place the yolks in the bowl of an electric mixer and add the sugar syrup to it. Beat on high speed for 5 to 6 minutes. It should about triple in volume and become very fluffy and light. Add the bittersweet chocolate. Beat the egg whites until firm, and, using a whisk, stir half the whites into the chocolate mixture. Fold in the remaining whites, using a large rubber spatula. Work fast or the whites will break down and become grainy.

2. Cut a piece of parchment or wax paper large enough to line a 12- by 16-inch cake pan. Spread butter on the cookie sheet so the paper will stick to the pan. Then butter and flour the paper.

3. Pour mixture on top of the paper, trying not to work it too much so it won't deflate. Spread to about ½ inch thick. Bake in a preheated 375-degree oven for about 15 minutes. Cool at room temperature.

4. Place a piece of parchment paper on the table and invert the cake on it.

5. Remove the paper from the back of the cake, then place it back loosely. Roll the cake between the two sheets of paper. Refrigerate until ready to use. It will keep for a few days.

6. Prepare the filling. Combine the instant coffee with the boiling water and sprinkle the gelatin on top. Mix the cream and sugar together and whip until the cream holds a peak but is still soft. When the gelatin has been absorbed by the water (about 1 minute), mix in until smooth. Quickly pour the gelatin mixture into the whipped cream and whisk fast until well combined. The cream will harden almost immediately.

7. The cream stiffened and holding a peak well.

8. Unroll the cake and remove the top layer of paper. Spread with a ½-inch layer of cream.

9. Use the bottom paper to help roll the cake. Don't press down on the cake too much or the cream will seep out. Continue rolling.

10. When the cake is rolled, the seam should be underneath.

11. Make the *ganache*. Combine the cream with the melted chocolate and the rum and beat the mixture with a whisk until it holds a peak, about ½ minute. Do not overbeat or the mixture will get too hard and grainy.

12. Spread the *ganache* ¹⁄₁₆ inch thick all around the yule and, using large spatulas or the bottom of a removable-bottom cake pan, lift up the yule and place it on a board covered with a towel or on a platter.

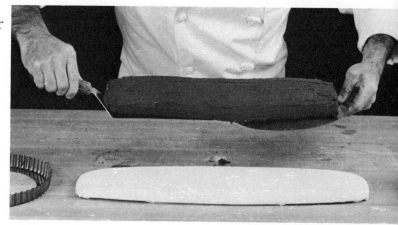

13. Sprinkle the top with the cocoa powder.

14. Place the bark around the cake. If the chocolate is too stiff to fold, warm with your hands to soften. Then remove the paper.

15. Place another length of bark on the other side, folding the ends so the cake is wrapped all around. Cut more bark into pieces and decorate to look like a log. Refrigerate until ready to serve.

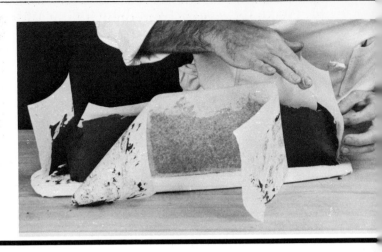

126. Chocolate Bark *(Écorce en Chocolat)*

WHEN YOU BUY chocolate to make leaves, bark, curls or any other decoration, get the best available. Good-quality chocolate is usually higher in butter fat content (cocoa butter), which makes it more elastic and therefore easier to work with and helps it remain shiny. Unfortunately, it is not easy for the home cook to find large blocks of the quality chocolate restaurants use, although some specialty stores do carry 5- and 10-pound bars. We use a bittersweet chocolate for all the chocolate techniques. Sweeter chocolate can be used if you prefer.

1. Melt approximately 1 pound of chocolate in a double boiler, or place it in a gas oven with the pilot light on and leave it overnight so it melts very slowly. Be careful when melting chocolate not to heat it too much or it will lose its shine. Be careful when melting chocolate on direct heat because it scorches easily. Lay out a length of parchment paper and pour the chocolate on it in two long lines.

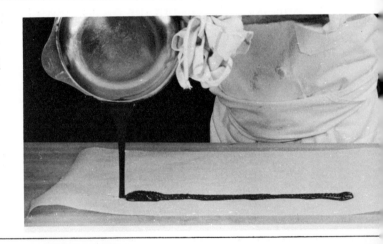

2. Spread out the chocolate with a spatula. If you are decorating a Christmas log (technique 125), make the strips about ¹⁄₁₆ inch thick. One edge of the chocolate strip should be pegged with curves and dents to imitate broken tree bark. Let set and harden in a cool place or refrigerate.

3. Lift the chocolate from the paper by sliding a spatula underneath or transfer directly onto the yule log while still attached to the paper and then remove the paper. Remember that if the strips are not wide or long enough, or if the shape is not attractive enough, the chocolate can always be remelted and used again. The strips can be prepared ahead and kept refrigerated.

127. Chocolate Leaves *(Feuilles en Chocolat)*

THE BEST and easiest way to make chocolate leaves is to coat real leaves with the chocolate. Natural leaves come in all shapes and sizes and make beautiful designs. Use dark chocolate, milk chocolate (which has a lighter color) or white chocolate. (See color plate 32, page 69.)

1. Select your leaves. Try to pick leaves all the same size. Decide whether you are going to coat the top or the underside of the leaves. The design on the underside is usually in more relief and will give more texture to the chocolate. Melt the chocolate in the oven or over hot water.

2. Dip a side of the leaf in the chocolate, making sure that it is coated all over.

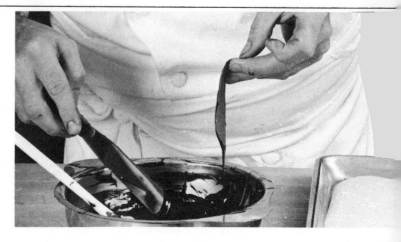

3. Place the leaves, chocolate side up, flat on a piece of parchment or wax paper, chocolate showing.

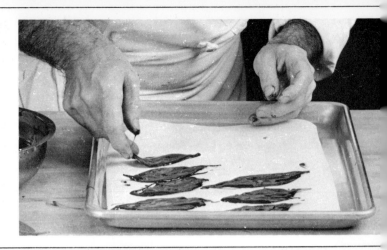

4. White chocolate is usually thicker. It is not runny enough to coat by dipping. Instead, use a spatula or a knife to spread it well. Place the coated leaves flat on the paper.

5. When the chocolate is almost set but still soft, place in a curved pan to mold. If the chocolate is still too soft it will run toward the center of the leaves; if it is too hard it will break when bent. Set the mold in the refrigerator until the leaves are set.

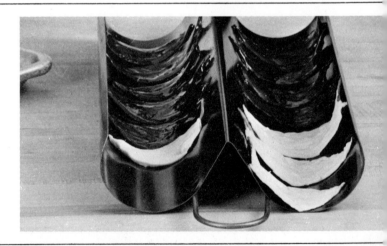

6. Pull the leaf from the chocolate. It should come off easily.

7. A white chocolate leaf. Arrange all your leaves on a platter or use to decorate a cake or a cold soufflé.

128. Chocolate Box *(Boîte en Chocolat)*

YIELD: 1 9-inch box

A ROUND CHOCOLATE BOX is very festive and decorative. Filled with chocolate truffles, it makes an ideal presentation for Christmas or Easter holidays. Melt about 1½ pounds of chocolate in the oven or in a double boiler.

1. To make the bottom and the lid, pour some chocolate on two pieces of parchment paper.

2. Spread it out with a spatula to about ⅛ inch thick. The disks should be at least 9 inches in diameter. Let set to harden either in the refrigerator or in a cool place.

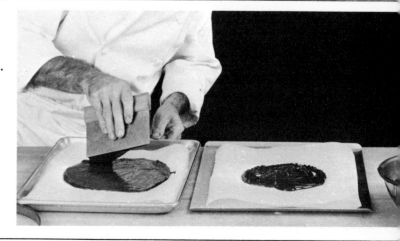

3. Meanwhile, cut a long strip of waxed paper and pour a line of chocolate on it. This will be the sides of the box. Be sure that the strip is long enough to go around the disk. Let set in the refrigerator.

4. When the chocolate disks have set—they should be hard enough not to run but not too brittle—set a 9-inch flan ring on top and trim into a neat circle.

5. Remove the trimming. Remember that if anything goes wrong, the chocolate can be remelted and the process started again.

6. The disk should lift easily from the paper.

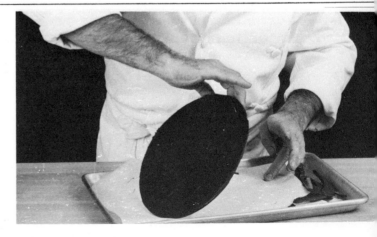

7. Trim the strip on both sides to have a clean length about 1 inch wide for the side of the box.

8. Lift the strip with the paper and fold it around the disk so it encases the whole bottom. If the strip is too long, trim so the ends abut.

9. Remove the wax paper and, using a paper cone, squeeze a bit of melted chocolate inside, at the joint.

10. With the tip of your finger smooth out the melted chocolate. When it hardens it will secure the sides to the bottom.

11. Use the second disk for the cover. Etch a design free hand with a nail or the point of a knife.

12. Fill a paper cone with melted chocolate and pipe a line on the design.

13. Place a chocolate rose or carnation in the center (technique 129) with a bit of melted chocolate under it to secure it to the lid.

129. Chocolate Flower *(Fleur en Chocolat)*

PROFESSIONAL CHOCOLATE WORK is an art which requires special equipment. However, if you have a large chunk of chocolate to carve from and a vegetable peeler, you can make curls and flowers. Buy a piece of chocolate thick enough to be held and worked with. It should be quality chocolate that's high in butter content, which makes it more malleable. Most important is the temperature of the chocolate. Keep overnight in a place no warmer than 90 degrees; not hot enough for the chocolate to melt but hard enough so it can withstand a knife or peeler, yet soft enough so it can be molded into shapes.

1. When you work with chocolate, work fast and be sure to have dry hands. Using a vegetable peeler, cut strips of chocolate. Use each strip right away before it hardens.

2. To make a rose, roll a strip so it is pointed on top. This will be the heart of the rose. (For more information on rose making, see technique 139.)

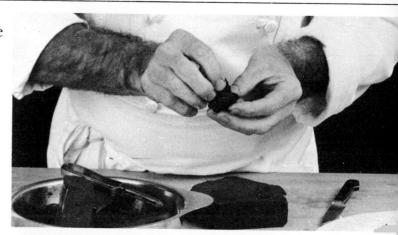

3. Peel another strip and wrap it around the center. Curl the edge outward. Continue cutting strips to make more petals. Wrap them around the rose which will get larger and larger. Curl the edges outward.

4. Five or 6 strips should make a big enough rose. Work fast so the chocolate doesn't melt in your hands.

5. Make other roses of varying sizes and degrees of openness. When the roses are done, place them on a plate with the nicest part showing and let them cool in the refrigerator until hard and brittle. The chocolate will be dull rather than shiny.

6. To make a carnation, use the point of a knife and scrape the top of the chocolate over and over to build up a long wrinkled strip of chocolate on the end of the blade. Then roll the strip into a curl around the point of the knife. (This technique is similar to the one used to make butter decorations on page 16 of *La Technique*.)

7. Make a second and a third curl smaller than the previous one and combine to make a large flower.

8. To make chocolate rolls, peel a strip with the vegetable peeler. Sometimes the chocolate will curl by itself.

9. If it does not curl, roll gently into a curl with the tip of your fingers.

130. Chocolate Truffles *(Truffes en Chocolat)*

YIELD: 3 to 4 dozen truffles

CHOCOLATE is sometimes tricky to use and is always very sensitive to heat. It can scorch, curdle, change color and go from the brightest to the very dull, depending on the amount of heat. It contains cocoa butter, which, like other fats, is not easily incorporated into liquids. Sweet chocolate is easier to work with. Because of its milk and sugar content it absorbs liquid more readily than unsweetened chocolate, which is pure fat and cocoa powder.

These chocolate truffles are conventionally served to guests around the Christmas holidays in France. They are called truffles because of their similarity in shape and color to the expensive truffle found in the southwest of France.

Make the basic truffle recipe, then divide it and flavor each portion differently. We used three flavors and coated each differently so as to recognize one flavor from another. The basic recipe will yield three to four dozen truffles. However, they can be made smaller since they are very rich.

Basic mixture

¾ pound (12 ounces) bittersweet chocolate
4 egg yolks
⅔ stick (2⅔ ounces) sweet butter, softened

First flavor

1 tablespoon rum
1 tablespoon coffee extract

Second flavor

½ cup pralin (see technique 114)
2 tablespoons Cognac

Third flavor

Rind of 1 orange (about 1½ teaspoons)
1½ tablespoons Grand Marnier

1. Melt the chocolate in a double boiler or in an oven until the chocolate is lukewarm. Add the egg yolks and stir with a whisk for a few seconds. It will probably curdle.

2. Add the butter in pieces and whisk well. The mixture may become smooth or it may remain somewhat separated. Do not worry about it. Divide the basic mixture into three small bowls.

3. In one bowl add the coffee and rum, in the second the *pralin* and Cognac, and in the third the Grand Marnier and orange rind. Work each flavor in with a whisk. At this point the mixture should become smooth. If it doesn't, add 1 teaspoon of hot water to each bowl and whisk until it does. Keep adding water a few drops at a time until smooth. It should not require more than 1 tablespoon of water at most. Cover each bowl with plastic wrap and re-frigerate for a few hours.

4. With a spoon, divide the mixture into little balls the size of extra-large olives or smaller.

5. Roll in the palm of your hand to smooth. Keep each flavor separate and refrigerated until very cold.

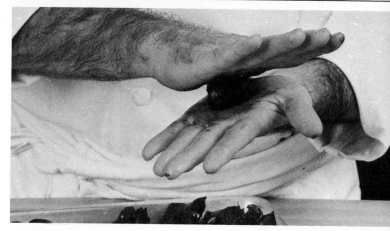

6. For the first coating, melt chocolate. Secure a toothpick in each ball (we used the Grand Marnier-flavored balls) and dip each one into melted chocolate. As you lift the ball out, roll it slightly on the side of the bowl to eliminate the excess.

7. Secure the toothpicks in a piece of foam rubber or styrofoam so the chocolate drips along the toothpick. If the balls are placed on a plate they will flatten on one side and the chocolate will accumulate at the base. Let set until very hard.

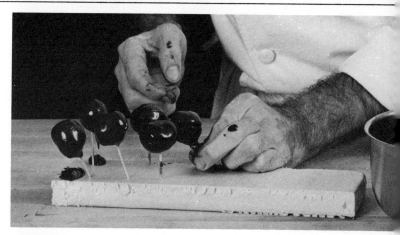

8. Roll the rum and coffee-flavored balls in unsweetened cocoa powder. Shake the pan so the balls roll around and get coated.

9. Use a vegetable peeler to grate some chocolate on top of the third batch of truffles.

10. Or roll balls in slivered almonds and chocolate shavings for another effect.

11. The three types of chocolate truffles.

12. Slice off the excess chocolate that accumulated around the toothpick, then remove the toothpick. Arrange the different flavored truffles in a chocolate box (technique 128). Truffles will keep in the refrigerator for a couple of weeks.

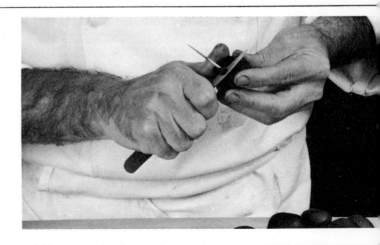

131. How to Peel and Glaze Chestnuts *(Épluchage et Marrons Confits)*

WHEN BUYING chestnuts, select carefully, checking for small holes which indicate that the chestnut is wormy. Choose them plump and shiny. Fresh chestnuts are delicious just plain roasted in the oven, over charcoal or in the fireplace. However, after roasting and peeling they can be braised and served whole or boiled and puréed. Although dehydrated chestnuts are readily available, they do not compare to fresh ones. Before braising chestnuts with a roast pork or turkey, both the outer shell and inside skin have to be removed.

For a purée, usually served with a red wine venison stew or other game, cover the peeled chestnuts with water (or water and chicken stock), add a dash of salt and a rib of celery and simmer, covered, for about 40 to 45 minutes until tender. Then purée through the fine blade of a food mill and finish with butter, salt, pepper and a bit of heavy cream.

For a dessert purée, such as the celebrated Mont-Blanc (a concoction of meringue, whipped cream and purée of chestnuts), peel the chestnuts, then cook in milk with a dash of sugar and vanilla. Purée in the food mill and sweeten with a sugar syrup.

For a stuffing, peel the chestnuts, cook in water for about 30 minutes, then mix with the other stuffing ingredients. If the chestnuts are not cooked in water first, they will be tough in the stuffing.

Regardless of how they are served, the chestnuts must be peeled first.

To glaze chestnuts

12 *cups water*
2 *cups sugar*
1 *teaspoon vanilla extract*
1 *pound chestnuts*
1 *tablespoon rum or Cognac*

1. Make a slice against the grain on both sides of the chestnuts. Be careful to slice only the outer and inside skins without going into the flesh.

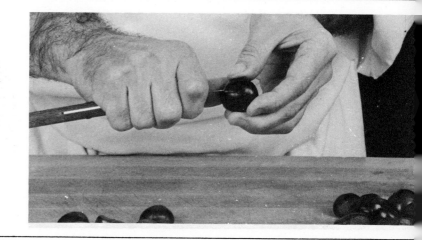

2. Place on a cookie sheet and roast approximately 15 to 20 minutes in a preheated 400-degree oven. Press the chestnuts to crack them open.

3. The chestnut should come out in one piece. Put the ones that don't peel easily back into the oven for a few minutes. Don't roast too many at one time unless you have helpers to peel them with you while they are hot. As they cool, they become hard to peel.

4. Pieces of glazed chestnuts are mixed with ice cream, Bavarian cream or whipped cream and served as dessert. Whole, they are served as bonbons or dipped into caramel (technique 133). To glaze the chestnuts, place the water, sugar and vanilla in a large shallow saucepan, bring to a boil and boil for 1 minute. Add the chestnuts.

5. Bring the water to a bare simmer and cook gently, covered, for about 3 hours. Uncover and cook slowly for another hour, or until a heavy syrup has formed and all the chestnuts are coated with it.

6. At least half of the chestnuts will be broken. Fortunately, most recipes call for pieces of candied chestnuts. Let the chestnuts cool then place in a jar. Add 1 tablespoon of rum or Cognac to the syrup. Cover with the syrup. Keep refrigerated and use when needed.

132. Almond Chestnuts *(Marrons en Pâte d'Amandes)*

YIELD: About 8 to 10 "chestnuts"

THE ALMOND "CHESTNUTS" are the perfect decoration for the chocolate chestnut cake (technique 134). They could also be arranged as a centerpiece or presented in the chocolate box (technique 128). They are not chestnuts but little balls of almond paste dipped in chocolate to look like unpeeled chestnuts.

About ¾ pound almond paste
½ pound bittersweet chocolate, melted
2 to 3 drops green coloring for leaves
About 2 to 3 tablespoons powdered sugar
About ½ teaspoon egg white for the icing

1. Work the almond paste until it is smooth. Divide into little balls the size of an olive and roll in the palm of your hand, making them slightly flat on one side to imitate a chestnut.

2. Pierce each ball with a skewer or, as pictured here, a piece of metal hanger. Incline the pan of melted chocolate on one side and dip the almond ball in. Coat about three-quarters of it.

3. As you lift each ball from the chocolate, the excess chocolate will drip into a point at the end of each one, making it look even more like a chestnut. Let the "chestnuts" dry over a bread pan so they harden without changing shape.

4. Mix the remaining almond paste with green food coloring. While the chestnuts harden, make leaves and shells with the green almond paste. Press pieces down with a spatula to flatten and shape into the form of leaves. (See Almond Paste Flowers, technique 139.) Use powdered sugar to prevent the paste from sticking. Use a fork to make indentations in the "leaves." Mold little shells around your thumb.

5. Mix the powdered sugar with egg white and, with a wooden spoon, work for about 1 minute into a smooth, thick, shiny icing. Place in a paper cone. Decorate the shells with dots of icing squeezed from the paper cone.

133. Caramel Glazed Chestnuts
(Marrons Glacés au Caramel)

THE "CHESTNUTS" in technique 132 are made from almond paste dipped in chocolate. In this technique we use actual pieces of chestnuts although little balls of almond paste could be substituted. Instead of glazing the chestnuts with chocolate, we dip them into a chocolate-flavored caramel. The caramel drips in a long thread which hardens into a very decorative ornament for a cake or for a buffet centerpiece.

12 *of the best candied chestnuts (technique 131)*
1 *cup sugar*
1 *tablespoon unsweetened cocoa powder*
¾ *cup water*

1. Mix the sugar, cocoa powder and water in a sturdy saucepan and bring to a boil. Cook until it turns into a caramel, for about 12 to 15 minutes. The temperature should be at least 325 degrees. Check the temperature by dipping the point of a knife or fork into the caramel and then dipping it into cold water. The caramel should harden immediately. The mixture will be dark in color because of the cocoa powder, and you won't see, as you usually do with a caramel, when it changes color and is ready. Let the caramel cool a few minutes until it thickens. Impale the chestnuts on skewers and when the caramel stops bubbling and is thick, dip each chestnut in the mixture.

2. Let the chestnuts hang from the side of a pan until they are hard. To free the skewer, use a pair of scissors to cut and crack away the caramel around the skewer.

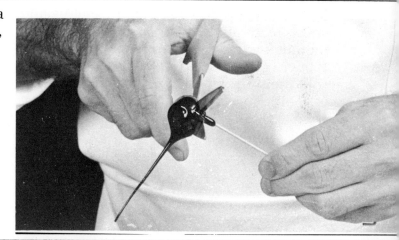

3. The caramel chestnuts can now be used for decoration.

134. Chestnut Chocolate Cake *(Turinois)*

YIELD: 18 to 20 servings

THIS IS A RICH CAKE, made with melted chocolate, purée of chestnuts and butter. It should be served very cold, cut in thin slices, plain or with a chocolate sauce or a *crème Anglaise*. Leave plain or decorate with powdered sugar and glazed or almond chestnuts (techniques 131 and 132). If you decorate the top with powdered sugar do it at the last moment because the sugar will dissolve within 20 to 25 minutes because of the moistness of the cake.

---

2 *pounds peeled chestnuts (about 2¾ pounds un-*
peeled)
2 *sticks (8 ounces) sweet butter*
¾ *cup sugar*
1 *pound bittersweet chocolate, melted*
2 *tablespoons dark rum*
½ *cup pieces of candied chestnuts, optional (tech-*
nique 131)

---

1. Place the peeled chestnuts in a kettle and cover with water. Bring to a boil and simmer gently for 40 to 45 minutes until tender. The 2 pounds of chestnuts will absorb moisture during cooking which will bring their weight up to about 3 pounds when cooked.

2. Drain the chestnuts (most will have broken) and pass through the fine blade of a food mill while still hot.

3. Mix the butter and sugar together and work with a whisk until smooth. Add the chocolate, the purée of chestnuts and the dark rum and mix well until the mixture is smooth. Then add the pieces of candied chestnuts (optional).

4. Line a loaf pan with a large strip of parchment paper. Place the mixture in the mold.

5. Refrigerate for at least 3 to 4 hours before unmolding. Run a knife all around the cake, unmold, then remove the paper.

6. To decorate, make a rectangular stencil with a piece of wax paper and place on top of the cake. Sprinkle powdered sugar over the stencil, then remove.

7. Decorate the top with almond or candied chestnuts. Serve plain or with a custard sauce flavored with rum (see recipe in technique 121).

135. Cream Puff Cake *(Croquembouche)*

THE *croquembouche* is a cream puff cake usually served at weddings in France. The puffs are sometimes built around a bottle or arranged in a special conical mold made for *croquembouche*. We built ours in the bowl of an electric mixer. If the cake has to be transported somewhere, it should be transported in the mold. For a big party, instead of building an extra large *croquembouche* which is delicate and difficult to move, make a small *croquembouche* and arrange the leftover puffs around. Avoid making it on a humid summer day because the caramel will stick and melt and the cake may collapse, especially because the stuffed puffs are heavy. The *choux*, which should be fairly small, can be cooked ahead and so can the cream. This recipe yields about 80 small cream puffs.

Puff dough

1½ cups milk
1 stick (4 ounces) sweet butter
1 teaspoon salt
1½ cups all-purpose flour
6 large eggs

Crème patissière (cream filling)

2 cups milk
8 egg yolks
1 tablespoon vanilla extract
¾ cup sugar
½ envelope unflavored gelatin
⅔ cup flour
¾ cup heavy cream
½ stick (2 ounces) sweet butter, at room temperature

Caramel glaze

2 *cups sugar*
½ *cup water*
¼ *teaspoon cream of tartar diluted in 1*
    tablespoon water

When ready to assemble the *croquembouche*, make a second batch of caramel.

1. To make the cream puff dough, place the milk, butter and salt in a heavy sauce-pan and bring to a boil. As soon as it boils, add the flour in one stroke and mix rapidly with a wooden spatula. Keep cooking the mixture (*panade*) on low heat for about 1 minute to dry it out. Place the mixture in a clean bowl and stir about 1 minute to cool it off slightly. Add 2 eggs and mix well until blended. (You will notice that the mixture will stay loose for a while and suddenly tighten. When tight add the other eggs. Re-peat the process each time you add eggs.) Add another egg and mix until smooth. The eggs are added to the *panade* in 4 addi-tions. At the third addition the mixture should be worked a little more to give it the proper texture. The mixture can also be made in an electric mixer. Very lightly but-ter and flour 2 or 3 cookie sheets. (If the sheets are coated too thickly the puffs will not stick.) Using a pastry bag fitted with a plain tube with a ¼-inch opening, form the *choux*.

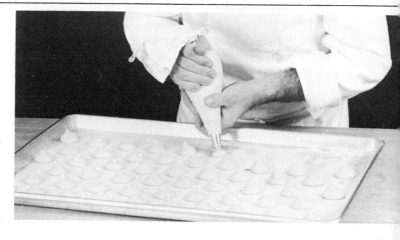

2. To form the *choux* hold the pastry bag straight down and squeeze without moving your hand. Then stop squeezing and lift up the bag in a sudden short upswing. The puffs will have small tails. Wet a towel and press the tail down to make the *choux* rounder. Place in a preheated 400-degree oven and bake for 30 to 35 minutes until the puffs are well browned and dry.

3. Keep the door of the oven slightly ajar during the last 10 minutes of baking so the *choux* dry out and don't collapse. If the weather is humid, let cool in the turned off oven with the door ajar. For the *crème patissière,* place the milk in a heavy saucepan and bring to a boil. Combine the yolks, vanilla, sugar and gelatin in a bowl and work with a whisk until pale yellow and foamy, about 1 to 2 minutes. Stir in the flour. Pour the boiling milk on top of the egg mixture and mix carefully. Then place the mixture back in a saucepan and bring to a boil stirring constantly with the whisk until it boils and thickens. Let boil for 15 to 20 seconds, then stir in the cream. Pour into a bowl. Cover with plastic wrap and refrigerate until it reaches room temperature. Then add the softened butter with a whisk, piece by piece, and let cool.

4. Fit a pastry bag with a small fluted or starred tube and fill with the cream. Twist the flat bottom of the puff on the tube to make a hole and squeeze the cream inside. If the tube is plain it will not pierce the puff. In which case, make a hole with the point of a knife in each puff before filling.

5. Make the first batch of caramel by mixing together the sugar and water, stirring just enough to moisten the sugar. Place on heat and bring to a boil. After 3 minutes, add the cream of tartar dissolved in the water. Cook until it turns into a light caramel, about 10 minutes. Remove from the heat (it will continue to cook and darken for a few minutes). If it darkens too much, place the saucepan in lukewarm water to stop the cooking. If it gets too thick, remelt it on top of the stove. Holding the *choux* by the bottom, dip the top into the hot caramel.

6. Slide the top of the *choux* against the side of the pan to remove the excess caramel. Glaze all the *choux* on top. Then make the second batch of caramel to build the *croquembouche*.

7. This time the caramel should be light in color. As soon as the sugar mixture gets slightly blond, remove from heat. Use any type of metal mold you have but be sure to oil the inside. Begin by making a crown or ring for the top of the cake. Dip a side of a *chou* into the caramel, then stick it to another *chou*. Repeat to form a crown, about 6 to 7 *choux* around.

8. Place that crown in your oiled mold so the caramelized top of the *choux* touch the metal. Then start building up the sides of the mold. Try to stack the *choux* tightly, with the least space possible between each. Dip each *chou* in the caramel and fit it into the space.

9. Keep building. When you get to the top try to make it the same height on all sides. Remember that the *croquembouche* will be turned upside down. If too high on one side or the other, cut a *chou* in half to even out. It can go one or two layers above the side of the bowl. If any of the *choux* are not holding properly, dab some caramel in between with the point of a knife.

3. Make little almond paste balls and place in the center of each prune. Press with your finger to flatten and make it fit nicely. Cut the figs in half. Put a piece of almond paste on the bottom half and use the top half as a hat.

4. Mark a crisscross pattern on the round almond paste shapes and stripes on the oval shapes. Make eyes and noses on the little "Santa Clauses." Stick each stuffed fruit with a toothpick.

5. Place the sugar in a clean stainless steel or copper saucepan. Moisten with the water and shake the pan lightly so all the sugar gets "wet." Do not stir anymore. Boil the sugar and water for about 1 minute and add the cream of tartar diluted with water. With a wet brush, clean around the saucepan while cooking to melt the crystallized sugar—if any. (Another method is to cover the boiling sugar with a lid for 1 minute. The steam will melt the crystals.) The sugar must be cooked to the hard-crack stage (approximately 300 degrees).

6. Incline the pan and dip the whole fruit in the syrup. Lift and brush gently against the side of the pan to remove the extra syrup. Place on a lightly oiled cookie sheet until set and hard. Then twist the toothpicks back and forth to loosen and remove. If the fruits get sticky in very humid weather, put in front of a fan to dry out.

137. Caramel Cage *(Cage en Caramel)*

THESE EXCEPTIONALLY DECORATIVE caramel cages can be placed atop desserts such as *oeufs à la neige,* poached fruit, different coupes, ice cream, and whipped cream-filled shells. The cages can be made in different shapes.

1. Make the caramel from technique 135, Cream Puff Cake. When the caramel is ready, let it cool off a bit until it is thick enough to form long threads. If it hardens too much, it can be remelted. Use Pyrex or stainless steel bowls. Oil the outside of the bowl, then, using a teaspoon filled with caramel, drape long threads on the top and sides of the bowl.

2. The threads should be long enough to weave back and forth from one side of the bowl to the other. If the threads are too short, the cage will break when unmolded.

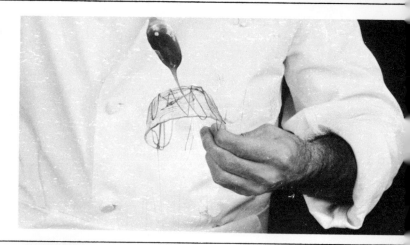

3. A large stainless steel bowl can be used to make a cage large enough to cover a cake or mousse.

5. Pour the mixture onto an oiled slab of marble. The heat of the caramel will damage most other surfaces. It will even buckle stainless steel.

6. Use a spatula coated with oil to spread the *nougatine* on the marble and turn it upside down.

7. After about 1 minute the *nougatine* should be workable. Roll it with an oiled metal rolling pin. (A piece of cast-iron piping, 1½ inches in diameter, works perfectly.) Roll while it's still hot. Work as fast as possible because once the *nougatine* cools off it gets hard and can't be rolled any longer.

8. Using a sturdy knife and the rolling pin as a hammer, cut the *nougatine* into 2 or 3 pieces.

9. Place the pieces on an oiled cookie sheet in a preheated 225-degree oven to soften a bit. Take one piece out at a time and place on the marble.

10. Roll each piece as thin as possible (about ⅛ inch thick) and cut into shapes before it becomes too brittle. In this case we cut triangles.

11. Place the triangles on the rolling pin to shape them. If too hard, soften in the oven for a few minutes. Let the triangles harden on the roller. You can also make *barquettes* or plain flat shapes.

12. To make the base of the decoration, place a piece of rolled, soft *nougatine* on a small inverted cake pan and press around with your fingers as fast as you can until it takes on the shape of the pan. Trim around using the knife and the metal roller. Work as fast as you can.

5. Lift the flat piece with a spatula and roll it around the center cone.

6. Roll another piece flat and place around the flower bud. Continue the process, adding more petals. Turn the petal edge outward.

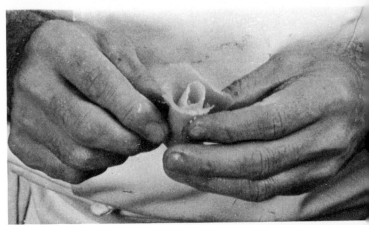

7. To make a carnation, use pink almond paste. Roll in a long cylinder about ¼ inch thick and flatten with a spatula, pressing forward so that one edge of the strip is ultra thin. Use powdered sugar to prevent sticking.

8. Using a fork, make ridges on one side of the strip. The tines of the fork must go through the almond paste.

9. Slide a flexible metal spatula under the strip to loosen it.

10. Fold the strip left to right on top of itself into wave-like pleats.

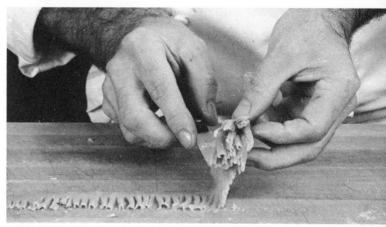

11. Roll the end of the strip around the flower to encase.

12. Press the bottom together gently between your fingers.

3. Let the sugar cool a bit, then lift each side with an oiled spatula and fold onto itself.

4. Keep lifting and folding the sugar onto itself until it is solid enough to hold.

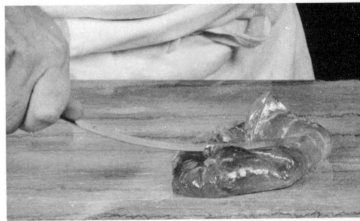

5. Oil your hands, grab the sugar and start pulling it. It is hot and you have to work fast. Note that the sugar is still transparent and clear.

6. Keep pulling and folding for about 1½ minutes. Note that the sugar becomes shiny and opaque.

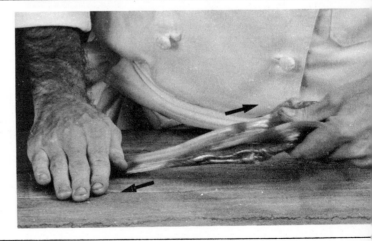

7. When the sugar is very shiny and glossy it is ready to be shaped, however it will be too hard. Place on an oiled tray in a 180 to 190-degree oven for a few minutes to soften a bit.

8. Remove from the oven and pinch the top of the sugar lump with both thumbs and forefingers and pull it apart to open out and spread the sugar into a thin "veil." Grab the center of the veil and pull out.

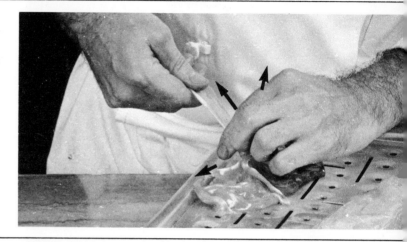

9. Twist and break into a very thin petal. The petal will have the imprint of your thumb.

10. Roll the petal into a cone to simulate the bud or heart of a rose (see step 3, technique 139).

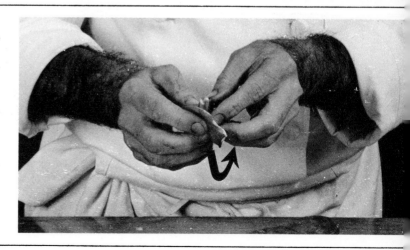

11. Pull out a second petal and roll it tightly around the center of the rose. Continue pulling out petals and placing them around the rose to enlarge it. Fold the edges outward. Work as fast as you can. When the sugar becomes too hard, let it soften slightly in the oven or under the infra-red lamp.

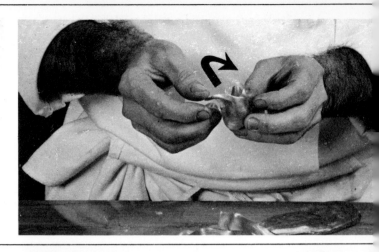

12. When the rose is completed, set in a small glass so it keeps its shape while hardening. The ribbon is made from loops glued together into a bow. Each loop is made by pulling a strip of sugar, folding it in half, side by side, then pulling and folding again (side by side). Each time the ribbon will get wider and wider. It should be about 1½ to 2 inches wide. Cut sections and fold them on themselves to make loops.

13. Pull strips and fold to imitate leaves.

14. Pull thin long strips from the sugar.

15. Roll into tendrils to simulate vines and stems of flowers.

16. To make a bow, pass the ends of the loops over a flame to melt, then glue the loops together. Use the flowers, bows and leaves to decorate a cake.

141. Cake Glazed with Fondant
(Gâteau Fondant)

Cakes, especially wedding cakes, are beautiful glazed with a shiny *fondant* (sugar icing). To make a cake, layer a *génoise* with a butter cream or *ganache*, then cover with a layer of almond paste so the top is absolutely smooth for the *fondant*.

1 8- to 10-inch diameter cake about 3 inches high
About 1 pound almond paste

Fast *fondant*

3 cups powdered sugar
¼ cup hot water
1 tablespoon light corn syrup

1. Place the cake on a cardboard round. Roll the almond paste to about ⅛ inch thick. Use powdered sugar instead of flour to help in the rolling.

2. Roll the almond paste back onto the rolling pin, lift it up and place it on the cake.

3. Press the paste all around the cake so it adheres well. Trim the base. If there are any cracks, patch closed. Brush the cake. It should be smooth all around and on top.

4. To make the fondant, mix all ingredients together well. Work it for about 1 minute with a whisk. The mixture should be glossy and smooth. Use right away or cover with a wet towel or else it will crust on top very rapidly.

5. Place the cake on a wire rack and pour the fondant on top.

6. Spread with a spatula so the fondant runs all around. Work as fast as possible.

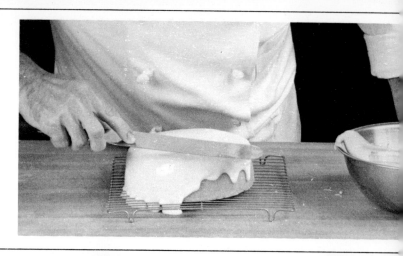

7. Lift the cake and bang the wire rack on the table a few times to encourage excess to drip off.

8. Lift the cake and run your fingers around the bottom edge to make it smooth. The cake can now be refrigerated or served, plain or with the sugar flowers described in the previous technique.

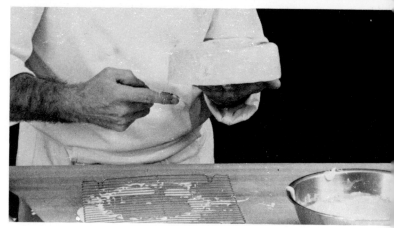

General Conversions

WEIGHT

American	British	Metric
1 ounce	1 ounce	28.4 grams
1 pound	1 pound	454 grams

VOLUME

American	British	Metric
1 U.S. teaspoon	1 U.K. level teaspoon	5 milliliters
1 U.S. tablespoon (3 teaspoons)	1 U.K. dessertspoon	15 milliliters
1 U.S. cup (16 tablespoons)	$^5/_6$ breakfast cup (8 fluid ounces)	236 milliliters (about ¼ liter)
1 U.S. quart (4 cups)	$^5/_6$ Imperial quart	1 scant liter
1 U.S. gallon (4 quarts)	$^5/_6$ Imperial gallon	3¾ liters

LENGTH

American	British	Metric
1 inch	1 inch	2½ centimeters (25 millimeters)
12 inches (1 foot)	12 inches (1 foot)	30 centimeters

Note: All conversions are approximate. They have been rounded off to the nearest convenient measure.

Oven Temperatures

Fahrenheit	Centigrade	British Regulo Setting	French Setting
212°F	100°C		1
225°F	107°C	¼	2
250°F	121°C	½	3
275°F	135°C	1	3
300°F	149°C	2	4
325°F	163°C	3	4
350°F	177°C	4	4
375°F	191°C	5	5
400°F	204°C	6	5
425°F	218°C	7	6
450°F	232°C	8	6
475°F	246°C	8	6
500°F	260°C	9	7
525°F	274°C	9	8
550°F	288°C	9	9

Selected Measurements

American (spoons and cups)	British (ounces and pounds)	Metric
BREAD CRUMBS		
1 cup	2 ounces	60 grams
BUTTER		
1 teaspoon	$1/6$ ounce	5 grams
1 tablespoon	½ ounce	15 grams
½ cup (1 stick)	4 ounces	115 grams
1 cup (2 sticks)	8 ounces	230 grams
2 cups (4 sticks)	1 pound	454 grams
CHEESE (*grated*)		
1 cup	3½ ounces	100 grams
FLOUR (*all-purpose, unsifted*)		
1 teaspoon	⅛ ounce	3 grams
1 tablespoon	⅓ ounce	9 grams
1 cup	4¼ ounces	120 grams
3⅔ cups	1 pound	454 grams
HERBS (*fresh, chopped*)		
1 tablespoon	½ ounce	15 grams
MEATS (*cooked and finely chopped*)		
1 cup	8 ounces	225 grams
NUTS (*chopped*)		
1 cup	5½ ounces	155 grams

ONIONS (*raw—chopped, sliced, or minced*)

1 tablespoon	⅓ ounce	9 grams
1 cup	5 ounces	140 grams

PEAS (*fresh*)

1 pound unshelled = 1 cup shelled	1 pound, unshelled	454 grams, unshelled

RICE (*raw*)

1 cup	7½ ounces	215 grams

SPINACH (*fresh, cooked*)

1¼ pounds, raw = 1 cup, cooked (squeezed dry, chopped)	1¼ pounds, raw	550 grams, raw

SUGAR (*regular granulated or superfine granulated*)

1 teaspoon	⅙ ounce	5 grams
1 tablespoon	½ ounce	15 grams
1 cup	6½ ounces	185 grams

confectioners' (*powdered, unsifted*)

1 teaspoon	⅛ ounce icing sugar	4 grams
1 tablespoon	⅓ ounce icing sugar	9 grams
1 cup	¾ ounces icing sugar	100 grams

TOMATOES (*fresh*)

¾–1 pound, whole = 1 cup, peeled and seeded	¾–1 pound, whole	340 grams

VEGETABLES (*raw—chopped fine, such as carrots and celery*)

1 cup	8 ounces	225 grams

A Note to the User: All conversions are approximate. The weights have been rounded off to the nearest useful measure for the purposes of the recipes in this volume. Weights and measures of specific ingredients may vary with altitude, humidity, variations in method of preparation, etc.

Index